THE SANS-CULOTTES

THE
SANS-CULOTTES

The Popular Movement and Revolutionary Government 1793-1794

ALBERT SOBOUL

Translated by

REMY INGLIS HALL

Princeton University Press
Princeton, New Jersey

Originally published by
Editions du Seuil, Paris, 1968.
Anchor Books edition: 1972
Princeton University Press edition: 1980

Library of Congress Catalogue Card Number 80-7818
ISBN 0-691-05320-0
ISBN 0-691-00782-9 pbk.

First Princeton Paperback printing, 1980

The translator wishes to thank Dr. Helene Zahler for her many helpful suggestions during the translation of this work, and Miss Ro Lee for her kind assistance in the preparation of the manuscript.

TABLE OF CONTENTS

officers: civil and revolutionary
commissars and militants——The
preponderance of artisans and shopkeepers——Ideological consequences: property, work, bread——
Contradictions and unity among the
Parisian sans-culottes.

Practical demands and theoretical
statements, 1793 to the year III——
Popular egalitarianism: from foodstuffs to other staples——The sans-
culottes: the willingness to share.

Restrictions on property rights over
agricultural products: the nationalization or municipalization of foodstuffs——Criticism of the free exercise
of property rights: protection of
small ownership, restrictions on
large ownership——The extent to
which these were new ideas.

Against trading in coin——Against
joint stock companies——Against the
monopoly of war matériel: criticism
of large enterprise protection of
small independent production——
The clothing factories in the sections: the people's aspirations and

vote imposed by the Robespierre
Commune——Denunciation as a
civic duty.

havior: the familiar *tu*——Living conditions: house and furniture, the
question of rents, food (bread, meat,
wine)——Intellectual level: the popular press and the dissemination of
literature——Social morality: republican virtue, free love and natural
children, solidarity.

Revolutionary government and direct
government, liberal democracy and
popular democracy——Social contradictions: economic freedom and controlled economy——Employers and
employees, national defense and popular demands——Contradictions inherent in the composition of the
sans-culottes: artisans and shopkeepers, journeymen and day laborers——The effect of the "maximum"
——The absence of class consciousness——The disintegration of the
popular movement: exhaustion,
psychological weariness, the war effort, the bureaucratization of the
revolutionary cadres——Why the
bourgeois revolution would have
failed without assistance from the
popular movement.

Equality for social man
means equal rights.
*Vergniaud, March 13, 1793
(Ventôse, year 1)*

Bring an end to inequality
of incomes.
*Félix Lepeletier, August 20,
1793 (Fructidor, year 1)*

FOREWORD

Les Sans-Culottes, in an expanded and somewhat more
scholarly form, first appeared in 1958. This edition repre-
sents the second part of a doctoral thesis submitted to
the Sorbonne. It is devoted to the rise, halt and finally
the decline of the Paris popular movement from the fall
of the Girondins on June 2, 1793 (13 Prairial, year 1),
to that of Robespierre on 9 Thermidor, year 11, which
toppled the revolutionary government and which finally
brought about the downfall of the popular movement
as well. I believe that the political significance of this
work will still prove to be of interest, if we take this to
mean the contemplation of the past for the enlightenment of the present, and vice versa.

This book is in fact concerned with the study of the
all-important social force within the revolutionary process in France between 1793 and 1794, during the period
of the Jacobin dictatorship of Public Safety, that is to
say, with the Paris of the sans-culottes, organized in forty-
eight sections: history seen "from below," as I was taught
by master, Georges Lefebvre. Needless to say, I have not
explored all the problems and some, such as the war, are
only mentioned briefly. The fundamental problem of the
period was political; but surely the course of politics is
influenced by social pressures of the time. All studies of
political history entail a study of social history. The year
11 saw the birth of modern revolutionary politics in all
its epic grandeur and tremendous surge of fraternal
spirit, in its manipulations and in its baseness: in Ventôse of the year 11, Hébert was denounced as an "English

patriot"; two months later, the popular militants were to be denounced as "Hébertists."

Although the past may govern the present, history can also illuminate the past and in turn nourish present action. At the heart of the complex and terrible political and social struggle of the year II lies the problem of over-lapping powers, not only of the necessary transformation from cadres to working groups, but also of the revolutionary bureaucracy and the new brand of conformism. How can one fail to recognize in these problems some of those confronting revolutionary movements of the second half of the twentieth century?

The historian may either hide a subjective point of view behind his erudition, or take a more relativist point of view and project himself and the present onto the past, thus interpreting the past, which results in a definitive and immobile history, instead of a moving and fluid one. Or again, he can consider the essence of history as being attained only through many avenues, hence different systems of interpretations and histories.

The French Revolution was a total phenomenon, stemming from a process that embraced every aspect of historical evolution. Its historiography reflects the movement of history; various aspects of the totality are revealed to successive historians who bring out new data previously concealed behind the enormity of the total phenomenon. Furthermore, the Revolution opened a number of possibilities: whenever a new one is brought to light, it reveals another aspect of the revolutionary past, thus enlightening the historian, and also the politician, if he has eyes with which to see.

The history of the French Revolution will never be fully explored, nor will it ever be completely written. From generation to generation, as history, which it made possible, unfolds, it will never cease to cause men to reflect, to give rise to enthusiasm.

Albert Soboul
January 1968

INTRODUCTION: BOURGEOIS
REVOLUTION AND POPULAR ACTIVITY

The French Revolution together with the revolutions that
took place in England during the seventeenth century
constitute the culmination of a long economic and social
revolution that made the middle classes the masters of
the world.

This fact, which seems commonplace today, was ac-
knowledged by the more perceptive historians of the middle classes during the nineteenth century. Guizot wanted
to use history as a justification for the Charter,[1] to prove
that one of the basic characteristics of French society was
the emergence, growth and ultimate triumph of the
bourgeoisie. Existing between the people and the aristocracy, the bourgeoisie gradually created cadres and formulated the ideas of a new society which were validated
by the events of 1789. "The great role played by the Third
Estate in France cannot be ignored; it was the most
vigorous and the most decisive element of French civilization, and the one that in the last analysis determined
its direction and its character. From a social point of
view, in its relations with various classes that co-existed
on our territory, what was given the name of the Third
Estate progressively spread, grew, and at first greatly
changed, then defeated and finally absorbed, more or less,
all the others."[2] The Third Estate, according to Guizot,
meant the bourgeoisie. After Guizot, Tocqueville, regarding the gradual rise of the middle class, spoke with "a
kind of religious dread," "of this irresistible revolution ad-
vancing century by century over every obstacle and even

[1] Translator's note: The Charter of 1830.
[2] *Histoire de la civilization en France depuis la chute de
l'Empire romain*, 4 vols. (1828-30), p. 592 of the 1839 edition.

now going forward amidst the ruins it itself created."[3] Taine also sketched out this slow scaling of the social ladder by the bourgeoisie, the resulting inequality of which struck him as intolerable. "Since the nobility had lost its special powers, and since the Third Estate had acquired its own wide-ranging power—this leveling off being achieved through education and through skill—the inequality that continued to separate them became offensive in its pettiness."[4] However, so sure were these historians that the birth and progress of the bourgeoisie were primarily the result of the emergence and development of mobile capital, of commercial and later of industrial enterprise, that they never bothered to make a detailed study of the economic origins of the Revolution, or of the social classes who led it.

Yet during the revolutionary era, Barnave pushed his analysis further. Living as he did in the province of Dauphiné, in the midst of industrial activity, which—if one is to believe Roland, the inspector of manufacturing, writing in 1785—made this region, on account of the variety and density of its enterprises, one of the first provinces in the kingdom, Barnave came to believe that *industrial* property brought about the political rise of the class that controlled it. In his *Introduction to the French Revolution*,[5] after having posited the principle that property influences institutions, Barnave states that the institutions created for and by the landed aristocracy counteracted and held back the advent of a new era. "The moment the arts and commerce begin to be disseminated among the people, placing a new means of wealth at the disposal of the productive classes, a revolution in politi-

[3] *De la démocratie en Amérique* (1836–39), Complete works, Vol. I (1951), Introduction, p. 4.

[4] *Les Origines de la France contemporaine. L'Ancien Régime* (1876), Book IV, Chap. III, p. 412.

[5] *L'Introduction à la Révolution française* was published in 1843, in the first volume of Barnave's *Works*, edited by Berenger de la Drôme. Jean Jaurès talks of this work at great length in his *Histoire Socialiste*, I, 98.

cal laws comes into being; a new distribution of wealth
produces a new distribution of power. In the same manner
that the possession of land elevated the aristocracy, industrial property elevates the power of the people," that
is to say, the bourgeoisie. With great clarity, Barnave
asserts that the antagonism between landed property and
mòbile property was the same as that between classes
dependent upon them. Following the same line of
thought, further illustrated during the course of the first
half of the nineteenth century by the Utopian Socialists,
Marx and Engels stressed in the *Communist Manifesto*
of 1848 that at the end of the eighteenth century, with
the regime still feudal in terms of property, the organization of agriculture and industry no longer corresponded to
productive forces in full swing, and hence hindered the
development of the economy. "These chains had to be
broken," wrote the authors of the *Manifesto*. "They were
broken."[6]

Inspired to a certain extent by historical materialism,
but only to a certain extent (did he not in fact write in
his General Introduction that his interpretation of history
would be "at the same time materialist with Marx and
mystical with Michelet"?), Jaurès restored to the history
of the Revolution its economic and social foundations.
A vast fresco, his eloquent *Socialist History* remains a
monument.[7] "Involved in the feverish existence of assemblies and parties," Jaurès was likely, to a greater extent
than Albert Mathiez has suggested in his 1912 preface to
the new edition of the *Socialist History*, "to revive the
emotions, the thoughts, clear or obscure, of revolutionaries." "We know," wrote Jaurès, "that economic conditions,
the nature of production and of ownership, are the very
foundation of history." Perhaps Jaurès is guilty of over-
simplification: according to him, the Revolution unfolded
almost smoothly; its cause lay in the economic and intellectual power of the bourgeoisie, which had reached its

[6] See in particular the first part of the *Manifesto*, "Bourgeois
and Proletariates."

[7] *Histoire Socialiste*, 4 vols. in-8, s.d. (1901–4).

xx

maturity; the result was the legitimation of this power into law. But this explanation does not take into account either the date of the Revolution or its violent character, which makes the episode the most dramatic of the struggles of the bourgeoisie.

Albert Mathiez, going further, described, after Philippe Sagnac, the aristocratic reaction of the eighteenth century that culminated in the years 1787–88. He uses the ambiguous expression *the revolt of the nobility,* by which he means the frantic opposition of the nobility to all attempts at reform, and more particularly, the monopoly a privileged minority had on all the offices of state, and its obstinate refusal to share power with the upper middle class.[8] This explains the violent character of the Revolution: the advent of the bourgeoisie was not the result of a gradual evolution, but of a sudden and fundamental change.

The dramatic vicissitudes of the Revolution can likewise be explained by the resistance of the aristocracy if one stresses the rapid disintegration of the Third Estate, a fact that Jaurès and Mathiez in particular were justifiably insistent upon. The antagonisms that rapidly manifested themselves between the various strata of the bourgeoisie as well as between the bourgeoisie and the sans-culottes, artisans and shopkeepers, then, account for the complexity of revolutionary history and the succession of its various stages. Albert Mathiez went so far as to distinguish between four successive revolutions, the last of which, that of June 2, 1793 (13 Prairial, year 1), ended in an attempt at a social democracy. Without subscribing to these distinctions (the Revolution was essentially one, and remained essentially bourgeois in its various ups and downs), I must however stress the importance of Mathiez's work from the point of view of our present concern.

Turning aside from the Parisian and urban scenes, which until that time had engrossed the attention of his-

[8] Albert Mathiez, *La Révolution française* (1922), Vol. I, Chap. 1, *La crise de l'Ancien Régime,* and Vol. II, *La révolte nobilaire.*

torians, Georges Lefebvre undertook to study the peasan-
try. (France was, after all, essentially rural at the end of
the eighteenth century). Prior to Lefebvre's study, peasant activity had been considered a repercussion of urban
movements essentially directed, in agreement with the
bourgeoisie, against feudalism and royal power; hence the
homogeneity of the revolt of the Third Estate and the
majesty of its progress. Taking as his point of departure
a detailed social analysis, Georges Lefebvre points out
that within the cadre of the bourgeois revolution there
evolved a peasant current which was autonomous in its
origins, its conduct, its crises and its trends. The value of
Lefebvre's work lies in its evidence and the example it
sets.[9]

Is the picture it presents therefore complete and trust-
worthy? I think not. One social group to be found both
under the ancien régime and in revolutionary France is
not given its true place—a group which since that period
has been called the sans-culottes.

Every historian of the Revolution has stressed the role
played by the urban masses, particularly by the people of
Paris; the Revolution was to a large extent their making.
From the spring of 1789 to the spring of 1795, from the
fourteenth of July to Prairial, year III, they consecrated
their energy to it. They placed all their hopes in it. They
lived and suffered for it.

The people are the principal actors in Michelet's
History of the French Revolution.[10] Not the sans-culottes
but the "people," a term he did not attempt either to
define or to analyze; the people, that is to say, the whole
nation, France arisen in one mythical person. But during

[9] It suffices here to refer the reader to Georges Lefebvre's
own summary of the result of his researches, made in 1933: "La
Révolution française et les paysans," *Cahiers de la Révolution
française*, No. 1, p. 6; republished in *Etudes sur la Révolution
française* (1954), p. 246.
[10] *Histoire de la Révolution Française*, 4 vols. (1847–53).

the changing course of the Revolution, was the role of the
people of Paris sufficiently stressed? Have historians given
it its proper importance? Have they not tended more or
less to consider its action as being determined by that of
the bourgeoisie, to characterize it as being directed essentially against the aristocracy and feudalism, royal power
and the ancien régime? Did the sans-culottes, particularly
the Parisian sans-culottes, act only in full and perfect
accord with the revolutionary bourgeoisie?

Actually, the question has been anticipated. First by
Thiers, who, here and there, stresses the role played by
the Parisian sections and the autonomy of their activity.
In regard to foodstuffs, for example, he briefly points out
the antagonism that existed in February 1793 between
the sections, which demanded price-fixing, and the Jacobins, who condemned it as being dangerous to the freedom
of commerce.[11] His account is essentially political; economic life, the social struggles that formed the background
of the popular revolution do not come into the picture.
His information is based on official documents and
memoirs, and he did not even glance at the enormous
repository of the papers of Parisian sections of the time.

Michelet went further. In his preface of 1868, he mentions how his book was "carried in the womb of the
Archives." "For the great tragedies of revolutionary Paris,
the archives of the Hôtel de Ville opened the door to the
Commune registers; and the Prefecture of Police provided
me with the immense variety of verbatim reports of our
forty-eight sections." Michelet was not satisfied with studying the opposition of the municipality, that is to say, the
people's elected representatives; he observed the people
themselves, in their sections. For May 31, he tells us how
he took "religious care in reading and copying the registers of the forty-eight sections"; on 9 Thermidor, he followed *step by step* the thirty-one verbatim reports of sections that still existed.

Although Michelet was interested in almost nothing but

---

[11] *Histoire de la Révolution Française* (1823–27), 7th ed.,
1838, Vol. VII, Chap. IV, p. 310.

the *great tragedies* of revolutionary Paris, when the sans-
culottes erupted into the foreground, let us nevertheless
acknowledge the results of his research. Having introduced
the people into history, Michelet dispensed with a study
of their everyday actions. What were their fears and their
hopes, their needs and their means? And who were these
people? Were they a homogeneous group? Did journeymen and master workmen have similar interests? What
was the actual composition of these sections, these committees, these popular societies that suddenly appeared
amid the turmoil of troubled days to retire almost immediately to the shadows?

Having handled the documents themselves, having obtained from eyewitnesses a living acquaintance with the
Revolution, Michelet managed to capture the very soul
of the people who had created it, with both their enthusi-
asms and their illusions. He speaks of the great hopes of
1789, the rage of the people who created the notion of
the aristocratic plot, patriotic fervor in the year 1792. He
lived among the people, in the areas of the city where
the memory of Marat, of Jacques Roux and of *Père
Duchesne* was still very much alive, and he conceived an
admiration for Hébert and the Intransigents; he came to
appreciate the great disillusionment of the masses during
the spring of 1794. In making Jacques Roux one of the
first socialists, did he quite understand the real bearing
of the political and social aspirations of the Parisian sans-
culottes? "In the heart of Paris itself, in the dark, narrow,
working-class streets (Les Arcis, Saint-Martin)," he wrote
in his 1868 preface, "socialism bred a revolution within
the revolution." Is not Michelet transferring his
nineteenth-century preoccupations to the end of the
eighteenth century to serve the needs of his dispute with
Louis Blanc over Robespierre?

While Michelet brought understanding and human
warmth to his study of the papers of the Paris sections,
Mortimer-Ternaux adopted a tone of systematic dispar-
agement. For his *History of the Terror*, he thoroughly
searched the verbatim reports to find everything that

might support his political prejudices and prove that the Parisian sections were indeed "forty-eight centers of perpetual agitation."[12] Nevertheless, his work at least preserved transcripts of documents that have since disappeared.

Taine, in turn, in his *Origins of Contemporary France* —and more often than not without referring to the sources themselves—culled from his predecessors, particularly from the work of Mortimer-Ternaux, all hostile evidence in order to support his preconceived ideas: his description of the people of Paris, "that beast wallowing in a carpet of purple,"[13] was little short of caricature. Nevertheless, Taine did point out areas of fruitful research. He brought to light the social nature of the pressure from the sections and the manner in which this threatened the bourgeoisie. Bent on describing the popular movements with as much contempt as fear, he stressed, in showing the intertwining social forces, the complexity of personal interests and collective passions. In these respects, he remains an innovator.

Although Taine's class prejudices diverted him from this area of research, another historian, Ernest Mellié, in a modest contribution, did pursue it and showed the way, although his work does not bear comparison with his illustrious predecessors. In 1898, Mellié published *The Sections of Paris during the French Revolution*. He took particular care in studying their organization and their functioning. He wanted to show them, not only in the streets, during the course of the "high points" of the Revolution, or before the bars of the National Assembly, but "at home, in their everyday encounters, in the midst of their various occupations." Observed at meetings of assemblies, committees and societies, popular action no longer seemed to be sporadic, restricted to public demonstrations, but a continuous daily manifestation, attentive

[12] *Histoire de la Terreur*, 1792–1794, (1862–69), 3d ed., 1868, Introduction, I, 27.
[13] *Les Origines de la France contemporaine. La Révolution*, Vol. III, *Le Gouvernement révolutionnaire* (1885), Preface, p.1. Taine writes, "This volume, like its predecessors, is only for specialists in moral zoology."

to all the needs of existence; thus popular social support
once again becomes political action. This is a vast proposition, which, if it had been realized, would have formed
a tableau of daily life in revolutionary Paris. In fact, Mellié
contented himself with a study that was essentially concerned with institutions: when the sections were established, which laws they dispensed, the manner in which
they organized themselves, fulfilled their tasks, gradually
extended their powers, and how the electoral bodies transformed themselves into autonomous municipalities capable of bringing pressure upon the Parisian authorities
and national assemblies.

Mellié follows the sections in their various activities,
shedding light on their manner of operation and the complexity of their functions. Does he also shed light on the
specific nature of the popular movement, the cadres of
which were formed by the people of Paris? "Writing a
history of the sections virtually means going back to writing about the Revolution," writes Mellié, which is to ad-
mit implicitly that popular action developed only as a
function of the bourgeoisie and possessed no specificity,
no autonomy. Although it is true that the Parisian sections not only influenced the course of the Revolution
during its great "high points," but intervened daily during
the debates of the national and municipal assemblies—
and hence that their history is often confused with that
of the Revolution itself—it is also true that they were
autonomous to some extent and had characteristics of
their own. To write a history of the sections of Paris is
not just a matter of talking about the Revolution, but,
at least from 1792 onwards, of writing a history of the
Parisian sans-culottes.

The history of the sections, which Mellié did not pursue,
is well handled, for the period extending from June to
December 1792, by F. Braesch. His thesis is devoted
as much to the Commune of August 10 as to the history
of Paris. "It struck me that the most important historical
figure of the French Revolution . . . this personality with
a hundred heads and a million arms which we call Paris,

deserved in its turn to be placed in the center of the Terror."[14] The real nature of municipal politics, and therefore, in many instances, of general politics, must be sought in the sections, more than in the central body of the Commune itself.

Braesch also wanted to "follow in detail the complicated game of the politics of the sections," to write their history, to make an original and positive study. But this work is not without limitations. Although he says himself that he gave an important place to economic and religious factors, he nevertheless strove to consider them *only from the political point of view*. Referring to Michelet, he called the economic question "a result, an essential progression, of freedom," in other words, freedom *precedes all*. This statement of principle, a false analogy to the social problems of the twentieth century, leads to an error of perspective. "The struggle was, as it is today, between the workers and powerful bourgeoisie." But this is to forget that for the sans-culottes the aristocracy was the basic enemy; it confuses the journeyman artisan with the factory worker. This is not a "simple question of differences of modality"; it is a very fundamental difference.

Albert Mathiez goes to the heart of the matter in *The High Cost of Living and the Social Movement under the Terror*: he makes economic freedom and control the stakes of the struggle between the sans-culottes and the propertied classes when he shows how the Intransigents were opposed to the right of property and to the right to live. But hadn't many Montagnards made the same distinction? Mathiez, who puts the question of foodstuffs above all, and rightly stresses a *violent and profound antagonism* between the system of "overall maximum," the economic terror the sans-culottes wanted, and the "aspirations of a society passionately taken up with the idea of liberty,"[15]

[14] *La Commune du dix août 1792. Etude sur l'histoire de Paris du 20 juin au 2 décembre 1792* (1911), Introduction, p. ii.

[15] *La Vie chère et le mouvement social sous la Terreur* (1927), Conclusion, p. 611.

which were the aspirations of the bourgeoisie, neglects the political incompatibility between the sans-culottes' democracy and the revolutionary government, overestimating the role of Robespierre.

In contrast, Daniel Guérin, in *The Class Struggle under the First Republic*, calls Robespierre the precursor of Thermidorian reactionism. He saw the Parisian sans-culottes as a vanguard and its attempts during the year 11 as an embryo of proletarian revolution; thus he verifies the theory of permanent revolution according to which the proletarian revolution of the twentieth century can already be seen in the framework of the bourgeois revolution of the eighteenth century. "In 1793, the bourgeois revolution is an embryo of a proletarian revolution, the one riding on the back of the other."[16] Thus we find the problems of our time transferred to the eighteenth century: the sans-culottes artisans and shopkeepers are placed in a proletarian factory environment, are transformed, taken for a proletarian vanguard, when actually they occasionally formed a rear guard, defending traditional economic positions. This denies the very specific character of the popular movement under the Revolution.

Therefore, most of the historians, whether they considered popular action to be under the wing of the bourgeoisie and essentially directed against the aristocracy and the ancien régime, and thus integrated perfectly into the bourgeois revolution, or whether they saw it as a precursory movement of the social struggles of the nineteenth and twentieth centuries, have a tendency to underestimate the original and specific character of the popular revolution.

It is quite evident that the sans-culottes had always fought against the aristocracy and royal absolutism. The events of the fourteenth of July prove this, as do Valmy and the patriotic enthusiasm of the volunteers. The sans-

[16] *La Lutte des classes sous la première République. Bourgeois et "bras nus"* (1793-1795), 2 vols. (1946), I, 8.

culottes furnished the revolutionary bourgeoisie with the indispensable manpower for bringing down the ancien régime and for routing the coalition. They also constituted an element that, in many respects, was in opposition to the bourgeoisie. They could not change the general direction of the Revolution, but this did not mean they did not pursue their own objectives, often in alliance with the bourgeoisie, occasionally in opposition. The sans-culottes, like the peasants, tended to look beyond the downfall of the aristocracy, toward goals that were not precisely those of the revolutionary ruling class. A specific sans-culottes current also developed in the same way that a current of peasant autonomy existed.

We must look for the origins of the position held by the artisan and shopkeeping class in the heart of the society of the ancien régime during the course of the economic crisis on which the work of G. E. Labrousse has thrown new light, that is, the deterioration of living conditions among the working classes in Paris well before 1789. The sans-culottes were set in motion as much by the aristocratic plot as by the food crisis. This popular current is specific in its origins and even in its procedures and political organizations: general assemblies and Parisian sections, where the sans-culottes were all-powerful in the year II, and especially in those sectional societies founded during the autumn of 1793. What a difference there is between these and the popular societies of the *censitaire* period! What a greater difference still, even in the year II, between a sectional society and a Jacobin club! Finally, the sans-culottes movement was specific and autonomous in its crises: for example, that of the summer of 1793, which ended in September 5 and 6, described by Mathiez as being *forced by Hébert*, by Daniel Guérin as specifically a workingman's demonstration, and which was really "sans-culottes days," which Hébert, Chaumette and the Paris Commune took part in rather than led. These events had no precedent in the general trend of the Revolution: the sans-culottes claimed rights to the taxation of foodstuffs and over the regulations regarding their commerce, which the Jacobin bourgeoisie granted them on September 29, 1793 (Vendémiaire, year II), but under pressure.

Thus in the last analysis the specific nature of the sans-culottes' activities is brought to light. Insistent upon controls, upon taxation, which were characteristic of the ancien régime system of production and exchange, they remained on the whole hostile to the values of the bourgeoisie, which took part in the assemblies and staffed the ministries, and did not falter until it had installed the brand of liberty favorable to its enterprises. The thinking of the Parisian sans-culottes was often identical to that of the peasants, who, faced with the advances made by capitalist agriculture and imbued with a spirit of agrarian individualism, were desperately eager to defend their rural communities and the collective rights that ensured their survival. In addition to the conflict between the Third Estate and the feudal aristocracy, two Frances appeared to be confronting one another: that of the artisan and journeyman, of the shopkeeper, of the peasant smallholder, and that of the large farmers, powerful merchants and leaders of industry.

Social antagonism in the meantime increased twofold as a result of opposing political factions. Since 1789, the popular movement tended toward decentralization and local autonomy—a distant possibility, deeply felt, and for a long time suppressed by the overriding necessity of strong monarchical power which was to come to the surface under the Revolution. Little concerned with sounding public opinion, Tocqueville did not touch upon it: it was opposed to the central thesis of his book,[17] which attributes the whole course of the ancien régime to centralization. The war once again made centralization necessary. During the spring of 1793, the need for national defense restored the unity of the remaining revolutionary *tiers*, who alone were capable of guaranteeing public safety. The people forced a revolutionary government, a mass uprising and a

[17] *Souvenirs.*

controlled economy, which had to feed the cities and bolster the armies. But the bourgeoisie, who from the beginning had held the reins of the Revolution, saw in the Montagnards another attempt to assume control. Would the sans-culottes be content to obey? The revolutionary government had been created to conduct the war on the frontiers and thereby to bring about the downfall of the aristocracy: but having brought a strong and centralized government to power, would the sans-culottes support it? The conflict grew because of the differences of background and political behavior: could the sans-culottes have the same concept of democracy and revolutionary dictatorship as the bourgeoisie?

The social and political struggles became complex. The evolution of history cannot be reduced to a mechanical schema; rather, it is a dialectical movement. Lest they distort by simplifying, historians must be aware of the complexities that make history so rich, as well as the contradictions that give it its dramatic character.

Although the sources of the history of this popular current, which from the spring of 1789 to the spring of 1795 animated the Revolution and often carried it forward, have suffered irreplaceable losses and exist only in the form of incomplete series or disparate collections of papers, they are nevertheless numerous enough, and appear to have been hardly referred to.

Essentially, they consist of the papers of the Parisian sections that survived the fire that destroyed the Archives of the Prefecture of Police in May 1871. Organized by the municipal law of May 21–June 27, 1790, the forty-eight sections of Paris were dissolved on 19 Vendémiaire, year IV; they succeeded the sixty districts created by royal decree on April 13, 1789. To the papers they received from the districts, the sections added a collection of important archives: records of the debates in the general assemblies, verbatim reports of the sessions of civil, revolutionary, military, charity and saltpeter committees, correspondence with other sections and various administrative authorities (Commune, *département*, National Assemblies), enrollment registers, security cards, passports, not to mention the papers of numerous popular societies, gathered when they disappeared during the spring of the year II or during the year III. In the year IV, these archives were transferred by the disbanded sections to the twelve municipalities that replaced them; many were subsequently catalogued.

During the previous year, the revolutionary committees of the sections likewise had handed over their papers to the twelve committees of district surveillance, according to the law of 7 Fructidor, year II.

In the meantime, the archives of the revolutionary committees, and those of the sections, were not transmitted to the new organizations without considerable pruning. After the execution of Hébert, and later still, after Thermidor, when the course of the Revolution, for a while deflected on account of the popular movement, began once again to reflect the particular quality of the men of '89, the sans-culottes officials of the Paris sections and committees were particularly careful to take certain precautions. We find mention of this in documents of Prairial, year III, when warrants for the disarmament and arrest of former Terrorists were tampered with. The commissions of inquiry named for this purpose hastened to lay claim to the papers of the year II, in order to see whether there were any motives for the repression of Terrorists. Registers often were burnt, or compromising pages torn out. Whatever the importance of the destruction of documents after 9 Thermidor, there was a considerable mass of files and registers which the revolutionary committees in Vendémiaire, year II—and a year later the sections themselves—transferred to the organs that replaced them, the committees of surveillance and municipal districts.

What happened to this invaluable collection? It is difficult to follow the history of the archives of the forty-eight sections of Paris with any accuracy. On what date and according to what system were these papers, first re-

grouped at the twelve municipalities incorporated during
Vendémiaire, year IV, transferred, either to the National
Archives, where a collection of registers of some importance is to be found, or to the Archives of the Prefecture
of Police, where, although it is reasonable that the series
of verbatim reports of the police commissars of the sections should have been found almost intact, it is curious
that the registers of the general assemblies should be
found to have been deposited as well? It is virtually impossible to answer these questions. One thing is sure, however: between September and November of 1834,
Barthélemy Saint-Hilaire removed certain valuable documents from the Archives of the Prefecture of Police, where
there used to be "more than 300 registers from the sections." These verbatim reports from the sections gave
Michelet the tremendous variety of their accounts of "the
great tragedies of revolutionary Paris." Finally it was also
at the Prefecture of Police that Mortimer-Ternaux consulted the sections' papers for his *History of the Terror,*
thereby discovering the absence of the registers of three
sections. Some were in fact kept in the archives of the
municipalities where they had been placed in the year II,
as were those of the *Postes* section, discovered at the town
hall of the second arrondissement and deposited in 1891
in the Seine Archives. A major portion of the sectional
papers kept in the archives of the Prefecture of Police
were destroyed during the fire of May 1871. Only the
verbatim reports of the police commissars and the pages
that Barthélemy Saint-Hilaire, in order not to have to
transcribe them, had cut out with scissors from the registers themselves, escaped this disaster. The majority of
the latter, along with the collection of Saint-Hilaire's papers, are to be found in the Victor Cousin Library. The
losses incurred by the May 1871 fire are irreplaceable.

In the meantime, the haphazard distribution of the
archives of the sections, the lack of scruple on the part of
Saint-Hilaire and the existence of an important collection
formed from sectional papers at the Bibliothèque Na-
tionale permit further reconstruction of an imposing col-

lection of documents essential for those who wish to study
the history of the Parisian sans-culottes. Numbers of sectional papers are to be found elsewhere, distributed in the
various revolutionary series of the National Archives: these
papers have still to be sorted, in order not to overlook
documents of crucial importance. Thus, in the archives
of the revolutionary assemblies that compose Series C, the
motions, addresses and petitions of the general assemblies
and of the popular societies are still to be found, though
less frequently, among the papers of the Legislative Committee of the Convention. Series F7, and in particular the
funds of the Public Safety Committee and its inexhaust-
ible alphabetic series, form a group of documents of great
importance, especially for the study of the revolutionary
activists of the Parisian sections. Lastly, one must mention
the archives of the revolutionary tribunal and of the military commissions of the year iii, grouped together in Series
W. The collection of revolutionary archives between 1790
and the year iv appears to be the necessary complement
to the various sectional deposits—a vast field, where the
joy of discovery often offers recompense to the patience
of the decipherer.

Although today the collection of papers left behind by
the Parisian sections and by their various committees upon
their dissolution appears to be in a mutilated state, it
attests to the tremendous activity of the sections and committees and their basic roles in the Revolution. Nevertheless, we find by piecing together the bills and documents
divided among various repositories, that these reports are
many and varied. The study of these papers cannot but
shed light upon the history of the Revolution and allow
us to determine the real role of the Parisian sans-culottes,
without whose co-operation the bourgeoisie would not
have been victorious.

To the study of the Convention and its committees
and to that of the Paris Commune, which up until now
have held the particular attention of the historian, I in-

tend to add that of the Parisian people in its general assemblies and its sectional societies; by shifting focus, new aspects will appear, which will further our knowledge. The history of the "great tragedies of revolutionary Paris," to use Michelet's expression once again, developed on various levels: that of the Convention and its committees, that of the Commune, the sections themselves, that of the general movement of the Revolution and that of the popular current. Between 1793 and the year ii, one confronts two sets of problems. The first is political: how to reconcile the sans-culottes' concept of appropriate behavior with the exigencies of the revolutionary dictatorship and the necessities of national defense. In other words, how to resolve the problem of the relationship between popular democracy and the revolutionary government. Another problem, of a social nature, also becomes apparent: how to reconcile the economic aspirations and demands of the sans-culottes with the exigencies of the bourgeoisie, which remained the leader of the Revolution. In other words, how do we resolve the problem of the relations between the masses and the propertied classes?

It is important that we should at this point show, within the Parisian cadre, that the popular current possessed its own autonomy and specificity, and that we should grant it an important place in the history of the Revolution, first, to enrich our understanding of the period, but also to integrate this understanding more accurately with the perspective of the origins of contemporary France, and thereby contribute to the stress on the original characteristics of French national history.

THE REVOLUTIONARY CALENDAR

VENDÉMIAIRE	(Sept. 22–Oct. 21)
BRUMAIRE	(Oct. 22–Nov. 20)
FRIMAIRE	(Nov. 21–Dec. 20)
NIVÔSE	(Dec. 21–Jan. 19)
PLUVIÔSE	(Jan. 20–Feb. 18)
VENTÔSE	(Feb. 19–Mar. 20)
GERMINAL	(Mar. 21–Apr. 19)
FLORÉAL	(Apr. 20–May 19)
PRAIRIAL	(May 20–June 18)
MESSIDOR	(June 19–July 18)
THERMIDOR	(July 19–Aug. 17)
FRUCTIDOR	(Aug. 18–Sept. 16)

Each month was composed of thirty days, with five supplementary days falling at the end of each calendar year.

This calendar was used from September 22, 1792, through year IV.

THE PARISIAN SECTIONS

(from a 1790 map)

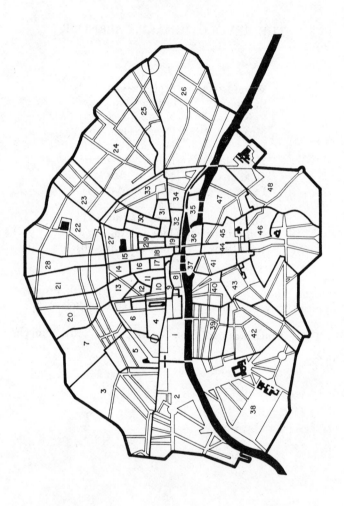

Historical Table of the Parisian Sections
May 21, 1790–19 Vendémiaire, year IV

1. *Tuileries* section (1790–year IV).
2. *Champs-Elysées* section (1790–year IV).
3. *Roule* section; renamed *République* (October 1792–30 Prairial, year III); restored to *Roule* (30 Prairial, year III–year IV).
4. *Palais-Royal* section; renamed *Butte-des-Moulins* (August 1792–August 1793); becomes *Montagne* section (August 1793–21 Frimaire, year III); restored to *Butte-des-Moulins* (21 Frimaire, year III–year IV).
5. *Place-Vendôme* section; renamed *Piques* (September 1792–5 Prairial, year III); restored to *Place-Vendôme* (5 Prairial, year III–year IV).
6. *Bibliothèque* section; renamed *Quatre-Vingt-Douze* (September 1792–October 1793); renamed *Lepeletier* (October 1793–year IV).
7. *Grange-Batelière* section; renamed *Mirabeau* (August–December 1792); renamed *Mont Blanc* (December 1792–year IV).
8. *Louvre* section; renamed *Muséum* (May 6, 1793–year IV).
9. *Oratoire* section; renamed *Gardes-Françaises* (September 1792–year IV).
10. *Halle-au-Blé* section.
11. *Postes* section; renamed *Contrat-Social* (August 18, 1792–year IV).
12. *Place Louis XIV* section; renamed *Mail* (August 1792–September 1793); became *Guillaume-Tell* section (September 1793–Messidor, year III); restored to *Mail* (Messidor, year III–year IV).
13. *Fontaine-Montmorency* section; renamed *Molière-et-Lafontaine* (October 1792–September 12, 1793); became *Brutus* section (September 12, 1793–year IV).
14. *Bonne-Nouvelle* section.

15. *Ponceau* section; renamed *Amis-de-la-Patrie* (September 1792–year IV).

16. *Mauconseil* section; renamed *Bon-Conseil* (August 1792–year IV).

17. *Marché-des-Innocents*; renamed *Halles* (September 1792–May 1793); became *Marchés* (May 1793–year IV).

18. *Lombards* section.

19. *Arcis* section.

20. *Faubourg-Montmartre* section.

21. *Poissonnière* section.

22. *Bondy* section.

23. *Temple* section.

24. *Popincourt* section.

25. *Montreuil* section.

26. *Quinze-Vingts* section.

27. *Gravilliers* section.

28. *Faubourg-Saint-Denis*; renamed *Faubourg-du-Nord* (January 1793–year IV).

29. *Beaubourg* section; renamed *Réunion* (September 1792–year IV).

30. *Enfants-Rouges*; renamed *Marais* (September 1792–June 1793); became *l'Homme-Armé* section (June 1793–year IV).

31. *Roi-de-Sicile* section; renamed *Droits-de-l'Homme* (August 1792–year IV).

32. *L'Hôtel-de-Ville* section; renamed *Maison-Commune* (August 21, 1792–Fructidor, year II); became *Fidélité* (Fructidor, year II–year IV).

33. *Place-Royale*; renamed *Fédérés* (August 1792–July 4, 1793); became *Indivisibilité* (July 4, 1793–year IV).

34. *Arsenal* section.

35. *l'Ile Saint-Louis* section; renamed *Fraternité* (November 1792–year IV).

36. *Notre Dame* section; renamed *Cité* (August 1792–21 Brumaire, year II); became *Raison* section (21–25 Brumaire, year II); restored to *Cité* (25 Brumaire, year II–year IV).

37. *Henri IV* section; *Pont-Neuf* (August 14, 1792–September 7, 1793); became *Révolutionnaire* section (September 7, 1793–1 Frimaire, year III); restored to *Pont-Neuf* (10 Frimaire, year III–year IV).

38. *Invalides* section.

39. *Fontaine-de-Grenelle* section.

40. *Quatre-Nations* section; renamed *Unité* (April 1793–year IV).

41. *Théâtre-Français* section; renamed *Marseille* (August 1792–August 1793); became *Marseille-et-Marat* (August 1793–Pluviôse, year II); became *Marat* section (Pluviôse, year II–22 Pluviôse, year III); restored to *Théâtre-Français* (22 Pluviôse, year III–year IV).

42. *Croix-Rouge* section; renamed *Bonnet-Rouge* (October 3, 1793–Germinal, year III); renamed *Bonnet-de-la-Liberté* (Germinal–Prairial, year III); became *Ouest* section (Prairial, year III–year IV).

43. *Luxembourg* section; renamed *Mucius-Scaevola* (Brumaire, year II–Prairial, year III); restored to *Luxembourg* (Prairial, year III–year IV).

44. *Thermes-de-Julien*; renamed *Beaurepaire* (September 8, 1792–20 Pluviôse, year II); *Chalier* (20 Pluviôse, year II–Pluviôse, year III); restored to *Thermes-de-Julien* (Pluviôse, year III–year IV).

45. *Sainte-Geneviève*; renamed *Panthéon-Français* (August 1792–year IV).

46. *Observatoire* section.

47. *Jardin-des-Plantes*; renamed *Sans-Culottes* (August 1792–10 Ventôse, year III); restored to *Jardin-des-Plantes* (10 Ventôse, year III–year IV).

48. *Gobelins* section; renamed *Finistère* (August 1792–year IV).

I

POPULAR MASSES AND MILITANT SANS-CULOTTES: THEIR ATTITUDES AND SOCIAL COMPOSITION

From June 1793 to February 1794, the Parisian sans-culottes movement allowed the consolidation of the revolutionary government and the organization of the dictatorship of public safety, while at the same time imposing upon a reluctant Convention economic measures considered right for ameliorating the lot of the masses. If over and beyond these aspects one attempts to examine the precise motive for the movement of popular action a problem presents itself—the social definition of the Parisian sans-culottes, that is, an analysis of its composition.

This is particularly difficult. The economic or fiscal documents that would permit a detailed analysis are absent. The few statistics available are characterized by a lack of thoroughness and precision. One can grasp the social characteristics of the sans-culottes mainly through political documents, particularly the dossiers of the anti-Terrorist repression of the year III. On the other hand, the antagonism between two social classes allows us to define the outlook and behavior of the Parisian sans-culottes in terms of what they opposed. As far as can be discerned, the absence of class consciousness accounts for the social opposition of the Parisian population, and also for the social composition of the political officials of the sections.

2

1. THE POPULAR CONSCIOUSNESS OF SOCIAL ANTAGONISMS

If we are to attempt to discern the social characteristics of the sans-culottes, it is important first to draw attention to the manner in which they defined themselves. Texts of this nature abound, giving us an approximate idea.

Ostensibly, the sans-culottes were recognizable by their costume, which set them apart from the upper strata of the former Third Estate. Robespierre used to differentiate between *golden breeches* and *sans-culottes*. The sans-culottes themselves made the same distinction. Noting the intrigues that undermined the Sceaux Committee of Surveillance, the observer Rousseville, in his report on 25 Messidor, year II, stresses the antagonism between the "silk-stockings" and the sans-culottes. Conventions of dress also pitted sans-culottes against the *muscadins* [royalist sympathizers]. Arrested on 4 Prairial, year III, for having said that "the blasted muscadins'll soon have a spade up there . . .", and questioned as to what he meant by these words, Barack, a clockmaker's assistant of the *Lombards* section, replied that "as far as he was concerned, muscadins were those who were well dressed." Gunner Fonatine, from *Réunion*, was arrested on 5 Prairial: he spoke of nothing but revenging himself against the muscadins, describing them as "those who on guard duty strike me as being better dressed."

Costume was accompanied by particular social behavior. Again, on this subject, the sans-culottes declared their stand through opposition. In the year II, the manners of the ancien régime were no longer acceptable. The sans-culottes refused to adopt a subordinate position in social relations. Jean-Baptiste Gentil, timber merchant, arrested on 5 Pluviôse, year II, for not having fulfilled his duties toward the Republic, was reprimanded for his public demeanor: "One had to approach him with hat in hand, the word *sir* was still used in his household, he retains an air of superiority"; also he had never been regarded as being a good citizen. The principal charge against Gannal, iron merchant from the *Réunion* section, arrested on 7 Frimaire, was his "haughty manner toward his workers." Paul Bonjour, adjutant in the fourth division of the naval ministry, was denounced in Frimaire by the popular society of *Poissonnière*, less for having been first valet of the wardrobe to a former member of Court than for having preserved the tone and manners of Court; his face alone betrays "the movements of a heart gangrened with aristocratic sentiments."

The sans-culottes often estimated a person's worth by external appearance, deducing character from costume and political convictions from character; everything that jarred their sense of equality was suspect of being "aristocratic." It was difficult, therefore, for any person of the old regime to find favor in their eyes, even when there was no specific charge against him. "For such men are incapable of bringing themselves to the heights of our revolution; their hearts are always full of pride and we shall never forget their former grandeur and their domination over us."

These were the motives for the arrest by the revolutionary committee of the *République* section on October 16, 1793 (25 Vendémiaire, year II), of the Duke of Brancas-Céreste, specifying he still enjoyed an income of 89,980 livres. The sans-culottes tolerated neither pride nor disdain; those were aristocratic sentiments contrary to the spirit of fraternity that existed between equal citizens and implied a hostile political stand toward democracy as practiced by the sans-culottes in their general assemblies and in their popular societies. These character traits appeared frequently in reports justifying the arrest of suspects.

On September 17, 1793 (Fructidor, year I), the committee of the *Révolutionnaire* section decided to arrest

Etienne Gide, clock merchant, who had supported the Brissotins; he was also accused of being haughty and proud and of often speaking *ironically*. On October 12, one bourgeois, a solicitor, was arrested by the revolutionary committee of *Réunion*: he had risen to support aristocrats in the general assemblies; more particularly, he demonstrated a "haughty manner toward the sans-culottes." Langlois, an architect from *Gravilliers*, was a partisan of liberty, but liberty "without equality"; he persistently demonstrated the greatest disdain toward the "poor sans-culottes." He was arrested on October 19, 1793. On 28 Brumaire, the committee of the *Marchés* section decided to arrest a music merchant, Bayeux. During the course of a meeting of the sectional general assembly, he had declared that it was "an abomination to see a cobbler acting as president of the meeting, and such a badly dressed one at that." According to the revolutionary committee of *Bon-Conseil*, Joseph Cataire, process server, was a snob, indifferent; more particularly, he was contemptuous of the sans-culottes. He was arrested for incivism[1] on 28 Frimaire. A hardware merchant by the name of Gence from the *Marchés* section had also "given evidence of contempt toward the sans-culottes." He was arrested on 22 Germinal, for "known incivism." In *Contrat-Social*, a clockmaker by the name of Brasseur was arrested on 23 Floréal; he was particularly reprimanded for having said that "it was most disagreeable for a man in his position to find himself in a platoon of guards among people one wouldn't choose to know."

Even more serious, according to the sans-culottes, than a haughty or disdainful manner toward themselves or straightforward indifference were statements referring to them as being of a lower social order. In its report of 8 Frimaire on Louis-Claude Cezeron, arrested for being a "suspect," the committee of the *Poissonnière* section made a particular case of a statement made during a meet-

---

[1] Editor's note: Word coined during the early years of the Republic applying specifically to the lack of loyalty to the principles of the Revolution.

ing of the general assembly on the preceding May 31 (12 Prairial): "that the poor depended on the rich and that the sans-culottes were never any more than the lowest order possible." Bergeron, a skin merchant from *Lombards*, said that "although he understood that the sans-culottes were fulfilling their duty as citizens . . . it would be better for them to go about their work rather than meddle in politics." He was arrested on suspicion on 18 Pluviôse.

The sans-culottes refused to tolerate others taking advantage of their social or economic status to impose upon them. Lawyer Truchon, from *Gravilliers*, denounced on several occasions by Jacques Roux in his *Publiciste*,[2] was finally arrested on 9 Prairial, year II: the revolutionary committee reprimanded him for having influenced "short-sighted" citizens, and for having stated that "for a place in government, one needed education, money and time to waste." Anthéaume, a former abbé, instructor of young pupils of the Patrie in *Guillaume-Tell*, was arrested on 16 Brumaire: he was reprimanded for "pride and intolerable pedagogy contrary to equality and the simplicity of a good republican."

The sans-culottes had an egalitarian concept of social relations. Their behavior also concealed realities which were more specific. To what extent were they seized upon and expressed?

The most clearly stated social friction in popular awareness was that which pitted aristocrat against sans-culotte: it was against the aristocrats that the sans-culottes addressed themselves from July 14 to August 10, and against whom they continued to battle. The address of the sans-culottes society of Beaucaire before the Convention of September 8, 1793, is significant: "We are sans-culottes . . . poor and virtuous, we have formed a society of artisans and peasants . . . we know who our friends are: those who freed us from the clergy and from the nobility, from feudalism, from tithes, from royalty and

2 *Publiciste de la République française par l'Ombre de Marat.*

from all the plagues that follow in its wake; we are those whom the aristocrats call anarchists, factionists, Maratists."

The nature of the class struggle was even more clearly stated in the address of the Dijon Popular Society on 27 Nivôse, year II: "We must be one people, and not two nations, opposed . . . all recognized aristocratic individuals without exception should be condemned to death by decree." According to mechanic Guyot, from *République*, "all the nobles, without exception, deserve to be guillotined."

At this point, the aristocracy was the main enemy of the sans-culottes. Ultimately, they managed to include in this term all their adversaries, although these might not necessarily belong to the quondam nobility, but to the upper echelons of the former Third Estate. In this way the role of the sans-culottes is imprinted upon the Revolution, and further demonstrates the autonomy of their action.

On July 25, 1792, the *Louvre* section announced the fall of the King, at the same time denouncing the hereditary aristocracy, "the ministerial, financial and bourgeois aristocrats, and particularly the hierarchy of recalcitrant priests." By the year II, the meaning of the word "aristocrat" was extended to embrace all the social classes against which the sans-culottes were struggling. Thus we have the significant expression "bourgeois aristocracy," which so often turns up in contemporary documents. Hence the specifically popular definition, coined by an anonymous petitioner in the year II, which has both political and social connotations: the aristocrat was one who regretted the passing of the ancien régime and disapproved of the Revolution, did nothing to further its cause, did not swear his allegiance to it, did not enlist in the National Guard; one who did not purchase expropriated land, although he might have had the means to do so; one who left land uncultivated without selling it at its true value, or leasing it, or giving a half share in the produce. The aristocrat was also he who did not give work to laborers or journeymen, although he might be in a position to do so, and "at a wage commensurate with food prices"; did not subscribe to contributions for the volunteers; and had done nothing to improve the lot of his poor and patriotic countrymen. The real patriot was he who took a contrary attitude on every possible occasion. The term aristocrat in the end, therefore, designated all the opponents of the sans-culottes, bourgeois as well as noble, those who formed "the class of citizens from whom one should take the billion we have to levy throughout the Republic." The most extreme sans-culottes did not use the term "aristocrat" for the old nobility, but for the bourgeoisie. On May 21, 1793, a popular orator from the *Mail* section declared that "aristocrats are all the people with money, all the fat merchants, all the monopolists, law students, bankers, pettifoggers and anyone who has something."

The economic crisis had contributed to bringing social clashes to a head: to the fundamental hostility between sans-culotte and aristocrat was added that of the sans-culottes and the upper sectors of the Third Estate, to the extent that it increased their differences and disunited the Patriotic Party of 1789. A note sent to the Public Safety Committee in Pluviôse, year II, pointed out the existence of two parties in the *Brutus* section: that of the people, the sans-culottes, and the other consisting of "bankers, money changers, rich people." An address delivered before the Convention on 27 Ventôse mentioned the brave sans-culottes, who were opposed not only to the clergy, the nobility, royal coalitions, but also to attorneys, lawyers, notaries and also all "those fat farmers, those egotists, and those fat, rich merchants: they're at war against us, and not against our tyrants."

Was this the "haves" against the "have-nots"? Not precisely. As far as the sans-culottes were concerned, artisans and shopkeepers belonged to the propertied classes. More particularly, the friction was between those who believed in the notion of limited and controlled ownership and the partisans of total ownership rights such as were proclaimed in 1789. Or the opposition between those who believed in controls and taxation, and those in favor of economic freedom; the opposition between consumer and producer.

Contemporary documents, over and beyond these basic reactions or distinctive statements, also allow us to explore the nuances of the social antagonisms expressed by the sans-culottes with some accuracy. They denounced "respectable people," meaning by this those who possessed, if not riches, then at least leisure and culture, the better-educated citizens, the better-dressed, those conscious if not proud of their leisure and their education. They denounced the propertied classes, that is to say, those who had unearned incomes. Finally, they denounced the rich in general, not only the propertied classes or the "haves," but also the "big men" as opposed to the "little men," which they were. The sans-culottes were not against property already owned by artisans and shopkeepers, and which journeymen aspired to possess, provided that it was limited.

The expression "respectable people" was first heard after June 2 (13 Prairial), when sans-culottes and moderates opposed one another on political and social platforms. The term was first applied to the bourgeoisie opposed to equality, but ended by having as wide a connotation as the term "aristocrat," and embracing all the enemies of the sans-culottes. On 12 Nivôse, year II, a certain Berberat was arrested. He was opposed to the events of 31 May (12 Prairial); he had referred to the patriots as lay-abouts; in short, "he tended to lean more toward the so-called respectable people or, to be more explicit, toward the aristocrats rather than the sans-culottes." Gence, a hardware merchant from *Marchés*, arrested on 22 Germinal, gave evidence, in June 1793 (Prairial, year I), of being partisan of "those formerly called respectable people." A certain Lamarre, lemonade vendor from the *Bon-Conseil* section, was arrested on 5 Prairial, year III; he consistently raised his voice against "respectable people," demanding before the assembly that they all be guillotined. As for washerwoman Rombaut, she stated that every single one of those so-called "respectable people" should be guillotined.

If the sans-culottes ironically called their adversaries "respectable people," the latter did not fail to treat them as rabble; thus, with two expressions, the lines for social clashes were drawn. On September 25, 1793 (4 Vendémiaire, year II), carpenter Bertout was arrested on the orders of the committee of the *République* section: he had declared a desire for "another government being established to oppose the rabble, because respectable people were lost." Among the charges leveled against a certain Appert, arrested on grounds of suspicion on 25 Brumaire, year II, the revolutionary committee of *Lombards* made a particular case concerning those patriots accused of "making attempts to replace respectable people with rabble." In documents dated year III, one occasionally comes across the expressions "respectable people" and "agitators" placed in opposition to each other, the latter being the political sans-culottes personnel of the year II. It is often difficult to qualify these expressions in terms of social attitudes among existing factions. On 16 Pluviôse, year II, the committee of surveillance of the sixth arrondissement mentioned the stormy scenes that took place between "respectable people" and "forty-penny men" in the *Lombards* section general assembly, proving the existence of opposition between the leisured and wealthy classes and those who worked with their hands.

This opposition was further expressed in the animosity between the sans-culottes and those who possessed unearned incomes, a situation that came to a head during the autumn of 1793, when the economic crisis and the difficulties of daily living resulted in increased class antagonism. The fact of being independently wealthy gave cause for suspicion. On September 18, 1793 (2d supplementary day of year I), the revolutionary committee of *Mucius-Scaevola* ordered the arrest of Duval, first secretary of the Paris Police, on two counts: for contempt toward the assemblies of that section, and for enjoying an income of 2,000 livres. The Duke of Brancas-Céreste was arrested on October 16, 1793 (25 Vendémiaire, year II), by the revolutionary committee of *République* on account of his status of former noble, but also because he still had an income of 89,980 livres. On 2 Germinal, the revolutionary committee of the *Mont Blanc* section issued a warrant for the arrest of Jean-François Rivoire, formerly a colonist in Santo Domingo: he had not signed the Constitution, he had never contributed to the funds, nor had he served in the Guard. Further, he had an income of 16,000 livres. In one extreme case a certain Pierre Becquerel from *Guillaume-Tell* was arrested on 19 Ventôse during a raid by the police in the Gardens of Equality, simply for having said he had a private income. On the preceding 2 Frimaire, the *Lepeletier* popular society adopted a petition to exclude from all government posts not only former nobles, the sons of secretaries to the king, brokers and dealers, but also all persons known to possess incomes of more than 3,000 livres. Posts vacated by this measure would be reserved for sans-culottes. These latter were not therefore opposed to all forms of income from investments, but only to the very wealthy. Among the sectional political officials of the year II there were numbers of persons with private incomes, retired artisans or small shopkeepers. Paper merchant Potin, police commissar from *Contrat-Social*, stated in May 1793 (Floréal, year I) that "it was necessary to apply an agrarian law to all incomes between 4,000 and 5,000 livres": according to the social ideals of artisans and shopkeepers.[3]

The sans-culottes' hostility toward those with large private incomes was merely one particularly stressed aspect of their instinctive opposition to the rich. Extreme sans-culottes like Babeuf in the year IV were not far from considering the Revolution as a declared war "between the rich and the poor." The nature of this clash to a large

[3] Translator's note: "Agrarian," in this sense, refers to heavy taxation on incomes above this level.

extent characterized Terrorist sentiments. On May 5, 1793, near the Church of Saint-Germain-l'Auxerrois, Mistress Saunier was arrested for having "shouted out loud that it was necessary to start August 10 all over again, and to assassinate and slit the throats of all the rich people." In the year III similar proposals, even if suggested during the previous year, would have provided a motive for arrest. Delavier, wigmaker from *Bonne-Nouvelle*, was arrested on 12 Germinal for having boasted he had led the rich condemned by the Revolutionary Tribunal to the scaffold. Viguier, from the *Poissonnière* section, also a wigmaker, arrested on 5 Prairial, had stated "no one would be happy until the rich and the dandies have been wiped out." In *Amis-de-la-Patrie* Pierre Portier was arrested on 10 Prairial: on various occasions "he had expressed jealousy toward the rich." When sectional power was in the hands of the sans-culottes, full of animosity or hatred toward the rich, they did not fail to take discriminatory action against them. Wealth was often the motive for suspicion. Although wealth was rarely the only motive invoked, it often lent support to vague accusations.

If one is to believe the evidence brought forward that resulted in his jailing, Jean-Baptiste Mallais, cobbler, revolutionary commissar of *Temple* on 13 Ventôse, year II, was particularly down on the rich. He declared to one citizen that "he hadn't arrested him because he had placed him among the ranks of the sans-culottes, but that he had arrested his master because he arrested all rich persons." To a woman he maintained that "if her husband had a fortune of 20,000 livres, he would be guillotined; but since he hadn't a penny, he considered him a sans-culotte." These remarks, made with the intention of provocation, are nonetheless significant for their Terrorist outlook.

In *Droits-de-l'Homme* in August 1793 (Thermidor/Fructidor, year I), a citizen was refused a certificate of loyalty on the sole allegation that he was "well-to-do." On October 10 (Vendémiaire, year II), the committee of

Révolution ordered the arrest of Bapst, a jeweler from the Quai d'Orfevres: he frequented the society of moderates and aristocrats and he was "presumed to be worth 80,000 livres." On 26 Ventôse, Godefroy, a textile merchant from *Lombards*, was arrested; he too had caused trouble on various occasions in the general assemblies. In his case it was above all his social position that made him suspect: at Vernon, in Eure, he owned a cotton mill where he employed 120 women, old men and children; his revenues were as high as 16,122 livres. The revolutionary committee of *Quinze-Vingts*, on the other hand, could find no political charge against Jean-Baptiste Gentil, timber merchant, arrested on 5 Pluviôse for not having fulfilled his duties toward the Republic. His character and income of 24,722 livres were duly considered by the committee. The same charges were made against one Santerre, a former butter-and-muslin merchant from *Faubourg-du-Nord*, arrested on 24 Germinal: he had a private income; "his relatives have always moved in moneyed, that is to say, aristocratic circles"; "he has grown fat off the sweat of wage earners."

Thus the instinctive reactions of the poorest became the general attitude among the conscientious, and a rule of political conduct. At the end of July 1793 (Thermidor, year 1), when it appeared that the "haves" supported the actions of the "federalists," and formed a majority in the moderate party, a petition from the *Sans-Culottes* section demanded that the rich aristocrats be stripped and reduced to beggary. The petition, prepared by the Commune and presented on 5 Frimaire to the Convention, urged that the rich who had left Paris for the country be obliged to return, and denounced wealth as "a form of gangrene which corrupts everything it touches or which is dependent upon it." On 9 Ventôse, according to the observer Charmont, a member of the saltpeter commission in the *Chalier* section insisted that "he had never seen anyone so stingy as the rich citizens of this section"; whereas the poor made more sacrifices than they could afford, the rich thought twice. "We must batter down the doors of these snobs who have no concept of fatherland."

This deep-rooted tendency among the sans-culottes to speak against the rich was encouraged in the year II by the ruling politicians of the time. "Herein lies the revolution of the poor," wrote Michel Lepeletier in the National Education Project which Robespierre read before the Convention on July 12 and 29 of 1793 (Messidor/Thermidor, year I). And speaking on 8 Ventôse, Saint-Just said: "The unfortunate are the powerful on earth; they have the right to speak as masters to governments who neglect them." Without wanting to go into the details of the social concepts of the Montagnards and the Jacobins, and the notion that they should establish contact between different classes, or to question the sincerity of the followers of Robespierre, it is important to recognize that there was a tactical necessity in such a policy. The crisis of the Revolution from the spring to the autumn of 1793 made the popular alliance necessary: the sans-culottes formed the cadre that was to permit the most advanced faction of the bourgeoisie to quell the aristocracy and its allies. "The hidden danger," wrote Robespierre in his diary during the June 2 insurrection, "lies in the bourgeois; in order to conquer the bourgeois, it will be necessary to rally the people." A few representatives on special service in the départements—such as Fouché in the Nièvre—realized these necessities and resolutely adopted a social policy favorable to the popular classes. Those who did not belong to the government openly exploited the antagonism between the rich and the sans-culottes for political ends.

Jacques Roux, and Hébert after him, orchestrated this theme with many variations. The sans-culottes formed an important mass of workers who could be pitted against government committees; there is no doubt that Hébert and his friends thought of using them to attain their goals. Jacques Roux had already written, "*Ut redeat miseris abeat fortuna superbis*," on the masthead of his *Publiciste*. In a popular style, *Père Duchesne* castigated the rich and exalted the sans-culottes. The rich snob, the

14

rich do-nothing, the useless rich: these themes were taken
up in various forms. In this manner, Hébert illustrated an
idea that was common among the masses; but he strengthened it and contributed to giving to the sans-culottes a
clearer understanding of the antagonisms between classes.

The differences between the sans-culottes and the rich
were rounded out by the former's hostility toward business enterprise, and this hostility constituted one of the
fundamental currents of popular opinion during the year
II.

Being urban consumers, the Parisian sans-culottes were
naturally against those who controlled staple food supplies. Retailers, they blamed the wholesalers. Artisans or
journeymen, hardly workers in the actual meaning of the
word, they remained essentially small independent producers, hostile toward those who had interests in commercial capital. The economic crisis and political struggles
intensified this inherent antagonism among the sans-
culottes. Scarcity and high prices spiraled, and every merchant was soon suspect of being a monopolist or a shark.
The struggle against the Girondins and subsequently, after May 31, against the moderates, was often, at least on
the sectional level, turned into a struggle against the merchant bourgeoisie. The sans-culottes were insistent upon
taxation and controls, and the conflict deepened; to the
extent that they defended freedom of enterprise, the merchants became suspect. Henceforth, the sans-culottes
included with the noble aristocracy and the religious hierarchy the mercantile aristocracy as well. Through a
natural reversal of things when, in the year III, the moderates were on top, one of the complaints most often
made against the former Terrorists was the persecution of
the merchants: a memorandum issuing from the purged
Gravilliers section on 20 Germinal, year III, reads in part:
"It was from the top of this mountain that commerce was
destroyed."

In 1793 and in the year II, popular hostility against the

merchants was marked, in its moments of paroxysm, by violence and pillage. It was also marked by a constant desire for repression. According to a denunciation made in the year III, "if there was the slightest noise in the assemblies [in the *Marchés* section], it could be attributed to the merchants, who were threatened with every arm of the law"; this section being largely composed of merchants, they were treated as aristocrats; "the pillaging of grocers was justified by saying the people had the right to counter the greed of the grocers." In March of 1793 (Ventôse/ Germinal, year I), during the recruitment of troops for the Vendée campaign, collections for volunteers were often an occasion for the sans-culottes to confirm their hostility toward the merchants. In *Lombards*, Jean-Baptiste Larue, journeyman mason and member of the revolutionary committee, declared that the volunteers were "idiots if they left without each having a hundred pistoles in their pockets, that we should cut off the heads of all these buggers, those merchants, and that after this operation, the sums of money required would soon be found."

Once popular power was on firm ground, the title of merchant alone was often reason enough for suspicion on the part of revolutionary committees. They were encouraged by the Commune, whose arrests of the nineteenth of the first month ranged among their suspects "those who felt sorry for needy farmers and merchants, against whom the law must take measures." Certain committees had not expected this encouragement. After September 14, the committee of *Lombards*, where hostility toward the merchants was particularly strong, arrested a certain Dussautoy; he was reprimanded simply for being a wholesale grocer. In the beginning of October, the revolutionary committee of *Brutus* decided to arrest a linendraper by the name of Launay, residing in Rue Neuve-Saint-Eustache, for being "among those merchants of this street who swell the ranks of the Federalist Party in this section." In *Bon-Conseil*, the committee justified the arrest on 25 Brumaire of Jean-Louis Lagrave, wholesale grocer, merely because of his social behavior: "He spends his time among business people, snobs like himself, not consorting with any patriot . . . always flaunting his rank among the wholesalers, censuring and even molesting citizens, like most wholesalers."

Merchants continued to be arrested until the spring of the year II: on 18 Ventôse, the *Lombards* committee again ordered the arrest of Duthu, on 1 Germinal, that of Garillaud, against whom no charges were leveled, apart from their indifference to public affairs or their status of wholesale grocer or dry goods merchant.

The hostility of the sans-culottes toward business was not restricted to measures against individuals; this was a war against an entire social class that, although it did not seek to eliminate that class from politics, at least sought to curb its powers, to put a halt to its prejudicial activities. On October 3, 1793 (13 Vendémiaire, year II), the *Unité* general assembly demanded that merchants, whatever the nature of their business, be excluded from the tribunals. On 30 Nivôse, year II, this same section decided to name six commissars to watch over *every type* of merchant. On 27 Pluviôse, the popular society of *Bonne-Nouvelle* heard a speech delivered by Citizen Jault, member of the General Council of the Commune, condemning the mercantile aristocracy. Attacks against commerce and the merchants were also among the favorite themes of *Père Duchesne*. After Hébert's condemnation, and that of Chaumette, the arrest of merchants ceased, as did denunciations of commerce. The Public Safety Committee inaugurated a new commercial policy: the Commune authorities were serious in putting an end to a campaign contrary to traditional class patterns and in rehabilitating an occupation considered indispensable to the war effort.

The reaction set in finally after the year III, and the merchants made the most of their revenge against former Terrorists for the maltreatment to which they had been subjected. During Germinal and Prairial, a simple remark was sufficient motive for arrest. The food shortage, worse because the "maximum" had been abolished, once again increased hostility toward commerce among the sans-culottes. The dossiers of the anti-Terrorist repression offer ample evidence, allowing us to determine the precise nature of public opinion on this subject; this varied, circumstances permitting, from a simple expression of hostility to a suppressed desire for the elimination of a social class.

For having said, in year II, "Neither the merchants nor the rich are worth sparing," Davelin, a feather dealer from *Amis-de-la-Patrie,* was disarmed on 5 Prairial, year III. Jacques Barbant, from *Arsenal,* was arrested: he had made certain vague derogatory remarks about merchants. A harness maker by the name of Caillaud, from *Bon-Conseil,* was also arrested: he had said, "I trust that there will be an end to all this, and that the idiot merchants and fops will not always be our masters." Certain complaints give evidence of a deeper awareness of class warfare. In the year II, a man by the name of Barqui from *Bonne-Nouvelle* asked that the merchants be banned from the general assemblies and the popular societies, and from all civil or military functions. Employee Rose from *Lombards* was opposed to the admission of merchants to popular societies. Quéreau, a journeyman carpenter, declared, in Ventôse of the year II, that "no merchant, not even a match merchant, should be allowed on revolutionary committees."

From hostility toward commerce, the more aware or the more violent among the sans-culottes went on to justify pillage. If we are to believe a denunciation made in the year III, Gillet, one of the foremost militants of the popular society of the *Quinze-Vingts,* preached the pillage of commercial establishments to the workers of the Porte de la Rapée: "those merchants are rascals, scoundrels: to pity the lot of the unfortunate workers, to find that they earned too little, were the means he thought appropriate to inspire them with a taste for brigandage."

During the upheavals of February 25 and 26, 1793 (Ventôse, year I), cobbler Servière, revolutionary commissar of the *Muséum* section in the year II declared before the general assembly, in what was formerly the Germain church, "that he thoroughly approved of pillage and would be very much against having to oppose it." On 5 Prairial, year III, in *Gardes-Françaises*, Chesneaux, the former president of the Cordeliers Club, was reprimanded for having stated that "pillage had a moral goal." Carpenter Debon of *Quinze-Vingts* was rebuked "for having on several occasions incited pillage against the merchants, in claiming they were the cruelest enemy of the people." In *Bonne-Nouvelle*, water carrier Bergeron was arrested on 6 Pluviôse, in the year III, when "as a result of his provocations he incited the pillaging of the wood merchants." In some ways (Chesneaux stressed it when he said it had a moral goal), pillage corresponded to the fundamental egalitarianism of the sans-culottes: individual action was legitimated by the inequality of living conditions.

Beyond the offensive remarks or the exhortation to pillage, Terrorist exaltation and the desire for punitive measures show the deep-rooted hostility of the sans-culottes toward the commercial bourgeoisie. Many militants considered the threat of the guillotine in times of shortages an excellent remedy. To oblige farmers to sell their grain according to the official price, they insisted upon the creation of a revolutionary army. When this army was created, the sans-culottes constantly demanded that it be accompanied by a mobile guillotine, in order further to insure its efficaciousness. This outlook can be traced throughout all the Terrorists' abusive remarks made in the year II against the merchants. Widow Barbau, from *Indivisibilité*, a veritable harridan according to her denunciators, had the habit of declaring "that until the snobbish merchants, the aristocrats, the rich, etc., are guillotined or dispatched en masse, nothing will work out properly." Widow Barbau quite naturally placed the merchants before the aristocrats. In *Unité*, a certain Roux asked for the erecting of guillotines "on every street corner in Paris, on the doorsteps of every merchant, so that, he said, we can have cheap merchandise." In the year II, Calvet, a barber and former member of the *Lepeletier* civil committee, declared that the "maximum" would be met when two hundred merchants were sent daily to the guillotine.

In *Invalides,* the clockmaker Fagère declared that "when the aristocrats are finished, we'll take up with the merchant class again. . . ."

In the year III, shortages and misery still exacerbated sans-culottes' hatred of the merchants. Terrorist remarks abound in the dossiers of the repression. On 19 Ventôse, Jacques Rohait, a job printer from the *Panthéon-Français* section exasperated by the high cost of meat, said that "all those wretched merchants deserve to swing." In *Fraternité,* a certain Berthaud was disarmed for having declared on 2 Prairial "that the merchants were going to have to jump." Seeing the body of Representative Feraud being dragged through the streets on 1 Prairial, Mistress Maudrillon cried: "Bravo, next it'll be the merchants' turn."

During those Prairial days, frenzied offensive remarks were not unusual. Nicolas Barrucand, dyer, former revolutionary commissar of *Arsenal,* declared that on the feast day of Corpus Christi "the streets should be carpeted with the heads of merchants." Baudit, a jewel engraver from *Gardes-Françaises,* stirred up the crowds in Rue Saint-Honoré with the words: "Blasted merchants! Blackguards! . . . I'll eat 'em up, every bit of 'em."

The still vivid memories of the year II suggested to many sans-culottes the need for a return to organized terror in order to put an end to the merchants, as they had done to the aristocrats. Ferrier, a hatter from *Gardes-Françaises,* remembering the uprisings in Lyons, Marseilles and Bordeaux in 1793, and the repression which followed, declared that "the large communes composed entirely of merchants and the wealthy must be destroyed, their inhabitants humbled and put down." Baillieux, a tailor from the *Muséum* section and one-time member of the former revolutionary committee of that section, declared "that during the first revolution, all priests, nobles and merchants would be killed in their homes." The Barbot sisters, who had a shop in the haberdashery quarter of the *Gravilliers* section, declared on 1 Prairial that "if the Jacobins gain control, guillotines will be erected at every street intersection to do justice to all the aristocrats, moderates and merchants."

These texts reveal that the sans-culottes identified themselves by opposition to the aristocracy, riches, and to commerce—antagonisms that account for the imprecise nature of the social disinctions within the former Third Estate and the difficulty of defining the sans-culottes as a social class. The sans-culottes can be clearly defined only when compared to the aristocracy; when compared to the bourgeoisie, the distinction becomes less clear. Composed of many socially disparate elements, the sans-culottes were undermined by internal dissent, which explains both their inability to establish a coherent program and, in the last analysis, their political defeat.

A fundamental hostility toward the aristocracy was not, however, unique to the sans-culottes. In 1789 it was also shared by all members of the former Third Estate. When the crises of the Revolution reached new heights, the Third Estate dissociated itself from it, certain factions among the bourgeoisie envisaging a compromise similar to the British Revolution of 1688. But, in the year II, the Montagnard bourgeoisie, and particularly its Jacobin faction, remained the determined leaders of the struggle against the aristocracy, both at home and at the frontiers. The necessities of this struggle determined the entire policy of the revolutionary government.

Lower-class hostility toward riches and commerce was not without certain contradictions, even to the extent that sans-culottes themselves sometimes owned a workshop or store. Doubtless they always took care to state explicitly that their hostility was directed toward large ownership, big business. Hence we have *Père Duchesne*, whose rage was inspired "by those big men who continue to swallow up the little men." After having declared, "Fatherland be damned! Merchants don't have one," Hébert swiftly explained: "Not that I should be looked upon as being against commerce. No one has a higher regard for the

'respectable man' who lives by his industry than I do."
By this he presumably meant the independent artisan
and shop owner, small production and small business.
Hébert had no notion that the interests of the artisans
might be opposed to those of journeymen and workers.

Such contradictions, which threatened the unity of the
sans-culottes, can be found in certain documents where
the sans-culottes took care to define themselves in a positive manner. These documents are rare because they came
from the lower levels of society, but they nevertheless
stress the heterogeneous composition of the sans-culottes.

In certain documents, the sans-culottes were identified
with those who had nothing, with the proletariat, in the
traditional sense of the word. Defining the "spirit of the
Republic" in Brumaire, year II, in his *Précis sur la Révolution et le caractère Français,* Didot, president of the revolutionary committee of *Réunion,* contrasts the rich with
"the real patriots, for the most part indigent." The sans-
culottes defended the property of the rich, "and every
day the rich aristocrat steals the property of the people:
their rights, their subsistence, their liberty." In a poster
dated 27 Pluviôse, Erimante Lambin from *Chalier* denounced lawyers, attorneys, priests and nobles, comparing
them to the sans-culottes, *who have nothing.* Soon, Babeuf
was to speak of the *propertyless* sans-culottes. The "haves"
were also aware that among the patriots, the sans-culottes
formed the majority of the "have-nots." On July 5, 1793
(17 Messidor, year I), Chabot read the Jacobins a letter
from Ramel, who wrote from Toulouse that men of property alone could save the nation. "How," he asked them,
"can you allow your interests to be entrusted to others?
Should your weapons be given back to the sans-culottes?"
The clearest description of this situation, emanating from
the sans-culottes, comes in an indignant report from Pétion
delivered April 10, 1793 (Germinal, year I), before the
Convention: ". . . when we speak of the sans-culottes,
we do not mean all the citizens, except for the nobles
and the aristocrats, but men who have nothing, to distinguish them from men who have something."

Having nothing, the sans-culottes worked to keep alive; to be more precise, they worked with their hands. In certain texts, the meaning of the word is even more restricted, and at the time clarified. That the sans-culottes composed the mass of workers and that they constituted the "most precious class" of the nation, was a theme often exploited by Hébert, who knew that this was the way for him to reach his constituents. "Only the sans-culottes are worth considering," he wrote in September 1793 in *Père Duchesne;* "it is they who manufacture the fabrics of the clothes we wear, they who work the metals and manufacture arms that serve for the defense of the Republic." Opposed to "these hardworking artisans, exhausting themselves with their labors," are the bankers, financiers, merchants, monopolists, lawyers, "in a word, all the leeches feeding on the sans-culottes."

In its address to the Convention of September 24, 1793 (3 Vendémiaire, year II), the *Poissonnière* section drew a sharp distinction between rich snobs and "that hardworking segment of the population who live solely by their work." On 16 Messidor, year II, the revolutionary committee of *Bon-Conseil* suspended three saltpeter commissars: "they were men of substantial incomes and a pride which set them at odds with the needs of their workers," who were, of course, real sans-culottes. When arrested on 17 Germinal, year III, and questioned about his section, *Sans-Culottes,* Vingternier replied that it contained no other than "the people and the workers."

During the repression of the year III, the former militants were often reprimanded for having exploited class warfare to their own political ends, while the "haves" had had reason to conceal their identity. According to a note dated 17 Nivôse, the former revolutionary committee of *Bonne-Nouvelle* had sought "to lead astray the numerous workers lodged in chambers." Damilot, wine merchant and ramparts commissar of *Gardes-Françaises,* was accused of having been "the advisor and activist among the poor workers of the section." In denouncing on 20 Germinal "the faction that coined the absurd words muscadins and sans-culottes," the "respectable people" of *Bon-Conseil* reproached it for having ranged the citizens in two opposing classes. "In the first class, as if there should be two classes among republicans, these men of ill will grouped lawyers, those of independent means, men of letters, clerks and artists. In the second . . . they admitted only those worthy citizens accustomed to working with their hands. . . . They were constantly telling them that the richest, the better dressed, or the better educated were their enemies and were counterrevolutionaries, and, as if patriotism lay only in occupation and dress, they have so firmly established the privileges of the caste they call the sans-culottes, that they claim no other group can be patriots."

In spite of the malevolent intentions and the obvious exaggeration of the denunciators, this document indicates clearly that a small number of sans-culottes tended to give first place to "haves–have-nots" warfare, whereas the moderates, who returned to power in the year iii, tended toward the traditional Third Estate–aristocracy confrontation. The confused awareness of this confrontation was bound to contribute to the dissolution of the sans-culottes coalition, excluding artisans and shopkeepers who, although small owners, were nonetheless "haves."

Very much aware of the fundamental hostility of the ancien régime toward themselves, and full of hatred against the aristocracy—but here resembling the Montagnard bourgeoisie—the sans-culottes could not, of course, have a class consciousness. Divided into various categories, with aspirations that were on occasion divergent, they did not constitute a class as such; their unity was only negative. One last characteristic emphasizes this: the masses considered social characteristics insufficient to define a sans-culotte; a counterrevolutionary worker could not be a good sans-culotte, but a patriotic and republican bourgeois was willingly labeled one. Social classification was qualified by political tendencies; one meant nothing without the other. "Neither virtue nor patriotism," declared *Père Duchesne*, "is to be found except among the sans-culottes; without them, the Revolution would be lost . . . only the sans-culottes will save the Republic." Thus sans-culotte becomes synonymous with patriot and republican.

For the sans-culottes, this did not mean a verbal declaration of patriotism or a mere intellectual bent, but was a matter of political behavior. The sans-culottes took park in all the great events of the Revolution; they fought for the democratic Republic. To the general assembly of the *Marchés* section, which on 9 Prairial, year II, reprimanded him for having been a Terrorist, Hébert, tisane peddler and sans-culotte that he was, replied by listing his services to the nation: "Doubtless I am a Terrorist, but I gave proof of this only before the castle of the tyrant Capet on August 10, 1792, where my terrorism cost me my left arm. . . . I am a man of blood. But I was lavish only with my own blood on August 10, the loss of which I have regretted only because it kept me from fighting at the frontiers with my brothers."

The sans-culottes' position is even more clearly stated by Brutus Magnier, president of a military commission attached to the armies of the West during the year II. Having criticized, in an intercepted letter, "the government, which has vowed to exterminate the sans-culottes," he was asked, during his interrogation on 21 Messidor, year III, what he understood by the word sans-culottes. "He replied, the conquerors of the Bastille, of August 10 and of May 31, notably those against whom it would appear we have declared a perpetual war; that further, he understood it to mean those who had been described as Terrorists and drinkers of blood, by cannibals who really merited these titles themselves." Thus the sans-culotte defined himself as much by his political behavior as by his social condition; the former was more easily comprehended than the latter.

One document, dated May 1793, brings up all these points in reply to "the impertinent question, 'But what is a sans-culotte?' " "He's a being who always travels on foot . . . and who lives quite simply with his wife and children, if he has any, on the fourth or fifth floor." Jacques Roux was also to speak of the attics inhabited by the sans-culottes, and *Père Duchesne* was to write: "If you want to become acquainted with the finest flower of the sans-culottes, then visit the workers in their hovels." The sans-culotte is productive, "because he knows how to work a field, how to forge, to saw, to file, to cover a roof, make shoes. . . . And since he works, you can be sure that he'll never be seen either in the Café de Chartres, or in pot-houses where conspiracies are hatched and people gamble, or at the Théâtre des Nations when they're performing 'L'Ami des Lois.' . . . In the evening, he goes round to the headquarters of his section, not powdered, scented, booted, with the hope of being noticed by all the citizen-wives of the tribunes, but to support good motions with all his might. . . . Besides, a sans-culotte always has his sword, with an edge ready to cut the ears off the malicious. Sometimes he walks out with his pike; but at the first sound of the drum, he can be seen leaving for the Vendée, for the armies of the Alps, or for the Army of the North."

2. STATISTICAL DATA

If one attempts a statistical study outside the range of political documents of the Parisian sections during the year II, one runs into the same difficulties in defining the sans-culottes and determining their numbers in terms of the rest of the population.

How many were they? It is impossible to say with any certainty. It is even more difficult to estimate the pro-portion of sans-culottes in terms of numbers of inhabit-ants in each section. The law of August 11, 1793 (Ther-midor, year I), ordered a census of the population of each commune. Begun in the year II in the Parisian sections, this work proceeded at a very slow pace; by Thermidor, only ten sections had accomplished the task. The tabulation dragged on through the year III. On 11 Fructidor, the Division Committee proceeded to apportion bread ration cards according to the registers of the sectional committees. Its *Tableau Sommaire* of the Parisian population records a total of 640,504 inhabitants, a higher figure than the 1789 census (524,186) made by the States General, and doubtless exaggerated, the sections having reason to declare a larger number of mouths to feed than they actually had. This figure, however, more or less coincides with a count of the Paris population made on 13 Pluviôse, year III, in terms of food needed, a figure that seems, until this point, to have escaped researchers, and that gives the number as 636,722 mouths.

However tentative these figures may be, they allow for interesting arguments over the pressure of population on food supplies in the various sections. *Panthéon-Français* was the most densely populated section, with 24,977 inhabitants, closely followed by *Gravilliers*, with 24,774. It is remarkable, however, that the sections located in Faubourg Saint-Antoine and Faubourg Saint-Marcel were not among the most populated. In the case of the first, *Quinze-Vingts* is fifth with 18,283 inhabitants, but *Montreuil* is only seventeenth, with 13,479, and *Popincourt*, thirty-sixth, with 10,933. The *Finistère* section of Faubourg Saint-Marcel is classed thirtieth with 11,775 inhabitants. Two heavily peopled zones were to be found in the heart of Paris, on either side of the Seine. On the Right Bank, twelve sections of the Center grouped together more than 180,000 inhabitants. On the Left Bank, the four sections of *Unité*, *Bonnet-Rouge*, *Mucius-Scaevola* and *Marat* had more than 70,000 inhabitants. In the year II, these various sections appear to have had the largest population increases: the food problem in these sections was more acute than anywhere else. Ducroquet, commissar of monopolies in *Marat*, was a symbol of the pressure the masses exercised over the authorities, such as the confused remedies they proposed for the alleviation of their misery. The distribution of the working-class population corresponded to the foregoing pattern—the vast majority lived in the heart of the capital. F. Braesch's study, based on employers' replies on the subject of the exchange of large *assignats* (bank notes) for small, in order to pay their employees, allows us to make accurate estimates of the number of wage earners in forty-one out of forty-eight sections around 1791.[4] Their number rose to 62,743, or, counting four persons to the average family, 250,972 inhabitants. Braesch's final estimate of the working-class population for the whole capital was 293,820, approximately half the population of Paris. Two zones of dense working-class population occupied the center of Paris, one on either side of the Seine. On the Left Bank, the sections of *Unité*, *Marat*, *Bonnet-Rouge*, *Mucius-Scaevola*, *Chalier* and *Panthéon-Français* numbered more than 10,000 workers. On the Right Bank, a compact bloc of working-class people extended from the Seine to the city gates: almost 28,000 wage earners. The quarters most famed in revolutionary history, however, contained smaller numbers of workers than the heart of the capital. The three sections of Faubourg Saint-Antoine numbered only 4,519 workers, only 613 in the *Finistère* section of Faubourg Saint-Marcel, 3,441 if one includes the two neighboring sections of *Observatoire* and *Sans-Culottes*.

No less significant is the working-class concentration by workshop and section. Although the average number of workers per employer for the whole of Paris was 16.6, it fell to 14.9 for the sections of Faubourg Saint-Antoine; 16.1 for *Finistère*. In the working-class districts in the center of the city, it stood at 15.6 on the Left Bank, and rose to 19.6 on the Right Bank. The section with the smallest working-class population was *Fraternité* (305 workers), whereas *Amis-de-la-Patrie*, in the heart of Paris, numbered 5,288. The highest concentration was in the *Marchés* and *Faubourg-du-Nord* sections: the average number of workers per establishment rises to 27.9 and 31.98;

[4] F. Braesch, "Essai de statistique de la population ouvrière de Paris vers 1791," *La Révolution Française*, Vol. 63 (1912), p. 288.

it is 25.7 in *Sans-Culottes*. On the other hand, small artisan production prevailed in the *Brutus*, *l'Homme-Armé*
and *Révolutionnaire*, where the average fell to 10.2, 9.9
and 8.5.

The rates of exchange for paper money used by Braesch
do not, however, provide an accurate gauge of the social
structure of the Parisian working force, since only the
owners, who had to guarantee the salary of their employees,
had access to them. But how many small artisans worked
alone in their workshops without bothering a soul? How
many journeymen, living under their master's roof and
eating at his table, were to all intents and purposes paid
in kind? In fact, the small artisan workshop eludes
Braesch's statistics.

Proof of this is to be found in the guidelines announced
in June 1793 by the authorities of *Faubourg-Montmartre*
for lumber shops, the wheelwright trade, metalworkers and
carpenters situated in that section. The destiny of wage
labor in this area appears to have been considerably less
than can be calculated from the sources used by Braesch.
It varies according to occupation: higher for those businesses requiring larger capital outlays and heavier equipment, even more in the lumber than in the metal trade.
In June 1793, there were nine lumber shops in the
Faubourg-Montmartre section employing a total of eighty-
one workers, an average of nine per establishment. Registers for paper money exchange dated two years previously,
mention only five establishments employing an average of
seventeen workers. Although in June 1793 one firm employed thirty-one workers and another seventeen, seven
others had between three and seven employees. There
were fewer employees in the coach-making business: 146
employees for twenty-three businesses, or an average of
6.1 apiece. In the meanwhile only nine enterprises, employing an average of nine workers each, had exchanged
assignats in 1790–91. The largest firm employed twenty-
four workers; two, fourteen each; one, twelve; another,
eleven. But two wheelwrights had no employees at all,
two had only three; three workshops had two workers, two
had three. Three coach makers were associated in one work-

shop; four others, also associated, employed four workers.
As for carpentry shops, of which there were nineteen in
that section, the average number of journeymen employed
drops to 5.2 (but twelve shops employed at least nine,
according to records of *assignats* exchanged in 1790–91).
Although four shops employed twenty-four, twelve, eleven,
ten journeymen, respectively, four artisan carpenters
worked alone; one shop employed only one journeyman,
two employed two; two, three; one, four; three small
shops operated with five journeymen each; two with six.
The figures vary even more in the metal trades: fifty-
one journeymen for twenty-five workshops, or an average
of two journeymen in each workshop. (But nine firms
employed a minimum of 6.5 men, according to the documents Braesch used.) Although one workshop employed
sixteen journeymen, ten had none; five had only one; three
had only two.

These slender statistics allow us to interpret Braesch's
research on the density areas of the Paris laboring population. For *Faubourg-Montmartre*, he arrives at an average of
15.9 workers per employer; if we concentrate on the
quadruple occupational division in the guidelines of June
1793, this average falls to 5.5. Doubtless, the last figure
does not take into account the occupations where concentration of manpower was already high: in textiles, in cloth
or hosiery manufacturing. The data strike us as closer to
reality than those of Braesch, whose calculations are in-
accurate because they do not include small businesses
where the artisan worked alone or employed one or two
journeymen at most. The small artisan played a major
role in the Paris work force.

Paris also contained a miserable, starving mass of unemployed marginal workers, who exerted considerable influence over the whole population during periods of shortage. According to a report presented on 14 Germinal,
year II, to the General Council of the Commune by Dan-
jou, the administrator of hospitals, the number of unemployed recipients of relief for all Paris sections rose to
68,981, or if one goes by the population figures relative
to the food supply of 13 Pluviôse, year III, approximately

one in nine received assistance. The proportion of this wretched mass varied in each section. It was particularly high in the historic faubourgs, thus their political role becomes clear. The three sections of the Faubourg Saint-Antoine counted 14,742 such persons, or approximately one in three. Obviously the question of daily bread would have been the prime issue here. When the faubourg surrendered its arms on 4 Prairial, year III, to General Menou, he asked wheelwright Delorme, captain and leader of the first battery of the Popincourt Cannoneers if he were a republican; Delorme, at the muzzle of his gun, replied: "Have you got some bread to give me?"

The section *Quinze-Vingts* ranked first among the Parisian sections for number of relief recipients (6,601), followed by *Finistère*, with 4,951, that is, one pauper for every 2.3 inhabitants; the proportion was higher in the Faubourg Saint-Marcel than in the Faubourg Saint-Antoine. On the Left Bank, the four sections of *Chalier, Panthéon-Français, Observatoire* and *Sans-Culottes* counted 10,625 paupers, or one out of every six inhabitants. They reached their highest number in the year II. Again, still on the Left Bank, *Bonnet-Rouge* had 2,037 paupers, or one out of every eight inhabitants. The *Ouest*, on the other hand, had fewer. The proportion was higher in outlying northern sections: *Faubourg-Montmartre, Poissonnière, Faubourg-du-Nord, Bondy* and *Temple* had a total of 8,448 paupers, or one in every 6.4 inhabitants. In the Center, the highest concentration was in *Maison-Commune,* which, with 4,258 paupers, was third with a proportion of 2.9. On the other hand, *Gravilliers* had only 1,616 on the relief rolls out of 24,774 inhabitants, one in every 16.5.

Thus, the more detailed social statistics of the Paris sans-culottes affirm the basic factor in the popular movements: hunger.

Although, during periods of crisis, the mass of Parisian sans-culottes pushed the revolutionary movement to heights of paroxysm, in periods of calm, when less anxious about

their next meal, their involvement with politics was spas-
modic. Not all the sans-culottes were militant. A study of
the political officers of each section in the year II provides
a revealing portrait of the Parisian sans-culottes.

The chief source for this study is the alphabetically
arranged collection of dossiers of the Public Safety Committee. Most of the dossiers date from the period of repression during Prairial, year III, which, in certain respects,
tells us as much about the Thermidorian psychology of
the propertied classes as about the attitudes of Terrorist
sans-culottes. Many denunciations should not be taken at
face value: during the more exasperating incidents of class
warfare in the spring of the year III, the least remark was
exaggerated and could give rise to an arrest; many people
who had not participated in the massacres were denounced
and arrested for being Septembrists (participants in the
massacre of 1793). Rancor and personal vendettas were
the order of the day. To this should be added the fact
that, during the year II, the bourgeosie had feared that
they would be dispossessed of their social and political
supremacy; repressive measures were intensified. The
numerous dossiers giving accounts of disarmaments and
arrests are nonetheless valid records, indeed the only documents that bear on every sector of the sans-culottes' political officers.

This documentation is, however, far from complete.
The age of the militants is rarely indicated, their occupation is often omitted. The vocabulary is vague; one cannot help being aware of how many sociological aspects of
the sans-culottes remain obscure. At the end of the eighteenth century, the "haves," aristocrats or bourgeois, referred disdainfully to those who worked with their hands
as "the people." In his *Journal*, Hardy, the bookseller,
includes in the term "humbler classes" both the non-
propertied and the lower middle class, the latter more often
than not *having* property, including as it does owners of
small businesses and workshop owners as well as journeymen, manual laborers and the indigent. There are numbers of subtle differences between the lower middle class

and the wage earners, and as many hostilities. Jean-Jacques Rousseau had already written in the *Confessions* that he was born "into a family whose manners marked it as being not quite of the people"; his father was a clock-maker. Like an echo, there is the case of carpenter Duplay, Robespierre's host: the words of his daughter, the wife of National Convention member Lebas have often been quoted. Her father, mindful of the dignity of the bourgeois, never allowed one of his *servants*, that is, one of his workers, to sit at his table. Jaurès reminds us that carpenter Duplay had an income of ten to twelve thousand livres from renting houses, without counting the receipts from his business. Language thus underlines the elusive nature of class distinctions and the indelible mark the artisan's occupation imprinted upon the members of his group: the craft or guild carried the label, not the notion of work or the size of his business. Carpenter Duplay was very much involved in his work; but he nonetheless had a large business. Did he wield a plane in his youth? Or did his father? Or his grandfather?

These are only details perhaps, but it is necessary to clarify this point for a complete social history of the Revolution. The owner of a business cherished his craftsman's qualification and always called himself "carpenter" or "timber merchant," even if he employed several dozen workers. For instance, one has to examine closely the dossier of fan maker Mauvage, militant sans-culotte from *Faubourg-du-Nord*, before realizing that he was owner of a fan-making concern employing sixty persons.

Since the same word was used in fundamentally different contexts, one must ascertain the social position of each artisan and shopkeeper. When does an artisan become an entrepreneur? More often than not, it is impossible, reading the documents of the period, to discern the differences between journeyman, small artisan and entrepreneur; the movement between is too subtly scaled. All attempts to classify within a rigid structure an essentially mobile social order are arbitrary. Furthermore, since it is based entirely on political documents, the study cannot be entirely satisfactory. It is important to determine the wealth of these militants, but the absence of fiscal documents for the Parisian sections leaves the problem open. Detailed research into notaries' archives might, perhaps, give us this information, at least in the case of sansculottes who were members of the lower middle class—the humbler classes have disappeared without leaving a trace—unless it is to be found in the dossiers of the anti-Terrorist repression.

In the year II, the political officers of the Parisian sections fall by function and by origin into three categories, which demonstrate the social differences among sansculottes. The members of the civil committees were the oldest group, the most stable and the wealthiest. They were usually lower middle class. Officers of the revolutionary committees, which were formed later, and whose members were immediately put on salary, were of lower-class origin. From March 1793 to Fructidor, year II, these committees were subject to political vicissitudes; they became increasingly democratized until the autumn of 1793. As for the militant groups in the sectional societies, largely formed after the autumn, they represented the most popular elements of the sans-culottes.

Created by the municipal law of May 21–June 27, 1790, and manned by *censitaire* citizens, the civil committees were by and large retained after August 10, 1792. The majority of their commissars maintained their positions until the year III—numbers of them even escaping the Prairial repression; essentially administrative functions often allowed them to remain apart from Terrorist policies. Although the committees received their funds for office expenses from the municipality, for a long time the commissars did not receive any payment; not until 6 Floréal, year II, did the Convention allot them three livres a day for public service. This measure came too late for the staff of the committees to be democratized. The civil commissars by and large belonged to the upper strata of the sans-culottes: the receipts from a workshop or the

profits from a business allowed them to devote themselves
to their administrative tasks.

Of the 343 civil commissars counted in the year II,
ninety-one, or more than a quarter (26.2 per cent) had
independent means. Although only twelve (3.4 per cent)
had private incomes or owned property, seventy-seven
(22.8 per cent) had retired; living on profits amassed during the course of a career as artisans, shopkeepers or in
the liberal professions, they were a group of small investors. In the group, 7.8 per cent were former members of
the liberal professions: former employees, former lawyers,
former priests. Former artisans and shopkeepers were the
most important group: 14.1 per cent. Every trade was
represented. First were those who had been wholesale
grocers, then wine merchants, followed by tailors, barbers
or wigmakers. Retired shopkeepers and businessmen outnumbered those who had been artisans: thirty-six (10.4
per cent) to thirteen (3.7 per cent). Again, it is necessary
to determine the degree of prosperity of these retired men
of modest means. The documents do not allow this. Their
incomes, however, were sufficient to allow them to devote
themselves to sectional affairs without receiving any payment before Floréal, year II.

Among the 120 artisans (34.9 per cent), although thirteen tailors and twelve painters stood at the top of the
list, the group of thirty-four artisans involved in artistic
activities is the largest. There were sixteen artisans in
woodworking and furniture making, eleven in the leather
trade, ten in textiles and nine in building materials. We
should also add six wigmakers or hairdressers. Here, too,
one must determine the importance of these artisan enterprises. How many journeymen worked with the small employer? The individual dossiers are insufficiently detailed
to allow us to determine the social status of civil commissars. There are, however, two clues: Ladante, civil
commissar of *Amis-de-la-Patrie*, whose former occupation
is not listed, had a personal income of 1,400 livres; that
is, the annual salary of a lower-level employee. Furthermore, he also acted as unsalaried judge of the commercial

tribunal. Viern, civil commissar in *Lombards*, employed eighty men in *his own factory*—for his time this good sansculotte was a big businessman.

First indemnified and finally salaried after September 5, 1793 (21 Fructidor, year 1), the revolutionary committees recruited their staffs more democratically than the civil committees; they represented the lower segment of the sans-culottes population. Very few commissars had private means: twenty-one, or 4.6 per cent of the 454 commissars counted, whereas there were 26.2 per cent on the civil committees. Among the revolutionary committeemen, only four (0.8 per cent) were real investors living entirely off their investments; eleven (2.4 per cent) belonged to the liberal professions; six (1.3 per cent) were retired shopkeepers or artisans. Although there were few entrepreneurs, there were even fewer who could really be called working class. Manufacturers, entrepreneurs or master artisans numbered thirteen (2.8 per cent, compared to 2.3 per cent on the civil committees). On the other hand, there were twenty-two salaried men, workmen, journeymen or boys, and twenty-three servants or former servants, 9.9 per cent of the total. The liberal professions were represented by fifty-two commissars (10.5 per cent). At the top of the list were the artists, painters, sculptors and musicians; then the teachers; and relatively few lawyers. To this group could be added twenty-two employees, seven (4.8 per cent) of whom were attached to the postal service.

The majority of the commissars were artisans or shopkeepers by occupation: 290 out of 454 counted, or 63.8 per cent of the personnel of revolutionary committees. All together, 206 commissars (45.3 per cent) could be considered artisans; eighty-four (18.5 per cent), shopkeepers or businessmen. There was probably a larger number of artisans on the revolutionary committees than on the civil committees: the indemnity of three, then five livres per day represented for many some compensation for the decline or ruin of their businesses; in this respect, the large number of artisans involved in artistic or luxury work is significant. The twenty-eight cobblers formed the most important group (6.1 per cent), followed by eighteen carpenters (3.9 per cent). Then came the sixteen wigmakers or hairdressers (3.5 per cent). However, forty-two commissars (9.2 per cent) were members of the skilled crafts. The building trade was represented by thirty-seven commissars (8.1 per cent), woodworking and cabinetmaking by twenty-nine (6.3 per cent).

Among the eighty-four businessmen, forty-one labeled merchants (9 per cent) appear to have been more than simple shopkeepers. Businessmen or shopkeepers, ten wine merchants stood at the top of the list; to whom one could add six lemonade vendors; liquor stores played an important role in sectional political life. Another fifteen commissars were in the retail food business: six grocers, three pastry cooks, one baker, one greengrocer, to whom could be added two restaurateurs and two innkeepers.

Individual dossiers occasionally permit a closer look at the social status of these commissars. Numbers of artisans or shopkeepers, more or less ruined by the disappearance of their clientele, found a means of sustenance in the salaried position of commissar. Hence the large number of wigmaker-hairdressers and cobblers on revolutionary committees, and also of unemployed former servants—there was a particularly large number of these on the committee from *Bonnet-Rouge* in the previous Faubourg Saint-Germain. Having lost his job as wigmaker on account of the Revolution, Noël, from *Bon-Conseil*, became a commissar; he had three children and his old mother to support. Jean-Baptiste Moulin, also a wigmaker, was commissar in *République* and on the jury of the Revolutionary Tribunal after 22 Prairial, year II. Arrested in the year III, he justified himself by saying, "Having lost my job as wigmaker, I was forced to take a position on the surveillance committee in my section in order to eat."

In the *Marchés* section, according to the civil committee in Messidor, year III, Miel, under arrest since 5 Prairial, said he "only accepted a position on the revolutionary committee in order to procure enough to live on for himself, his wife and his children." In 1789, Grambau, commissar of *Lombards*, was a wholesale florist; his business was destroyed by the Revolution. Castet, a merchant from the *Guillaume-Tell* section, according to his denouncers in Prairial, year III, threw himself into the activities of the revolutionary committee "for the sake of a job." A former servant, Claude Gourgaud, "finding himself out of work on account of the Revolution," became an office boy for the revolutionary committee of *Poissonnière*. Nicholas Petit, a grease monkey in a textile factory in *Lepeletier*, was hired on October 16, 1793 (26 Vendémiaire, year II), as an office boy. Arrested on 19 Ventôse, year III, he was reprimanded for having taken this job; he could neither read nor write. He had the authorities write in his court transcript, "Since my job as a grease monkey did not give me enough to support my family, I was forced to look for a job and I obtained a position as an office boy. . . . Is it a crime to try to live?"

If many commissars found that they earned more than they could at their trades, others either had modest incomes or important positions. In *Arsenal*, Commissar Lambert was a former servant who lived on a small income. Etienne Fournier, commissar from *Indivisibilité*, formerly a craftsman in faience, had an income of 1,700 livres, the annual salary of an average employee. In *Révolutionnaire*, Commissar Tarreau was aware that his work as a jeweler had not got him "what one could call a fortune; it has given me only the bare necessities to support my wife and my children." We must understand that Tarreau's social position was between the leisured class and the lower class. Martineau, wood and wine merchant, member of the revolutionary committee of *Bondy* from its founding to 9 Thermidor, was a wealthy man. He had inherited *a considerable amount of money* from his uncle, and "he also had respectable means from his wife's dowry." Dyer Barrucand, from *Arsenal*, who had participated in the storming of the Bastille, commissar in charge of the making of pikes, member of the revolutionary committee, declared a fortune of 21,600 livres; he had bought a house for 47,300 livres; doubtless, he had to borrow money and sell his silver to do so; still, he remained well off.

Other commissars owned large businesses. In *Gardes-Françaises*, a plaster manufacturer by the name of Maron employed twenty workers in his quarry. Mauvage, commissar in *Faubourg-du-Nord* and active militant, was the owner of a fan-making business that employed sixty workers. He nevertheless called himself quite simply, a fan maker. Some committee members profited from the situation to establish themselves in business and thus moved up the social ladder. If Condelle, a former porter, commissar in *Arsenal*, became only a simple wine merchant, Larue, who was on the revolutionary committee of *Lombards*, and who was a mason in the year 1789, had become an entrepreneur by the year 11. According to his denouncers, "he was employed in several different capacities by the former Commune, which contributed to the making of his career."

Compared to the civil committees, the members of revolutionary committees were recruited on a far more popular basis and at the same time comprised the same variety of social backgrounds, from salaried worker to big businessman. Indeed, the sans-culottes formed a coalition of heterogeneous social elements.

The same can be said when one examines the third group of sectional political officers of the year 11, the militants, with the qualification that here the salaried group was larger. Out of 514 militants counted (and by "militant" we mean all citizens who played an active political role, either in working-class society, or in the general assembly, and who therefore suffered during the repression of the year 111), sixty-four (12.4 per cent) were wage earners, journeymen, errand boys or day laborers. If one adds to these the forty servants, hawkers, office boys and store clerks (7.7 per cent), the lowest order constituted 20.1 per cent of the group of militants, whereas they formed only 9.9 per cent of the members of revolutionary committees and 0.8 per cent of civil committees. On the other hand, there was only one person of independent means and one landlord, eight retail shopkeepers or businessmen (1.9 per cent), whereas this class represented 4.6 per cent of the revolutionary commissars and 26.2 per cent of the civil commissars. At the same time there were only four entrepreneurs and manufacturers (9.7 per cent); whereas the proportion was 2.3 per cent for civil committees and 2.8 per cent for the revolutionary committees. There were thirty-five militants among the liberal professions (6.8 per cent), to whom forty-five employees could be added, raising the proportion to 15.5 per cent. The group of employees was particularly important; they made their presence felt in the meetings of sectional societies as often as possible.

There was a smaller proportion of shopkeepers and artisans on the civil or revolutionary committees: eighty-one merchants (15.7 per cent), 214 artisans (41.6 per cent). In the first category, thirty-four (6.6 per cent) were labeled merchants; the eighteen retail food store owners formed the most numerous group; but ten wine merchants stood in the top rank—thus once again the importance of their role in political sectional life is confirmed.

Among the 214 artisans, the cobblers formed a compact group of forty-one militants (7.9 per cent of the total number), followed by twenty-four hairdresser-wigmakers and twenty tailors. Can one establish a relationship between the militant activity of these small artisans and their occupational problems? The building trade produced thirty militants (5.8 per cent); the woodworking and furniture-making trades, twenty-nine (5.6 per cent); and the artistic and luxury trades, only twenty-three (4.4 per cent). In other words, the trades that required the least occupational skill provided the largest number of militants; the proportion was reversed for the civil and revolutionary committees. The artisans formed a veritable elite that in many sections formed the cadres of sans-culottes.

Although the majority of militants were wage earners, numbers of them were nevertheless well-to-do citizens. In the *Droits-de-l'Homme* section, one Varlet had an income of 5,800 livres; in addition to his job as employee in the Post Office, he had a small personal fortune—this militant was a member of the middle class. Frangeux, from the *Lepeletier* section, an ardent Jacobin, had a private income: "My income is the result of my savings of more than forty years before the Revolution." In *Marat*, François Mercier, formerly a clerk to a wholesale hatter, who was on the jury of the Revolutionary Tribunal, bought an annuity with the 12,150 livres he inherited from his mother in 1780; he said that he was occupied with "the business of various people" and that he had saved part of his income, and his fees as a member of the jury, thereby amassing 9,430 livres. In the year III, he declared he was worth 21,580 livres. Bouland, an active militant member of the Lazowski Society and residing in *Finistère*, who persistently "harassed the merchants," had bought a house on Boulevard de l'Hôpital in the early days of the Revolution. Damoye, a wholesale harness maker from *Montreuil*, was arrested in Pluviôse, year III, for having been a Terrorist; in his defense he declared that he was a man of independent means, and that "he had had to defend his property, and that he had suffered considerable anxiety as a result of being constantly arrested during the past two months"; in the year IV, Damoye was taxed three livres (in coin) in the form of a forced loan.

Therefore, if one turns to the composition of the sectional political officers in the year II, as to those of the Faubourg Saint-Antoine, and, to a lesser degree, of the Faubourg Saint-Marcel during the course of the Revolution and during all the important days from July 1789 to Prairial, year III, one must conclude that the revolutionary vanguard of the Parisian sans-culottes was made up not of the working proletariat, but of a coalition of small employers and journeymen who worked and lived with them. Certain characteristics of the popular movement, a particular kind of behavior, and also certain contradictions resulted from this ambiguous situation.

Working and living with his journeymen, often himself a former journeyman, the small artisan owner exercised a decisive ideological influence upon them. Through him, middle-class influences penetrated the working-class world. Even if master and worker were in conflict with each other, the journeyman working in small businesses—raised in the atmosphere of the master-worker relationship, often living under his master's roof and eating at his table—had the same ideas on the major problems of the time. The lower middle-class artisans shaped working-class attitudes. Perhaps this statement should be refined. Besides the independent artisan, one should consider, for the Paris area, the dependent artisan, whose classic type was the Lyons silk weaver. Juridically a free man and head of his own business with his own tools, even able to hire journeymen, he, to all appearances, was an employer. Economically, however, he was only a salaried man dependent upon the merchant who furnished him with raw materials and sold his finished product. The interests of the dependent artisan and the journeyman were the same; faced with merchant capitalism, they fought for the *tarif*, that is, minimum subsistence wages. However, they would not go so far as establishing a relationship between the value of work and the rate of wages; wages were defined by food prices, not by the value of work done; the social function of work was not clearly understood. The dependent artisan stood between the journeyman and the independent artisan who attached himself to the lower middle class.

In contrast, the factory wage earner, already specialized and anonymous—many of them were in the center of Paris between the Seine and the gates, fewer in the faubourg sections—occasionally showed more independent behavior, foreshadowing to some degree the proletarian in large business enterprises today. This explains the episode at the Reveillon wallpaper factory which led to a riot on April 28, 1789. However, most wage earners in large factories started out in small workshops and remained imbued with the artisan spirit, which was further strengthened by the milieu in which they lived, a weak minority among journeymen. On the whole, the attitudes of the working class were strongly influenced by the attitudes of lower middle-class artisans, and, like the latter, they shared bourgeois ideology. During the Revolution, the workers were unable, either in thought or in action, to form an independent group.

This position carried serious contradictions which bore on the image the sans-culottes had of work and of their social role, as well as of their political activities. Tied to their journeymen on account of their close working and living relationship, the artisans nevertheless owned their own workshops and tools and considered themselves independent producers. Their middle-class mentality was accentuated by their having control over journeymen and apprentices. However, the system of small production and direct sale pitted them irrevocably against the merchant middle class and commercial capital. Hence, there existed among these artisans and shopkeepers who formed the activist wing of the sans-culottes a social ideal that contradicted economic growth. They were against monopoly of the means of production, but they were themselves proprietors. When, in the year II, the more radical sans-culottes insisted upon a ceiling on private fortunes, the essential contradiction between their social position and this demand escaped them. The demands of these artisans were sublimated in passionate complaints, revolutionary postures, without ever offering a coherent program. The same could be said for the men and political groups who had the same outlook: Jacques Roux, Hébert, Robespierre and Saint-Just.

Since they had difficulty in defining their position in society insofar as they were workers, the sans-culottes did not have a clear notion about work itself; they did not believe that work itself could constitute a social function, rather, they considered it only in its relationship to property. During the Age of Enlightenment, the middle classes had certainly rehabilitated the arts and the trades, and had given a tremendous impetus to invention. The bourgeoisie, above all, sensitive to the problems of technology

and production, had no concept of work as a social function. From 1789 to 1794, they never comprehended the
problems of work as such either in themselves or as a
function of the worker, but thought rather in terms of
their class interests. The Le Chapelier law is proof of this.
Although on September 29, 1793 (8 Vendémiaire, year
II), the Convention conceded the general fixing of prices
insisted upon by the sans-culottes, the Montagnard bourgeoisie considered this only a tactical concession: fixed
prices were still essentially related to foodstuffs; wages
were never considered as representing work.

How was it possible for workers, divided between the
dominant artisan economy and nascent big business and
lacking any class consciousness, to pit their ideas against
those of the bourgeoisie? In their struggle against the
aristocrats, workers to a large extent entrusted to the bourgeoisie the representation and defense of their interests;
their attitude toward problems of work could be influenced only by the dominant social and political structures. In the case of the bourgeoisie, property was at the
heart of the social problem; the Declaration of 1793, like
that of 1789, placed it among the indefeasible rights of
man after the abolition of feudalism had made the right
to property absolute. In the year II, the sans-culottes did
not make the problem of work central to their social concerns. They were far more aware of their consumer interests. Strikes and wage claims were not the reasons for the
revolt of the sans-culottes; it was a matter of food. The
rise and fall of the price of the chief staples of the people, wheat, and particularly bread, which represented at
least half of a family's expenses, was the decisive factor in
easing or restricting a wage earner's budget. The sans-
culottes insisted on fixed prices for foodstuffs; the demand
for a wage scale was exceptional, which is significant of
the economic and social as well as ideological conditions
of the time.

Fixed prices for foodstuffs were clamored for with espe-
cial vehemence by the militants, who, in their respective
sections, were subjected to pressure not only from workers,

but also from a large mass of starving unemployed. Hunger, a fundamental element in the popular movement, bound together social groups as diverse as the artisan, the shopkeeper, the worker, in a common struggle against the big businessman, the entrepreneur, the monopolist, whether noble or bourgeois. The term sansculottes might appear vague to contemporary sociology; however, given the social conditions of the time it corresponded to a reality. Doubtless, political motives, too, played a role in popular behavior: above all, hatred of the nobility, belief in an aristocratic conspiracy, the wish to destroy privilege and to establish equality of rights. If this were not so, how could one understand the enthusiasm and self-sacrifice of the volunteers? But the riots of February 1793, and the popular movement of the following summer could not be described as taking the same general direction as the bourgeois revolution; Robespierre himself considered that the first uprisings were due to the public outcry against shoddy merchandise. The *maximum*, which was fought for so persistently and finally imposed on September 29, 1793 (Vendémiaire, year II), was not intended to assist national defense, but to guarantee the workers their daily bread. The permanent ferment of popular action was a result of hard living conditions; in the last analysis, economic fluctuations were tolerable only when balanced with revolutionary activity.

On 1 Prairial, year III, a tailor named Jacob Clique, from the *Gardes-Françaises* section, was arrested for having said: "It would appear that the buyers have an understanding with the farmers to sell everything for as high a price as possible in order to starve out the worker." When questioned, he declared: "I am crippled with misfortune; I am the father of three young children, penniless, and my daily work has to provide for five people; during the past hard winter I was barely able to find work."

Many, in a very confused manner, linked the need for bread with political demands. A carpenter by the name of Richer, from *République*, declared, on 1 Prairial, year III, "Under Robespierre, blood ran and we had bread; today blood does not run and we don't have any bread, and we ought to make some blood flow in order to get some." The sans-culottes did not forget that during the Terror, in spite of all the difficulties, bread was not lacking. Terrorist activity was irrevocably bound to the overriding need for daily bread. This dual factor cemented the unity of the Parisian sans-culottes.

II

THE SOCIAL ASPIRATIONS
OF THE PARIS SANS-CULOTTES

*The condition and circumstances of the sans-culottes ex-
plain why they placed bread at the heart of their social
demands. From these demands they evolved in a confused
manner the statement concerning the rights of existence:
every man must eat his fill. It would be impossible to discern in this a coherent doctrinal system; the demands were
made under the weight of circumstances. Their unity
stemmed from the basic egalitarianism that is characteristic of the outlook and behavior of the masses: that conditions of existence should be the same for everybody. To
the absolute right of property, the root of inequality, the
sans-culottes opposed the principle of "equal incomes."
Hence their various social demands, from the right to
public assistance to the right to education.*

1. FROM THE RIGHT TO EXISTENCE TO "EQUAL INCOMES"

The Declaration of Rights of June 1793 stated that the
goal of society is the common good. The sans-culottes went
further: the Revolution was brought about by the people
and should therefore first of all guarantee them equal opportunity. The documents available do not present us with
a single theoretical justification for this right; even the
most knowledgeable militant was not a theoretician. The
right to existence was asserted in response to the pressure

of events and the problems of daily living. Starting from these premises, the sans-culottes quite naturally came upon the notion of equal incomes.

During the first months of the year 1793 increasing food shortages led the militants to clarify their thinking about social issues. On February 7, the committee of *Gardes-Françaises* declared that the poor should not be at the mercy of the rich: "Otherwise men will no longer have equal rights *. . .* otherwise the very existence of the former will be forever endangered while the latter will impose the stiffest laws." In a petition presented to the Convention on March 9, 1793 (19 Ventôse, year 1), a citizen from *Arcis* included among the enemies of the Republic "those who under the pretext of freedom and property believe themselves free to suck the blood of the unfortunate and to satisfy their vile cupidity while barely allowing the needy either to breathe or to complain." Even more significant, and presented on the same date, is the petition of a citizen from *Marais*: "It is time that the bread of day laborers, this modest tribute to painful and laborious toil, be assured to them, that speculation on human existence be outlawed by a republican government."

These ideas were fundamental to popular thinking. Jacques Roux developed them in his petition of June 25, 1793 (7 Messidor, year 1): "Liberty is but a phantom when one class of men can starve another with impunity. Liberty is but a phantom when the rich man, through monopoly, possesses the power of life and death over his fellow-man." During the crisis of the summer of 1793, these same ideas were forcefully stated. Speaking in the name of the commissars of the first assemblies, Félix Lepeletier declared before the Convention on August 20 (3 Fructidor): "It is not sufficient that the French Republic be founded on equality: the laws, the citizens' mores must be in harmony and tend to put an end to inequality of incomes; happiness must be guaranteed to every Frenchman."

On September 2 (16 Fructidor), in defending the maximum for staples, the *Sans-Culottes* section stated:

"The Republic should also guarantee to each citizen the means of procuring staples, without which they will die." According to the temporary commission of the Commune-Affranchie, 26 Brumaire, year II, it was ridiculous constantly to clamor for equality "when vast differences of fortune have always separated one man from another." How far the right to exist and its corollary, even if they were not clearly formulated, corresponded to the fundamental aspirations of the sans-culottes is further proved by the activities of the *Quinze-Vingts* section during the shortages of the year III. In defending coercive measures against wheat growers before the Convention on 10 Floréal, the sans-culottes said: "The poor who have only *assignats* [depreciated paper money] have the same right to live as the rich."

The demand for equal incomes corresponded to one of the essential currents of popular thinking: egalitarianism. Particularly sensitive to the rampant inequality accentuated by riches during times of shortage, the sans-culottes first of all claimed equal distribution of staples. This stage was quickly superseded by another: equality means nothing if it is not applied to all the conditions of existence. The rich man should not live better than the poor; he should give what he does not need for himself to the latter and share his goods with him. "Expropriate everything that a citizen does not need," declared the temporary commission of the Commune-Affranchie, "because to have more than one needs is a flagrant and gratuitous violation of the rights of the people. Every man who has more than he needs, more than he can use himself, is only abusing the rest; thus, after leaving him with his basic needs, the remainder belongs to the Republic and to its less fortunate members."

The taxation on foodstuffs tended to reduce the advantages of the rich and favor the workers. The same holds for the law that obliged producers to sell their goods at the going rate: "without making distinctions between the rich and poor," all the consumers had to purchase supplies at the official prices. Egalitarian claims went further. The rich should not be allowed to procure, even at the fixed rate, better quality food supplies not available to the poor. After examining a decree issued by Fouché and Collot d'Herbois, who were attached to the Commune-Affranchie, the General Council, discussing the indictment of Chaumette, decided on 3 Frimaire, year II, that there would only be one kind of bread—equality bread. "Riches and poverty should both be banished from the regime of equality; and there will no longer be any bread made of fine flour for the rich and husks for the poor."

The unequal distribution of various foodstuffs gave rise to constant objections on the part of the sans-culottes. On 21 Brumaire, the *Finistère* section complained to the General Council "that the merchants provided poor quality goods under the maximum system compared to those goods for which they could get higher prices"; a stop must be put to "this discrimination, which favors the rich and oppresses the poor." Even more vehement were the popular complaints about the distribution of meat. On 20 Pluviôse, the committee of surveillance in the département of Paris denounced the butchers: "The poor who come to buy from you, rejected, humiliated, take home bones and scraps, whereas the rich get the delicacies because 'they can pay.'" The sectional authorities were particularly intent on abolishing distinctions of wealth when the purchase of foodstuffs was involved. When the charity committee of the *Observatoire* section ordered five bakers to provide bread for the unemployed, the revolutionary committee vetoed this decision, "determined to abolish all distinctions between unfortunate citizens forced to receive charity and those more fortunate who were sufficient unto themselves."

Popular egalitarianism extended not only to foodstuffs, but also to goods that confirmed the social superiority of the rich. Irrational reactions, one might say, pushed the sans-culotte, whether he was a "have-not" or a small proprietor, to covet what he did not possess—a behavior pattern indicative of public opinion at the time and of a particular understanding of social relations. Such reactions erupted spontaneously in the form of rude remarks or sudden outbursts which were promptly suppressed by police informers or a more fortunate eavesdropper.

According to the observer Prévost, on 9 Brumaire in the year II, he heard a woman saying she was a Jacobin and remarking to another, "that is a very beautiful peignoir you have got; just wait, in a little while, if you have two, you will give me one of them, and that is what we expect; it will be the same with everything else." Toward the middle of Ventôse, when the food crisis once again set the sans-culottes in motion, Ancard declared in a café in Rue de Thionville, "The rich must share their fortunes with the sans-culottes." Similar remarks were common in that period. According to Bacon, on 25 Ventôse a citizen declared before the general assembly of the *Contrat-Social* section: "We have arrived at the stage when the rich must pay up, when the man who has two dishes of food must give one to a man who has none"; his words were very well received.

It would appear that whenever there were shortages there was an increased tendency toward egalitarianism. Once again during the spring of the year III, on 1 Germinal, during the course of a large public disturbance on Boulevard Montmartre, Gervais Beguin, a carter, attempted to overturn a cabriolet belonging to a manufacturer of buttons for the army, saying to him, "You oughtn't to have one more cabriolet than I." On 12 Germinal, in the *Muséum* section, a certain Caillau, who had climbed on top of a temporary barracks, applauded pillage, saying "that there is no reason why he should fear those who have something; as for the rest they deserved what they could get." An officer of the National Guard invited him to climb down, since the temporary barracks were national property; Caillau replied, "then part of it belonged to him."

During the course of the anti-Terrorist repression, such remarks often served as motive for arrest. Thus, on 5 Ventôse, an employee at the War Office, Cordebar, was denounced in the *Halle-au-Blé* general assembly as being "a

friend of the Héberts and the Chaumettes" and for having
declared in Floréal of the previous year "that if he were
free, he would pay a visit to those wealthier than he and
would say to them: 'You are richer than I am, you must
give me a part of your fortune'; and that if they refused
to do so, he would force them." Paper merchant Popin,
former commissioner of police in *Contrat-Social*, was arrested on 5 Prairial, year I; in May of 1793 (Floréal, year
I) he had declared that "the agrarian law was essential
over and above a yield of between four and five thousand
livres." On 10 Prairial, Oudard, instructor from *Halle-au-
Blé*, was also arrested for having insisted that "all the rich
and all the aristocrats must be guillotined and their goods
distributed." Summarizing all the complaints of the
"haves" against the popular militants, the commissars of
Butte-des-Moulins wrote, in a report dated 30 Pluviôse,
year III: "Finally, since they met no resistance, they came
up with the notion of invading, assaulting not property
but property owners, in order to share the property."

2. From "Equal Incomes" to Restrictions on
   Property Rights

As asserted in the report of year III by the moderate
commissars from *Butte-des-Moulins*, the sans-culottes were
not in fact hostile toward property as such; they wanted
merely to profit from this right and prevent its abuses.
After demanding equal incomes they quite naturally proceeded to restrictions on the rights of property—not toward their suppression.

Being consumers, the sans-culottes first of all attacked
property rights over agricultural products. The right to a
minimum standard of living was never formulated in the
abstract, but always resulted from a concrete situation; to
legalize fixing prices of staples was the only means of as-
suring equality of purchasing power. Thus the sans-

culottes managed to restrict the property rights of a grower over his crop and to control the retail prices of agricultural products, two popular demands.

This principle was clearly formulated by the committee from *Panthéon-Français* on September 22, 1792 (1 Vendémiaire, year 1): "There is no pretext, no reason, no law, under which the right of property can be claimed without its being abused, particularly in these three categories of retail business [wheat, meat and wine], since they very much affect the life of the poor, all of society and the public peace." The inviolable nature of the right of property could not be invoked to legalize free trade in basic necessities that involved the people's very existence. On February 7, 1793 (18 Pluviôse, year 1), the committee from *Gardes-Françaises* asserted that agricultural products should be regarded by the grower or the retail businessman "as being goods placed in trust for which he is to render an account to the Republic."

Since the ownership of agricultural products was no longer an indefeasible right, the Convention could pass laws about them; which it was not afraid to do, particularly to restrict trade in, and fix a maximum price for, wheat. This measure would inconvenience only the speculators, "who want to fill their pockets with that which belongs to the people, who want to put a price on the survival of thousands of citizens." Even clearer is the declaration made by a citizen of the *Marais* section in March 1793: "Generally speaking all basic goods and food products belong to everyone." In his petition dated June 24 (6 Messidor), Jacques Roux justified fixing prices for primary foodstuffs in terms of the right to exist: "Are the properties of rogues more sacred than the life of a man?" According to Leclerc, writing in *Ami du Peuple*, August 14, 1793 (27 Thermidor, year 1), "Wheat and generally speaking all basic consumer products belong to the Republic, except for a reasonable compensation to be paid to the grower for the sweat and work he put into the cultivation of his crops." And again on August 17: "Basic products belong to everyone." In the petition presented by the *Sans-Culottes* section on September 2, 1793 (16 Fructidor, year 1), it is stated that "the foundations of property lie in physical needs." Guidelines set by the temporary commission of the Commune-Affranchie state, "Everything produced on French territory belongs to France, with a fee due to the grower; the people therefore have a guaranteed right to the fruits of his labor." In the year III, the *Quinze-Vingts* section declared on 10 Floréal: "The products of the earth belong to all men, only reasonable compensation is owed to the growers."

But there was still the question of exercising these rights. The most aware sans-culottes realized that fixed prices were only an inadequate palliative and understood that the radical solution would be to put the distribution of agricultural products in the hands of the nation. As always in periods of crisis, public thinking explored new avenues. On the principle that "all men have an equal right to a minimum standard of living and to all agricultural products indispensable for his [sic] survival," Leclerc concluded in *Ami du Peuple*, August 10, 1793 (23 Thermidor, year 1), that the Republic ought to become the chief purchaser: "henceforth, basic necessities may be sold only to the state." The Jacobins in the *Arcis* section on 18 Brumaire, year II, demanded a form of nationalization, not only of basic foodstuffs, but also of all consumer products.

Social laws were to determine the interpretation of freedom, particularly free enterprise; speculation and monopolies would only be broken by the establishment of nationally owned stores "to which the growers, estate owners and manufacturers should be forced to sell at a moderate price the surpluses of every kind of merchandise; the nation will distribute the merchandise."

During a discussion in Ventôse of the distribution of a supply of oil impounded from the cellars of an émigré, the *Champs-Élysées* assembly even questioned private enterprise: "What is a merchant? He is the trustee and not, as we have stupidly thought up until now, the owner of the basic necessities of life. He is the trustee of these goods, in the same way as other citizens are in part trustees of authority; he is therefore a public servant, and even more important, since he holds in his hands the means of survival." "A citizen declared: '[Nationalization] would in fact . . . be one of the best and easiest means of doing away with vested interests or counterrevolutionary activities among merchants, who will thereby bring to Paris and distribute in each section as much foodstuffs as will be possible and sell them to the citizens at a price fixed by law.'"

The crisis during the spring of the year III forced the sans-culottes to come up with other similar systems of nationalization of foodstuffs. Thus wheelwright Journet, civil commissar from *Indivisibilité*, proposed, on 25 Floréal, state control of the retail food business; he suggested buying from the merchants and distributing the goods "in equal portions to all citizens." The unemployed and workers earning less than 1,500 livres would pay half the price that the government had to pay for the merchandise, "and the rich will pay the full price." Journet justified this system not on theoretical grounds, but on grounds of immediate necessity: Paris, "whose inhabitants must receive an equal division of supplies," and the Republic were in a state of siege.

Journet's proposals, which emphasize the permanence of public agitation, were double-edged in their egalitarian approach: guaranteeing an equal minimum standard of living to all citizens and compensating for social inequalities by curbing the fortunes of the rich. Thus, under pressure from events, popular thinking crystallized, and daily living gave birth to a social theory. From the principle of equality of incomes, the sans-culottes concluded that it was necessary to restrict property rights over agricultural products; through a necessary logical sequence they came to criticize free exercise of property rights, at least as those had been defined in the Declaration of August 1789 and in that of June 1793.

The principle of property as such was never questioned; the sans-culottes were very attached to the idea of small holdings. But being small producers, they based their ideas on personal work. This idea of a worker's private property based on his own labor corresponds to the artisan structure, which was still characteristic of the latter half of the eighteenth century in France. It was a method of production that could flourish only if the worker was a free proprietor, a peasant with his own land or an artisan with his own premises and his own tools. In demanding on 27 Nivôse, year II, that the Food Ministry pay the indemnity due to a local baker, the *Poissonnière* society declared that "the small fortunes acquired through work that is useful to society cannot be respected enough and must be preserved at all costs." Work, according to the temporary commission of Commune-Affranchie, must "always be accompanied by leisure."

The sans-culottes attacked the rich and the wealthy merchants, realizing in a confused manner that if the empire of riches remained intact, from lack of restriction on the rights of property, the equalizing of incomes would be only an empty phrase. In their addresses and petitions, particularly during periods of crisis, their egalitarian notions took the form of plans and projects that more or less centered around the redistribution of wealth: there should be neither rich nor poor; appropriate legislations should make it impossible to concentrate property and the means of production. The sans-culottes saw nothing contradictory in maintaining private property that they already owned, or hoped to own, and its restriction within the narrow limits familiar to their social position.

On August 18, 1792, Gonchon, spokesman for the Hommes du Quatorze-Juillet and the Dix-Août, declared at the bar of the Legislative Assembly: "Create a government that places the masses above their feeble resources and the rich below their means. The balance will be perfect." A year later, Leclerc echoed the same idea in *Ami du Peuple*, August 10, 1793 (23 Thermidor, year I): "A nation is very near ruin when one can see extreme poverty alongside extreme wealth." And on August 20, Félix Lepeletier, in the name of the commissars of the district assemblies, stated: "The rich should be not so much owners of property as honored trustees of a surplus fortune consecrated to the happiness of their co-citizens." The temporary commission of the Commune-Affranchie eventually declared on 26 Brumaire, year II, that "if perfect equality were unfortunately to prove impossible among men, it is at least possible to narrow the gap [between rich and poor]."

It was a matter of time before utopian projects appeared. Having declared that the poor were entitled to a half share in the property of the rich, an anonymous pamphlet published in January 1793 declared that "no important formal agreement be signed, whether it be a question of purchase, or of a lease, or concerning manufactured goods or business societies, whether it be a marriage contract, or anything else, without a free distribution to the poor of a sum of money to be stated in said contract." During the spring of 1793, citizen Tobie urged the *Fédérés* section to adopt measures set forth in his "Essay on the Means of Ameliorating the Lot of the Needy." He reminded the authorities that "according to the Geneva philosopher [Rousseau]," the social state was of no use to man "unless everyone had something and no one had too much." "Whereas it is true that an equitable distribution of money can be looked upon as being an illusion by anyone of intelligence, it is nevertheless also true that the monstrous disproportion that exists between the proud millionaire and the humble wage earner cannot be permitted much longer in the new order of things."

But in order to lessen the inequalities of the system and to guarantee property to all citizens, the only suggestion offered by the author of the essay was to sell the former royal castles "and all their luxurious and scandalous contents," such as the jewels of the Garde-Meuble. The sums of money realized from these sales would permit making loans without interest to those who wanted to start a small business. This project clearly was aimed at artisans desirous of setting themselves up and living as small independent producers. It reflects the aspirations of the

58

social milieu from which it stems. In the *Lepeletier* section, the popular society adopted, on 2 Frimaire, a project whose declared aim was to "equalize fortunes insofar as it is possible." Large landholdings, "necessary for monarchial machinations," are dangerous in a republic. One must "destroy individual wealth, guarantee universal comfort and banish ignoble poverty. Fortunes remain piled up within a small group of people because the rich marry the rich. We propose a decree that men must unite, and not fortunes." This meant that when two rich people wanted to be united, they would be obliged to deposit a sum proportionate to their holdings at a government charity depository: "The yield of this just tribute would be used to give dowries to poor girls and to assist the hardworking and improverished artisan who has just married to set up house." This sumptuary law would certainly "spread wealth."

These projects were not precisely utopian visions. Rather, the petition presented by the *Sans-Culottes* section on September 2, 1793 (16 Fructidor, year 1), not only intended to limit "industrial and commercial profits" by general price-fixing and restricting the size of agricultural holdings, but also to impose a ceiling on fortunes. What was this ceiling to be? The petition does not go into detail on this point but lets it be understood that it would correspond to small artisan and shopkeeping property: "Only one workshop, or one store, would be allowed to each person." These radical measures, concluded the *Sans-Culottes* committee, "would gradually bring about the disappearance of the overwhelming inequality of fortunes and increase the number of proprietors."

At no other moment during the Revolution did there appear such a concise and interesting formulation of the popular social ideal: an ideal stemming from the artisans and shopkeepers who formed the cadres of the sans-culottes and who had a decisive ideological influence over their journeymen or their clerks. It was also the ideal of the mass of urban consumers and small urban producers, hostile to all dealers in staples and to all entrepreneurs, whose business dealings often threatened to reduce them to being dependent workers.

The ideas brought forward by the sans-culottes under the pressure of shortages were not particularly original. They were outlined in various different ways by the spokesmen of various factions of the Montagnard bourgeoisie, and their common source of inspiration was the philosophical thinking of the century influenced by Rousseau.

First of all, the cultivator should not have an absolute right of ownership over the yield of his land. In his speech of December 2, 1793 (12 Frimaire, year II), on foodstuffs—on the occasion of the disturbances in the département of Eure-et-Loire, Robespierre subordinated the right of property to the right to existence: "The primary right is that of existence; the primary social law is therefore that which guarantees to all members of society the means for existing; all others are subordinate to these laws." In May 1793 in his "Opinion on Fixing the Maximum Price of Wheat," Momoro, who although he was not a sans-culotte, nevertheless expressed their thinking, describing property, as usual, in terms of the right to use and to abuse, asked the question: "Does this right apply to the cultivator and his crop, to the fruit of his sweat? Obviously not. These crops are destined for society as a whole, for reasonable compensation, which should be the price"; this compensation must be commensurate with "the resources of the citizenry."

Hébert, here a sonorous echo rather than a theoretician, wrote in 1793, "The earth was made for every living creature, and everyone, from the ant to that proud insect who calls himself man, must find sustenance in the yield of this common mother." In conclusion, he declared, "The right of existence is paramount, one must at all costs eat."

During the course of the summer of 1793 these ideas were commonplace, and public pressure was so strong that on September 1 Dufourny, a supporter of Danton who was openly hostile to the sans-culottes, clearly outlined the confused aspirations of the masses: "Landowners and cultivators have no right to abuse their land, either by not planting it, or by destroying their crops—they are in fact the owners neither of the land nor of the crops." They are only the trustees of the harvests, solely at the disposal of the nation in return for compensation. Business should be returned to its primary purpose, serving the cultivator and the consumer. Foodstuffs should not be an object of speculation: "The man who speculates in foodstuffs for profit is a useless middleman, dangerous and guilty, a genuine monopolist, an enemy of society."

This was about all the sans-culottes had to say on this subject; their only originality was to want to put these ideas into practice and to force restrictions and fixed prices on the economy. The Montagnards refused to adopt the law of the maximum until they were forced to do so. Robespierre's silence on this serious problem throughout the summer of 1793 is significant. He was too knowledgeable a politician to underestimate the balance of social forces, to neglect the interests of the bourgeoisie, despite his love for the people. Contrary to the public declarations of unanimity, the clash of interests persisted.

The same could be said for property rights. The Montagnard and Jacobin leaders formulated similar propositions to those of the sans-culottes. But when did they attempt to put these ideas into law? Chaumette spoke on several occasions before the Tribunal of the General Council on this subject, Hébert often wrote on it; they wanted to be the common spokesmen for the sans-culottes. More of a theoretician, Billaud-Varenne, in his *Eléments de Républicanisme*, posited that property was the core of civil institutions. Therefore, "the political system should not only guarantee to each person the peaceful enjoyment of his possessions, but this system should be so worked out as to establish, insofar as possible, a division of goods which, if not absolutely equal, should at least be fair to each group of citizens." Although property rights were indefeasible, "they should serve every citizen of the nation";

thus no one will find himself "directly dependent upon another person."

On April 24, 1793 (5 Floréal, year 1), Robespierre spoke of property as not a natural right, but a social institution, which every citizen should enjoy. In his *Institutions Républicaines*, Saint-Just declared that it should be the aim of the Republic "to give to every Frenchman the means of getting the necessities of life, without his being dependent on anything except the law and without mutual dependence within the civil state." In other words, all Frenchmen should be small owners and independent producers. Furthermore, "Man must be independent . . . there should be neither rich nor poor."

From Montesquieu to Rousseau, it was commonly held during the eighteenth century that the Republic could survive only with a measure of social equality; the Montagnards leadership did not give any more evidence of original thinking than did the militant masses.

On one point, however, the Parisian sans-culottes did show a certain ideological audacity. The most enthusiastic Montagnards never went beyond restrictions on large landholdings. In his *Institutions Républicaines*, Saint-Just wrote that "only maximum territorial holdings should be determined." Although in his *Eléments de Républicanisme* Billaud-Varenne talks of "restricting the corrosive influences [of great fortunes] by an accelerated program of subdividing land allowing no possibility of future concentration," he was talking only about landed wealth. "No citizen should be allowed to possess . . . more than a fixed number of acres," averaging about thirty. Momoro was even clearer on the subject, although he was a militant friar and closer to the sans-culottes. His declaration of rights, published in September 1792, guaranteed only the rights of industrial property, property "which we falsely label 'territorial,' having been guaranteed only until the time laws shall have been passed on that subject."

On the border between the sans-culottes and the bourgeoisie, many revolutionaries, Jacobins or Montagnards, were more hostile toward landed wealth than toward other forms of property. Further proof of this is to be found in an essay on popular government that appeared in the summer of 1792, which states that although the nation must impose a ceiling of 120,000 livres per annum on income from landed property, it should nevertheless not "impose any restrictions on the increase of fortunes from purely mobile capital, such as money, government securities, merchandise, ships, etc."

The sans-culottes, consumers of agricultural products but also small urban producers, partisans of independence for their stores or their workshops, went further: fearful, above all, of being reduced to the ranks of the proletariat, they were as hostile to big business or industrial ownership as they were toward large landed estates. Thus we have the claims of the *Sans-Culottes* section that in order to prevent monopoly of the means of production no one should own more than one workshop or one store.

Popular thought, then, had an indefinite character and, to a certain extent, lacked originality. The indefiniteness stems from the very position of the sans-culottes in society. Composed of heterogeneous elements, their only common ground was hostility toward the aristocracy. Made up of artisans and businessmen, who sprang from the lower middle class and occasionally from the middle class, journeymen, who broke bread with their artisan masters and thought like them, workers from the few large industrial enterprises in Paris, not to mention intellectuals and artists and a few former aristocrats, it was impossible for the sans-culottes as a group to have either class awareness or a coherent social program. Thus their aspirations remained hazy and self-contradictory. Furthermore, they had no specific character. Their aspirations rose from that common source on which nearly all the revolutionaries drew, particularly the Montagnards and Jacobins. The sans-culottes' social ideal approached that of the Robespierrists: a community of independent producers to whom the state through its laws would guarantee an ap-

proximate equality. Hostile toward the Montagnard bourgeoisie, the militant sans-culottes insisted upon fixed prices
and controls; some of them demanded restrictions favoring
artisan and commercial property. They justified the maximum less on theoretical grounds than by pointing to the
needs of national defense, and as a means of restoring
balance between opposing economic interests. For this
reason they remained faithful to the Montagnard declaration of June 1793, which conceived of the nation as a
community where all citizens are equal and the goal is
universal happiness. In regard to social policy, the sans-
culottes therefore appear—except in certain cases and with
the contradictions already mentioned—to have followed
the lead of the Montagnard bourgeoisie and, particularly,
the Jacobins. Their originality lay elsewhere: in their political activities.

To what extent were these social ideas representative
of the sans-culottes as a whole? Debates, speeches and
petitions that have come down to us were produced by
the minority of militants who were sufficiently educated
to draw up programs; although numbers of them had no
direct knowledge of the philosophical thinking of the era,
they were nevertheless imbued with it. The ideas of
Rousseau in particular had spread among the popular
clubs and societies well before reaching the people. Muf-
fled echos of these ideas are to be found in documents
coming from sectional organizations. As many of these
show, numbers of militants who held political positions
in the sections could not read or write. The vast majority
of sans-culottes were moved to action by their miserable
living conditions rather than by the power of ideas.
Shortages were the permanent cause for public agitation,
from the Reveillon riots in April 1789 to the outbreaks
of Germinal and Prairial, year III. In the year II, every
sans-culotte tended confusedly to support the egalitarian
republic, which they called democratic or popular. If, because of insufficient education, only a few militants, following the lead of the Montagnard or Jacobin leaders,
could understand the essentials and justify them by ex-

pounding theoretically, the mass of sans-culottes were satisfied with struggling for their immediate demands.

In the final analysis, the social aspirations of the sans-culottes centered around their struggles for their concrete demands: for example, fixed taxes and rationing. In 1793, the grain maximum was insisted upon to fix the price of bread in proportion to wages, that is, to allow the workers to live. The right to exist was produced as a supporting argument. Social demands both obstructed and gave rise to theoretic justifications, thereby intensifying the struggle. Demands for action rather than declarations of principle best describe the social aspirations of the sans-culottes.

Sectional demands concerning various forms of speculation and particularly the monoply on war matériel by large entrepreneurs best demonstrate the popular idea of limited property and of small independent production which legislation would hold within narrow limits.

3. THE SANS-CULOTTES AND COMMERCIAL CAPITAL

The sans-culottes' hostility toward commercial capital is primarily symbolized by their persistent outcry against the trade in coin. There were reasons for this. The circulation of gold and silver coin helped to discredit the *assignats* and consequently further aggravated the economic crisis and the shortage of food. Hard money became the symbol of the social classes that were opposed to the egalitarian republic of the sans-culottes. Hence the frequent speeches against gold or luxury during the year II. A ban on the sale of coin was demanded in February 1793 in a strongly worded petition stressing the effect of depreciating paper money and its impact on the cost of living. On March 3 (13 Ventôse), a joint committee of the sections issued another proclamation on the same subject. The Convention finally agreed on April 11 (22 Germinal). The trade in silver coin nevertheless continued. On June

27 (9 Messidor), Representative Dentzel denounced the Rue Vivienne speculators. On August 29 (12 Fructidor), the committee from *Unité* brought to the attention of the General Council of the Commune the silver coin traders who were operating under the galleries of the Garden of Equality.

The Reign of Terror brought about an increase in repressive measures, which still appeared inadequate. On 7 Frimaire the General Council adopted a motion brought forward by the Cordeliers Club which would forbid circulation of coin until peacetime. The Cordeliers were particularly insistent that "every merchant, businessman and even every individual paid by an organization be forced to deposit at the Mint everything he owned in the way of gold and silver without exception, in order to change them for *assignats*." This would have given further reason for discontent in the financial and business community, so the petition was sent back to the Public Safety Committee.

It was not enough to root out the speculators. It was necessary to investigate the organizations that supported the interests of commercial capital. The sans-culottes demanded the closing of the Stock Exchange and the dissolution of stock companies. On May 1, 1793 (13 Floréal, year 1), the *Faubourg-du-Nord* section called for the closing of the Stock Exchange, the following day the *Contrat-Social* committee supported the action. Since the Girondins had been eliminated, the Convention conceded to this demand and on June 27, 1793 (9 Messidor, year 1), ordered the closing of the Paris Stock Exchange. But the action was taken only because of popular pressure and as a concession to sectional demands. On June 25, Jacques Roux had presented his threatening petition, and on June 26 the soap riots had broken out.

Equally indicative of the sans-culottes' economic stand was their hostility toward joint stock companies, whose numbers had increased toward the end of the ancien régime and that constituted the most highly evolved form of commercial capital. Toward the end of August 1793

(Fructidor, year 1), a citizen from the *Sans-Culottes* section was amazed to see "a public assistance office here, a business office there, somewhere else a savings bank, elsewhere on an old peoples' *tontine* [mutual aid association], over there a life insurance bureau, in this doorway a patriotic lottery of the Rue du Bac"—enterprises to swallow up money. "We have the most to fear from these rich men, masters and financiers"; they lower the standards of business and contribute to the problems of a republic. He also thought that the Convention should confiscate "the coffers of those wily old birds."

On August 24 (7 Fructidor, year 1), the Assembly banned financial companies; on 26 Germinal, amending its decree of 17 Vendémiaire, year II, it banned them all without exception.

The national defense policy on war matériel, although accommodated to the banning of stock companies, nevertheless required turning to private enterprise, nationalization having been adopted only for the manufacturing of arms. Bent on efficiency, the government committees were forced to concentrate their orders in the hands of large entrepreneurs or businessmen, instead of dividing them among many small workshops. All through the year II, this action was a source of conflict between the revolutionary government and the sans-culottes and contributed to the deterioration of their relations.

When war was declared, the sections, in order to relieve the misery of the masses and reduce unemployment, decided to reserve the outfitting of troops for their own members. On September 8, 1792, the General Council of the Commune asked that orders be equally distributed among the members of the forty-eight sections. The crisis of the early part of 1793 and the enlistments that followed increased the need for matériel. Sections opened workshops, like that of the *Tuileries*, which, in order to raise the necessary funds, established on February 4 (17 Pluviôse, year 1), "a civil contribution in money and in kind." The reasoning behind the decision of the *Tuileries* section is indicative of public hostility toward commercial

capital: "First of all, greedy, corrupt or inefficient suppliers
will no longer be able to hamper the movement of the
armies, to prevent our victory, and freedom will no longer
be at the mercy of speculators. Second, a small number of
wealthy entrepreneurs will no longer be able to reap all
the benefits from huge expenditures; they will be shared
among all our merchants, among all our workers, in short,
among all of us. Third, since small industry is always run
with intelligence and economy, by spending a small
amount we can offer them more in the way of supplies
and the supplies will be better." One could hardly say
more in praise of small independent production. But was
it compatible with the vast needs of national defense?

In fact the work was organized according to current
methods: the entrepreneurs received the raw material
from the government and manufactured the clothing. The
sections consistently protested against this organization,
but for lack of a program, they were hard put to it to succeed in their protest. On June 15, 1793 (28 Prairial, year
1), so that female workers could take advantage of the new
clothing manufacturing price scale, the *Finistère* committee decided to start a workshop under its own control.
It relied, however, on commissars capable of supplying a
guaranteed equivalent to the value of the raw material
handed over to the section and to advance the workers'
wages; two honest commissars would have to supervise the
operation in the name of the section and listen to complaints. Only one citizen came forward with a guarantee
of 6,000 livres; he was also an entrepreneur, but his enterprise was restricted by the powers of the commissars of
the section.

This system, which corresponded to popular demand,
ran counter to the needs of national defense, which desperately needed increased, therefore concentrated, production. The uniform supply department was forced to
organize large workshops, where production was run on a
rational basis. They constantly ran into objections from
workers accustomed to independent work, who persistently claimed the right to organize small sectional work-

shops. Thus two concepts of economic planning, and also government policy and popular demands, were pitted against each other.

On July 25, 1793 (7 Thermidor, year I), Bouchotte, Minister of War, once again attempted to reconcile these conflicting interests and, "for the sake of efficiency," to smooth out the difficulties between the sections and the Uniform Supplies Commission. On July 30 (12 Thermidor), the commissars of the forty-eight sections pointed out to the General Council of the Commune the number of "inconveniences that arise from grouping together a large number of citizens in a single workshop"; they considered the parceling-out among the sections a far more advantageous system. On August 9 (21 Thermidor), the Convention decreed the organization of no less than six large cutting workshops in Paris and of a distribution and delivery bureau near each workshop; the distribution of basting would be in proportion to the needs of each section.

The workers were even more incensed at the manner with which the administrators distributed the work. On August 25 (8 Fructidor, year I), a deputation of women demanded a reorganization of the garment industry workshops and "that the workers' transportation costs be paid." To silence these complaints, on August 30, 1793 (13 Fructidor), the Convention authorized the Ministry of War to increase the number of distribution bureaus to thirty-six, so as to avoid excessive travel for the workers; the general assemblies nominated one commissar for each section to supervise the distribution and delivery of material for the garment trade. Complaints continued to be made during the course of the year II, the sans-culottes having little patience with what they considered to be tight administrative control. They were against the entrepreneurs and subcontractors, a reaction they simply could not help. On October 2, 1793 (10 Vendémiaire, year II), the committee of *Faubourg-Montmartre*, "in the name of the unemployed women of this section," demanded that the Jacobins "find work for these women in making uniforms for the troops." At about the same time, the Hommes-Libres society of *Révolutionnaire* demanded that the distribution of work be entrusted to the sections, "who best know the real needs and patriotism of their citizens," and stated the right of equal working opportunities for the "unemployed and laboring classes."

Complaints against the entrepreneurs and subcontractors were far more virulent. On October 1, 1793 (9 Vendémiaire, year II), a deputation of cobblers declared before the Convention that they alone should be recognized as purveyors of shoes for the troops. On 4 Pluviôse, the popular society of *Unité* proposed "a law that would abolish and dismiss every subcontractor of the Republic who, by devious methods, managed to wheedle his way into supplying equipment for the troops." Who suffered? "It's the Republic that suffers, unemployed artisans suffer, as do poor workers who, in order to eat, are forced to go to the snobs and ask for work in the clothing industry at scandalous wages." To avoid having to have recourse to these middlemen, the society of *Unité* declared that "all merchandise necessary for equipping and furnishing the armies should be pooled without delay in the various independent warehouses, so that these goods be shared out among the clothing workshops of the sections," established by decree on August 30, 1793 (13 Fructidor, year I). In this manner the workers would be employed "and the bread they will eat will revive their republican sentiments." The petition denounced the profits of the monopolist subcontractors. The deals they made appeared to benefit the Republic; whereas in fact, "the monopolists forced the unfortunate to shoulder the whole weight of their cupidity." They paid between fifteen and eighteen sous for making a pair of gaiters, ten to twelve for a shirt, whereas the garments sold for thirty sous, and the thread the worker had to provide cost him almost half of his wages.

This petition was so in tune with public hostility toward commercial capital that it received widespread support from the section organizations, such as the *Lepeletier* society on 7 Pluviôse and the general assembly of *Invalides* on the fifteenth. The workers of the latter renewed the assault on 30 Pluviôse, presenting to the Assembly a petition that wanted "the uniforms to be made for the soldiers of the Republic to be given to the sectional workshops and not to the greedy subcontractors who to a large extent fixed the prices for work."

The Assembly considered that "it was fair that the profits to be made from public works benefit the largest number of poor people possible," at the same time naming commissioners to accompany the petitioners to the Jacobins. The popular society of *Unité*, which had unsuccessfully presented its petition to the Convention on 20 Pluviôse, managed on the twenty-fourth before the General Council of the Commune to get the support of all the sections and popular societies. Their commissars presented themselves at the bar of the Convention on 5 Ventôse; the petition was again sent to the Public Safety Committee. Since social problems were by now alarming, the petition became another warning to the government. Once the crisis was over and the Cordelier leadership eliminated, the committee no longer had to yield to popular demands, which would have alienated that faction of the bourgeoisie for whom the war market was a source of profit from the revolutionary government, at the precise moment when the committees were partially revising their commercial policies in a liberal direction.

The problem, therefore, persisted together with the demands of the people. The hardening of government policy after Germinal did not manage to prevent these problems from arising. On 15 Floréal the general assembly of *Bonnet-Rouge* denounced a new aristocracy, that of the entrepreneurs: "One single person, always the richest, is sure to absorb all lucrative enterprises, when a fair distribution of these enterprises would offer a vast number of good citizens legal benefits and the means of supporting their families." The establishment of the twelve executive commissions was to urge "the gathering together of a vast number of workers of all types." A few entrepreneurs must not monopolize all the work. In order to prevent the monopoly contemplated by these "financial entrepreneurs," the Convention should decree that no one be allowed to subcontract his various operations without obtaining a certificate of patriotism. Thus putting off all those greedy speculators, who would far rather stand aside than run the risk of a confrontation which would likely go against them. As for the sans-culotte, who would easily obtain the certificate he merited, he will take only "that portion of the work which belongs to him, without denying his brother sans-culottes." The militants of *Bonnet-Rouge* intended to turn the Terror against commercial capital: if the merchant entrepreneurs were refused certificates of patriotism, they would be placed in the category of being suspect. This petition had the same fate as previous ones: it came at the exact moment when the government committees were relaxing the economic terror, for the benefit of the propertied classes.

The sectional workshops manufacturing clothing for the troops were, however, not immediately done away with by the Thermidorian reaction; doubtless they rendered certain services. The crushing of the Parisian sans-culottes during the Prairial days of the year III finally brought about their suppression: on 25 Prairial the Public Safety Committee authorized the provisions commission to liquidate the cutting workshops and the distribution bureaus of the Paris Commune and to make contracts for outfitting troops with individual entrepreneurs.

History was repeating itself. It was impossible to give preferential treatment to small independent production when economic freedom had been restored and when the merchant bourgeoisie considered the manufacture of war matériel the particular domain of their capitalist initiative.

4. Popular Fiscal Law

Like the actions taken against monopoly in the manufacture of war matériel, sectional fiscal policies allow us
to discern the social aspirations of the sans-culottes and
to determine their limitations. They, too, were an attempt
to close the gap between the rich and the poor and to
equalize the conditions of existence.

In this instance, the social instinct was combined with
revolutionary fervor, the "haves" more often than not being moderates. Popular ideas on monetary matters sprang
from the same source as the Ventôse decrees. It was a
case of rescuing the less fortunate citizens by taxing the
rich; it was also essential to strike at the enemies of the
Revolution. The decree brought before the Commune-
Affranchie by Collot d'Herbois and Fouché on 24 Brumaire, year II, is particularly clear: the revolutionary tax
levied on the rich was to be commensurate with their
wealth and their incivism.

The social and political consequences of this popular
fiscal policy were identical, in their respective proportions,
to those that followed the Ventôse decree: the new law
pitted the "haves" against a system that attacked wealth,
and incited them to free themselves from the yoke of
sans-culottes democracy.

The outlook of the people who drew up the revolutionary tax system for the rich can be seen in L'Instruction
of the temporary commission of the Commune-Affranchie,
the majority of whose members were Parisian sans-
culottes. How were they to foot the cost of the war and
furnish all the needs of the Revolution if not by taxing the
rich? If they were aristocrats, it was only fitting that they
pay for a war that they brought on. If they were patriots,
they could but rejoice at seeing their fortunes serve the
Republic. Every citizen who was not in need must be sub-

ject to taxation. The reapportionment of public contributions "will not be the result of detailed mathematical calculations, nor will tentative measures help us." The tax collectors would impound everything for which a citizen had no use, since "having more than one needs is a flagrant violation of the rights of the people." Aroused by the spirit of sharing, the militant editors of *L'Instruction* attacked every form of property. The tax on the rich would not only be levied on their revenues: "Everything of which the rich have a surfeit and which can be useful to the defenders of the fatherland, the fatherland claims instantly; this means those people who have ridiculous stockpiles of sheets, shirts, napkins and shoes." All these articles were to be subject to requisition by the revolutionary government. And some people applied this literally.

That this concept, according to which the rich alone should bear the burden of the charges on the state and ease the lot of poor citizens, was characteristic of popular attitudes is further shown by its survival during the reaction of year III. The address of the *Piques* section before the Convention on 30 Germinal, which denounced the former Terrorists, demanded a constitution "which, above all, should not condemn a poor man to fulfilling the duties of a rich man who more often than not ignores them. The man who has property requiring extensive guarantees should therefore contribute more to the state." The address continues, "It is time to attack those rich egotists who share neither our anguish nor our dangers; hitch them to the shafts of the constitutional chariot; let them use their strength to pull it, so that the small farmer, the artisan and the poor can drive it effortlessly."

The sectional militants had several occasions between August 10 and 9 Thermidor to put these principles to a test. The loans, taxes or voluntary contributions put into effect by the order of general assemblies in the various sections were usually set aside for support of the war effort, either for arming and equipping volunteers or for organizing the collection of saltpeter, or giving assistance to the wives and children of soldiers. Less commonly, these levies were used to relieve the misery of the poor. In this instance, the social aspirations of the sans-culottes appear to have been directed by the demands of the revolutionary struggle rather than by their own principles.

The law of 13 Frimaire, year III, ordered an audit of the accounts of the legal authorities who collected revolutionary taxes and voluntary or forced contributions; the *Théâtre-Français* section, formerly *Marat*, protested it the moment it was announced. In September 1792, the Assembly had demanded a voluntary contribution for arms and uniforms. In March 1793, further voluntary contributions were collected on the occasion of the conscription of 300,000 men, and again in May, during the recruitment for the Vendée campaign. In Frimaire, year II, a subscription was started "for the relief of the persons who had suffered from a fire in the Rue Serpente." Another collection was made in Nivôse for arms and equipment for the Jacobin dragoons recruited by the section. In Germinal, there was still another for torches for the companies and for the expenses of the celebration planned in memory of the martyrs for freedom. In Floréal, the general assembly ordered a final collection "to meet its commitments to the defenders of the fatherland and to their families."

Taking the sections as a whole, the popular demands for fiscal changes were at first determined by the danger from outside. The militants began to tax the rich to arm or assist the volunteers. The class aspects of the tax became more pronounced as the power of the people increased. The first demand for a class-oriented tax came during the disturbances in September 1792. On September 2, the committee of *Montreuil* section demanded "a law which would force all persons with private incomes who could not pay for the defense of freedom through the sweat of their brow, to give part of their fortune to support the wives and children whose fathers were fighting the war." On the same day, the people of *Poissonnière* took notice of a resolution of the *Gravilliers* section proposing "that rich old men assume responsibility for the wives and children of citizens recruited for the front."

These demands obviously did not produce satisfactory results: the propertied class still had enough power not to
have to surrender in this matter. General assemblies, such
as that of *Théâtre-Français*, organized *voluntary* contributions in their own areas: it is impossible, however, to discern the precise nature of these levies.

In March 1793, after the recruitment of 300,000 men
had been decreed on February 24, there was an increase
in the number of revolutionary taxes: taxes for equipping
the soldiers, and assisting their wives and children. But
the sans-culottes still were not absolute masters of their
own sections; the "haves" fought them for power. Thus
taxation was not a mere matter of class warfare, but rather
was the result of a compromise. On March 9, the general
assembly of *Bondy* decided to clothe and arm all the volunteers of the section. Since, however, they considered
that "one of the reasons which, until this moment, had
delayed the movement of the intrepid defenders of freedom had been their uncertainty over the well-being of
their fathers, mothers, wives and children," the assembly
decided "that the wives, children, mothers and fathers of
poor citizens who left for the front would be fed and have
their rents paid by the citizens of the section." The section
left it to the propertied classes who were members of the
assembly to impose taxes upon themselves, "to lay aside
a small part of their wealth to compensate for the dangers,
the suffering, even the lives of those who were marching
on the enemy, in order to guarantee them all the advantages of our holy Revolution and their own wealth." The
section reserved the right to determine the amount of a
citizen's contributions only if it should appear grossly insufficient. This was in fact a compromise between the
"haves" and the sans-culottes, the former giving their
money and the latter their blood: a compromise which in
another form confirmed the privilege of substitution
(money payment to exempt a conscript), which the sans-
culottes were to protest against when they came to power.
On the same principle, the general assembly of *Temple*
decreed on March 11, 1793 (Ventôse, year 1), "that all

the citizens will contribute voluntarily and according to their means, which they will themselves evaluate, to the needs of those of our brothers who are leaving for the frontier."

After June 2, the ill will of the "haves" persisted in many sections which in the meanwhile continued to depend upon their generosity. This alone emphasizes the consistent weakness of the popular movement. On June 4, the civil and revolutionary committees of *Indivisibilité* alerted its general assembly: "Many wealthy citizens refuse to give of their person and wealth in support of freedom and equality"; others do not contribute in proportion to their ability. Meantime, the assembly decided to allocate 100 livres a month to each volunteer, plus assistance to his family, as long as the Vendée campaign lasted: in other words, 30,000 livres a month for the section's fifteen companies. The committees pointed to two means of fulfilling these commitments. "The first is that each rich person in the section must promise in writing that voluntarily and in good conscience, according to his abilities, he will donate his prescribed sum of money until the Vendée campaign is over; the second is a compulsory tax to be levied on rich citizens." The committees decided on the first solution. The sums of money pledged would be printed and posted. "If it appears that certain pledges do not conform to the presumed wealth [of an individual], the general assembly will be empowered to take whatever measures it considers appropriate to make the said citizens pay according to their means."

After the events of September 1793, the sans-culottes finally dominated their sections: that which had been left to the goodwill of the "haves" became a demand. Then taxation took on class characteristics and was considered revolutionary. Chaumette expressed this new state of mind when he declared on 19 Brumaire before the General Assembly of the Commune: "Since the rich have refused to contribute in any manner whatsoever toward the well-being of our brothers, it has been necessary to force them to pay for the activities and surveillance of the sans-culottes." If the "haves" failed to fulfill their potential, then they had to be forced to do so. Antoine Lebrun, a carpet maker, justice of the peace of *Bonnet-Rouge*, was arrested in Prairial, year III, for having declared in September 1793 "that we knew how to use the bayonet to get the money to provide for the pressing needs of the wives and children of the defenders of the fatherland." Antoine Maréchal, a carpenter, revolutionary commissar of the *Mont-Blanc* section, was denounced in Frimaire, year III. Throughout the year II he never stopped demanding "forced revolutionary taxes" on the rich. During a party given by the section in honor of Marat, to the comment that it would cost an awful lot of money, Maréchal exclaimed, "We have rich people in this section, suspicious people, we'll arrest them and, if necessary, impose a revolutionary tax of 100,000 écus."

When the law of 14 Frimaire, whereby the revolutionary government forbade levying similar taxes, was passed, the sans-culottes henceforth were satisfied with organizing *voluntary* subscriptions in their own sections. The rich still had to make their offerings, for fear of being suspected of incivism. They did this unwillingly. When the commissars of *Halle-au-Blé*, charged with collecting for the equipment of a Jacobin dragoon, turned up at the house of the assigned contributor, Petit, a doctor, he received them, crying out: "What, you again! When will it all end?" and gave them a ten-sol *assignat*, although it was generally known that he enjoyed an income of approximately 5,000 livres. When Petit was denounced in the general assembly, he was unanimously declared to be a bad citizen; this finding was published and posted.

During the course of the winter, *voluntary* collections were increased, creating further tension between the "haves" and the sans-culottes; equipping of Jacobin cavalrymen, collecting saltpeter, ceremonies celebrating the tenth day festival, civic festivals were also occasions for indirectly taxing the rich. Display of wealth would almost certainly give rise to suspicion by the popular authorities. At the beginning of Pluviôse, the *Lepeletier* society decided to equip a Jacobin cavalryman. They sent out a circular to wealthy citizens: "How fortunate you are to have more than they [the sans-culottes] and be in a position to give money! You would not wish to deny yourselves this favor which your brothers see without envy only because they all are prepared to offer their blood for the mother country as compensation." On 30 Pluviôse, the assembly of *Lombards* adopted a rule about the organization of the saltpeter industry. A collection was organized to subsidize setting up a workshop and paying ten livres per day to the sans-culottes assigned to this task. Article 3 of the authorization was amended to read that if the rich failed to give according to their means, the fact would be reported to the general assembly. On 30 Ventôse, the *Chalier* section decided on a collection for purchasing three copper caldrons necessary for refining saltpeter; on 5 Germinal, after having praised the sans-culottes, who had contributed as much as they could (poor journeymen gave as much as twenty livres), the saltpeter commissar "complained bitterly against these vile self-centered snobs, enemies of the Revolution, who keep everything for themselves and appear to insult the misery of the people by their ostentation and their sumptuous style of living"; rich people worth 40,000 livres, others with several servants, "individuals who once had their carriages," did not blush to offer only twenty sous or five livres. The general assembly ordered that the list of these wealthy people be sent to the revolutionary committee, "enjoining it to treat them as suspects according to the law."

Since the sections lost the power of levying revolutionary taxes by the law of 14 Frimaire, and since they proceeded to make only *voluntary* collections, only a few documents dated before 14 Frimaire give any idea of the principles of popular fiscal policy. The taxes levied from June 1793 to Frimaire, year II, were essentially aimed at paying back advances made by the Treasury, on the order of the Convention, and which allowed the sections to fulfill their commitments to the volunteers for the Vendée campaign.

On June 11, 1793, the general assembly of *Panthéon-*

Français decided, in order to liquidate its debt, to levy a contribution on all landed and mobile property in the section; this levy did not extend to the "poor class of workers." The tax was a moderate one; it was certainly not in any way progressive. Landed property was taxed 10 per cent of its income, with a deduction for legal costs and of 150 livres for each child under the age of fifteen. The tax was the same for mobile wealth, but calculated on house rent. Lawyers and men of the law would contribute a tenth of their rent; teachers, a twentieth; public servants, six deniers for each livre (2.5 per cent) of salary. Finally, those citizens "who lived entirely by the work of their hands" were taxed six deniers for each livre of rent over and above 100 livres; anyone earning less might contribute whatever he desired. Although workers and employees were favored, the taxes on landed and mobile property—in the absence of any progressive rate—were moderate: indeed, were not many sans-culottes themselves owners of workshops or land?

The *Gravilliers* section adopted a progressive system. On June 6–8, its revolutionary committee discussed "a method of assessing the rich," in order to repay the 180,000 livres borrowed by the section. Finally the assembly fixed the minimum tax from 1,200 livres on landed property to 300 on rents, the basic tax being 5 per cent "and rising progressively." Unfortunately the rate of progression was not mentioned. A verbatim report of the September 5 discussions in the *Lombards* section in favor of paying back the loan made by the national Treasury for the volunteers for the Vendée campaign, was identical in the incidence of taxation, but went into greater detail. All the citizens in the section whose income from government salaries, land or industry exceeded 1,200 livres per annum, either proved or presumed, were to be taxed. Citizens who were "well off and lived on their incomes," that is, who did not work, were to pay 50 per cent more than the taxes imposed on other citizens. Bachelors had to pay a surtax over and above the regular tax. On the other hand, every head of a household who had at least four children younger than twelve years had to pay only half the tax, and every aged or sick relative would count as a child. Finally, single "young businessmen, bank tellers, notaries' and lawyers' clerks, lodged at the expense of those for whom they worked" and who were not summoned for the Vendée campaign, were penalized: they were to pay ten to fifty livres, according to each individual case. Here again, the absence of two essential factors makes it hard to understand the impact of popular fiscal policies: the rate and the scale of progression.

Even more straightforward on this point was the project for *contributions* of the *Bonne-Nouvelle* section. Owners of apartment buildings and people with private incomes were to be taxed one fifth of the net returns on their buildings or their stocks: no minimum tax or progressive scale was specified for this category. A tax was to be imposed on every tenant; in order that this contribution not be too hard on the "poor class," the general assembly set a minimum; the scale was to be progressive; one sol for every livre (5 per cent) was the minimum tax on 300 livres of rent; one sol, six deniers for every livre (7.5 per cent) between 300 and 600 livres; two sols on every livre (10 per cent) between 600 and 1,000 livres; two sols, six deniers on every livre (12.5 per cent) for any rent over and above 1,000 livres. Civil servants, employees, pensioners were to be taxed according to their salaries: at the rate of one sol for every livre (5 per cent) up to a salary of 2,000 livres; one sol, six deniers on the livre (7.5 per cent) for salaries between 2,000 livres and 4,000 livres; two sols on every livre (10 per cent) of any salary over and above 4,000 livres.

The moderate character of this popular tax is particularly striking. The Parisian sections had repeatedly demanded from the Commune and the Convention progressive taxes on the rich under the name of forced loans. The Convention finally decreed an exceptional forced loan, but only reluctantly. When this loan project, already decreed in principle, came under discussion on June 21,

Robespierre declared that the measure did not spare medium-sized fortunes sufficiently, but at the same time he recommended that the rich should not be frightened. Popular fiscal policy shows the same contradiction: it took care to spare the "have-nots," but did so without crippling landed or mobile property, from which many sans-culottes, artisans or shopowners, to a certain extent benefited.

5. THE RIGHTS TO EQUAL WORK OPPORTUNITY AND TO ASSISTANCE

According to popular thinking, fiscal policy ought to rectify the inequality of living conditions, in default of a redistribution of property, by imposing a ceiling on fortunes. Demands for the right to work and to assistance tended to have the same aims: to guarantee every citizen independence and subsistence. The right to work and the right to assistance seemed corollaries of the right to exist: an attempt to guarantee economic equality.

On May 22, 1793 (Prairial, year 1), when the *Gravilliers* section presented its volunteers for the Vendée campaign, it demanded that the Convention guarantee the support of the sans-culottes, especially in public works. The Declaration of Rights of June 24 was less clear: there is no explicit mention of the right to work, only of the right to assistance. Popular thought held that the one went with the other. In its petition of July 27, 1793 (Thermidor, year 1), the *Maison-Commune* section deduced that both stemmed from the right to existence. Unemployment and high prices deprived "the less wealthy class" of its existence; legislation must give him back this right; this could be *easily* achieved "by work, and by moderate prices for foodstuffs." Consequently the committee of *Maison-Commune* demanded the opening of public works. "In a nation where freedom and equality reign," states a petition from *Hommes-Libres* in Brumaire, year ii, "public works are the property of the poor and working classes of society"; this was to claim the right to work.

The popular demands concerning the forms of assistance were more detailed and adamant.

Just before May 31, during their conflict with the moderates, the more progressive sections attached the utmost importance to the organization of public assistance; it was necessary to rally the poorest sans-culottes. The Convention, by its decree of November 26, 1792 (6 Frimaire, year 1), had already granted assistance to the parents and children of volunteers, a measure which, on May 4, 1793 (14 Floréal, year 1), was extended to the families of all ranks in the Army. The *Invalides* committee went further; on May 8, they demanded pensions for widows and orphans, for the wounded, for those who lost their means of livelihood; the funds would be provided by the contribution of one twelfth of the annual income of citizens old enough to bear arms. It was no longer merely a matter of granting assistance to the parents and children of the volunteers; once again one had to make the rich contribute to caring for those in need; the measures envisaged often gave rise to a certain class antagonism against the "haves." The forced loans levied on the rich that had been demanded by the people of Faubourg Saint-Antoine on May 1, 1793 (11 Floréal, year 1), were initiated in order to equip the volunteers, but also to assist the poor.

After June 2, the tone of these demands changed and became more insistent. On June 10, the gunners of the *Quatre-Vingt-Douze* section demanded a constitution "which would declare assistance from the nation to be the property of the poor." The Declaration of Rights complied: public assistance was declared a *sacred debt*. This program still had to be organized. During the preceding March, the Convention had indeed laid the groundwork for the general organization of public assistance. On June 28, it adopted a measure on the annual grant of money to children, old people, the poor; on October 15 it tackled the problem of suppressing beggars. No steps to apply these general decrees were ever taken and the demands continued.

When the Constitution was adopted, many of the Parisian primary assemblies, in particular those of the Faubourg Saint-Antoine, congratulated the Convention for having proclaimed the right to existence, but urged that it "fulfill its commitments." The *Quinze-Vingts, Popincourt* and *Montreuil* sections, which had the largest number of poor people, declared on July 4, 1793 (Messidor, year 1), that it was time that the poor, who until this time had alone supported the Revolution, "begin to reap the benefits"; they demanded "the establishment, so long desired, of workshops where workingmen, at all times and in all places, can find the work they need; hostels where the aged and the sick can receive assistance with the brotherly love which humanity owes them." On July 17, the Society of Republican Revolutionary Women demanded the *organization of public assistance*. On August 14, the whole body of the Paris sections delivered to the General Council a petition addressed to the Convention on the organization of hostels and hospitals. Upon the departure of the young men for the front, in early September, the same demands were made in patriotic orations. Speeches made in the *Montreuil* section on September 11 reminded the Convention of its *sacred promise;* "the nation's generosity owes [our parents] the assistance which our absence makes necessary." The same demands were made by the conscripted men of the *Popincourt* section on September 22.

In Brumaire, measures adopted by Fouché in the Nièvre, and commented upon with enthusiasm by Chaumette before the General Assembly aroused new demands. "On 11 Brumaire the Commune attorney declared, 'People have written to me to the effect that this country has no more nobles or priests, or wealthy persons; I say rich persons, because we have found a means of eliminating poverty in giving assistance to all unfortunate cripples and impoverished citizens.'" Chaumette demanded a plan for assistance, "to provide relief for the aged, the infirm, and to at least provide jobs for the poor so as to eliminate begging in Paris and to offer assistance to suffering humanity." The rich would foot the bill. "Ah, the rich! We must force them to do good and to contribute voluntarily or by force to the happiness of all." Once again, declarations of principle were not implemented by action. The *Mucius-Scaevola* section suggested to the Convention on 22 Brumaire that the necessary sums of money be raised by levying forced loans on the rich; this suggestion was rejected. Always "at the expense of the rich snobs," the popular society of the *Popincourt* section demanded on 28 Nivôse, that hostels be organized for poor and aged citizens: "being poor, this section grieves to see our brothers suffer without being able to help them."

The worsening of living conditions toward the end of the winter of the year II brought a new series of demands for the organization of public assistance. On 3 Ventôse, Hanriot pointed to the organization in the *Contrat-Social* section of a center "where pregnant women would be received and would get the food necessary in their condition." The *l'Homme-Armé* section adopted a resolution "on the assistance that ought to be given to the unfortunate," especially supported by the *Lepeletier* society on 14 Ventôse, and by the *Invalides* section on the fifteenth. Referring to Article 21 of the Declaration, the *l'Homme-Armé* section reminded the Convention that "it was time to give poor citizens their rights." It demanded the establishment of a center in each section, "so that the rich egotist, in his own house, can no longer hope for the special attention and comforts which poor brothers will not receive in the center and which will have been prepared for them by our republican hands." No healthy poor person should be granted admission to these centers: temporary assistance will be given them, particularly in finding work or the raw materials needed for their occupations. On 15 Ventôse, the popular society of the *Bonne-Nouvelle* section also offered the Convention its ideas "on the means of making the different classes of society contribute proportionately for the assistance of the poor." On the twenty-ninth, the popular society of the

Lombards section discussed a project for a local welfare fund: "each member, according to the projected plans, will be guaranteed, in the event of sickness, assistance from the society." Here were the principles of social security. The decree of 22 Floréal concerning the establishment in each département of a program of national relief outlined this system of social security which the sans-culottes demanded in their confused manner, but it was still poorly distinguished from the traditional concepts of charity. After Thermidor, nothing of all this survived; great hopes were dashed.

6. THE RIGHT TO EDUCATION

The situation was the same in the case of public education, the organization of which would also have contributed to achieving *equal incomes*.

As sons of their century, the sans-culottes attached as much importance to their demand for education as to their demands for other social rights. In it they saw a means of ameliorating their lot, to rise in society and to destroy the empire of wealth, since education, if the community failed to guarantee it to all, was the most valuable privilege of the wealthy classes. The sans-culottes also anticipated a strengthening of the Republic from educational progress; the future, they considered, would be secure only if the younger generation were nourished on their ideals. Thus the demand for free education was included in the social action of the sans-culottes and deserves to be examined.

After May 31, the more progressive sections insisted upon the organization of public education or tried to provide it themselves. On March 17, 1793 (Ventôse, year 1), the patriotic society of the *Luxembourg* section decided to establish "public and provisional education for children." In view of the great need for education, the society itself took on the task of teaching them to read and write; it would accept children, boys and girls, between the ages of six and twelve, twice a week. It paid special attention to instruction in ethics and civics. "Education will be based on explaining to children their duties and obligations toward their country and their parents, to inculcate the manners and attitudes which they must aim for in order to be useful members of society; we will nurture their natural goodness, teach them pity, respect for the aged . . . We shall show them by suitable simple examples the purpose of every society, and the various forms of government which might be adopted; above all, we shall teach them about government based on freedom and equality. We shall explain to them natural laws, political laws and civil laws. To this will be added the definition of sovereignty, of the will of the people, of freedom, of equality, of the Republic; and we shall tell them about the horrors attached to all tyrannical government and about the happiness which naturally emanates from republican government." The society of the *Luxembourg* section was above all concerned with teaching civics and politics.

These same concerns guided the *Observatoire, Finistère, Sans-Culottes* and *Panthéon-Français* sections when, in May, they demanded a national code of education conforming to the principles of the Republic. The *Gravilliers* section urged, on May 22, that the Convention guarantee the nation's unity and indivisibility through the means of national education.

After June 2, the organization of education more than ever appeared necessary to consolidate the peoples' victory. "On the one hand, ignorance and fanaticism negate four years of struggle and sacrifice," declared a citizen in the general assembly of the *Amis-de-la-Patrie* section on June 16, "on the other hand, education dissipates prejudice and makes us cherish a Revolution whose solid foundations are only to be found in virtue." The speaker insisted on the need "to give poor people every opportunity to receive instruction," and urged a prompt organization of primary schools. In recognizing the right to education the Declaration of June 24, 1793, gave theoretic support to popular demands. But as stated in the *Panthéon-Français* section on June 27, "it is not enough to make laws, we must also guarantee their enforcement." Since the Constitution had been won, we must now "erect the column which must serve as a barricade against the prejudices of the Church and of the nobility: we must decree the organization of a school system which will be both communal and republican; this institution, neglected too long, is an integral part of the great plans for public safety. Ignorance and fanaticism are far more of a threat than the Vendée rising, than the weapons of the rebels." Once again, the aims were essentially political: it was a question of organizing "a national system of education which would offer the sans-culottes the skills required for every kind of employment."

The congratulatory speeches made on the occasion of the ratification of the Constitution stressed the need for speedy organization of a system of public education. One such speech was made in the *Amis-de-la-Patrie* section on July 4. On the same day, the *Fédérés* section demanded "a well-structured educational system which would guarantee the well-being of our children"; the shopkeepers invited the Convention to organize "a national system of education according to popular principles." On July 7, the *Bon-Conseil* section demanded a system of national education which would germinate "the seed of patriotic virtues"; on the fourteenth, the *Droits-de-l'Homme* section demanded "a public education which would teach the citizens their duties and what virtues they should practice."

The sans-culottes, however, had no intention of being satisfied with a mere civic education for forming future citizens; they also wanted a practical education which, being professionally organized, would prepare the young for specific activities. Here the influence of the ideas of the century is notable, particularly Rousseau's *Emile*: one must instill into children moral principles and occupational skills rather than intellectual knowledge. On July 4, the *Faubourg-Montmartre* section demanded "not one of those metaphysical educations which weaken republican manners and virtues, but an education suitable for perfecting the arts and the trades, in order to provide a great boost to natural industry, to our factories, to our commerce, and to destroy tyranny forever." On the same day, the three sections of Faubourg Saint-Antoine declared that they were waiting with the utmost confidence for the law pertaining to education: "We are absolutely confident that in it we will find the means of making the small farmer happy . . . with all the new inventions which would simplify his work and increase his profits; that the artisan, the soul of commerce, will find in it a means of perfecting his skill, the worker his talent, and that you will banish anything which might allow the rebirth or the perpetration of superstitious ideas."

On July 13, Robespierre announced before the Convention a plan formulated by Lepeletier de Saint-Fargeau; on the twenty-ninth, in the name of the Committee of Public Education, he proposed the adoption of this plan. Nothing much happened after this, although the organization of public education served as grounds for agitation on the part of the opposition. On July 17, the Society of Republican Revolutionary Women clamored for action on the plan. On August 17 in *L'Ami du Peuple*, Leclerc thanked "the person who conceived of the idea of giving the same educational opportunity to all children," that is, Lepeletier. "Why is it that the National Convention has failed to adopt this wise measure in its entirety, why does it fear forcing parents to submit to this new level of equality in sending their children, regardless of their background, to the same educational institutions?" Hébert was more vehement: "Never will we have good generals, good magistrates, until a sound education has transformed man." He urged that the Convention hasten "to provide education for the sans-culottes, in order to free them from the tyranny of the legal profession and men with the gift of the gab."

Encouraged by these words, the sections renewed their assault. On August 25, the *Lombards* section presented a petition to the Convention which said that national education must be *mandatory and free*. On September 12, the *Panthéon-Français* section posited the following principle: "The law punishes, education persuades," and demanded that a free public school be opened in every section or district. However, it was not only a question of educating children and young people; it was important not to forget the adult population, who were still subjected "to the influence of traditional prejudices." On October 21, the Convention voted a decree establishing state primary schools, with programs which combined physical, intellectual, and cultural instruction with instruction in ethics, gymnastics and the practical arts. However, it came up for discussion again after 14 Brumaire. The movement in favor of de-Christianization felt the urgent need for organizing; their ends were not purely destructive. When the *Mucius-Scaevola* and the *Bonnet-Rouge* sections brought the Convention the spoils of churches on 22 Brumaire, they urged it to organize "a national educational system that would be the same for all." On 6 Frimaire, "the young children" of the *Mucius-Scaevola* section returned, and in no uncertain terms, asked that the Convention "promptly organize primary schools."

Government red tape occasionally forced popular sectional societies to take the matter into their own hands. The *Bonne-Nouvelle* section organized "a course in ethics and logic," and the Lazowski society opened "a school of ethics for young citizens." When the popular society of the *Réunion* section proposed, on 27 Brumaire, "a course in ethics conforming to the laws of nature and of truth," its general assembly adopted the same ideas and created a commission on public education.

On 29 Frimaire, the Convention adopted a decree that concerned public education and particularly primary schools. It established a system of free education, controlled by the state, and decentralized, which corresponded fairly well with public opinion. But again, it was a question of putting the law into effect and throughout the war, the revolutionary government neglected this task.

Recriminations persisted. In Pluviôse, Hébert said, in Number 349 of his paper: "*Père Duchesne* is enraged to see that public instruction is not getting off the ground and that there are monopolists of the spirit who do not wish to see the people educated, so that the beggars should still be poor." On 6 Pluviôse the pupils of the *Fontaine-de-Grenelle* section told the Convention that their teachers "languished in the most frightful poverty; they had not been paid in three years." On the seventeenth of the same month pupils from *Mucius-Scaevola* again came before the Convention to demand "that primary schools be organized immediately."

The question of school books was no less urgent and drew the attention of the sectional authorities. On 22 Brumaire, the revolutionary committee from *Lepeletier* denounced an aristocratic edition entitled *New Method Of Learning the ABC* and urged heads of families to check on their children's teachers, so that "they do not teach this reactionary text." The decree of 29 Frimaire gave the Committee of Public Education the responsibility of publishing "elementary books on subjects absolutely essential for the instruction of citizens." On 9 Pluviôse, the Convention opened a competition for publishing elementary textbooks. In the meanwhile the sections were getting impatient. On 17 Pluviôse, the pupils of *Mucius-Scaevola* demanded elementary textbooks from which they could "learn love for the fatherland, the principles of wisdom and of all the virtues." On the twentieth, the pupils of the *Finistère* section announced that they were still waiting "for elementary textbooks on ethics and other sciences."

During Ventôse, the anger caused by the delay in the organization of public education contributed to the general unrest of the sans-culottes. According to the observer Charmont, writing on 5 Ventôse, "We are weary of not seeing the children receiving this new education which one day must bring happiness to future generations"; primary schools should be opened at last. On the tenth, the *Sans-Culottes* section adopted a vehement petition; it has become *absolutely essential* that primary education be organized, "in such a manner that individuals acquire the talents and virtues necessary for enjoying the fullness of their natural rights." On the fourteenth, according to the observer Hanriot, "The desire for public education is so strongly pronounced that they are complaining that no schools had been opened anywhere for the teaching of republican ideas. It would seem, said a good citizen speaking at a meeting of one of the societies, that we wish to put the chariot of the Revolution on the skids." The petition of the *Sans-Culottes* section was sent to the General Assembly on 15 Ventôse; it was well received by the *Montagne* section. By way of reply to the unanimous demand, the département posted on the twenty-first a demand for speedy establishment of primary schools; according to one observer, "the enthusiasm with which the people read these posters proved the good citizens' desire for the prompt organization of republican schools."

It would appear that some action was taken on this demand by the département. However, in spite of the good intentions of the authorities, the problems were immense: everything was lacking, building sites, books and materials. Neither the sections nor the Commune had sufficient resources to organize schools. On 19 Germinal, the commissars of the *Halle-au-Blé* section informed the département that their section did not have a single school. In order to start an establishment for boys and girls, they demanded that they be given the use of two government-owned houses; as for benches and desks, they wanted to have those belonging to Duplessis College, which had been turned into a jail. The département was only able to assign one of its members to accompany the commissar to the Committee of Public Education. However, the committee was not empowered to make decisions about the distribution of national property.

This indicates the insurmountable difficulties faced by the public authorities in organizing sectional schools; many gave up the battle. The disappointment of the sans-culottes was the greater because they had placed so much hope in education, seeing in it a means of consolidating the regime and of improving themselves.

The notion of limited property rights, demands for action against monopolies in public enterprises, demands for the organization of a fiscal policy, for public assistance and for education which would have realized a situation of *equal incomes*, and that in the name of a right to exist, which, although never clearly expressed, was nonetheless very much felt: all these currents characterized a social ideal which corresponded to the economic conditions of the time.

Whether peasant or artisan, whether it was a question of personal freedom or the freedom to work at what they wished, the sans-culottes had first to cast off their feudal dependence on others, a dependence that tied them to the land, or made them prisoners in an industrial enterprise. Hence their hatred of the feudal aristocracy and their hostility toward the ancien régime and its corporate organization; without their assistance, the bourgeoisie would never have triumphed. Visibly productive, they based the foundations of property on individual work and dreamed of a society of small owners, each with his own field, his own workshop, his own store. In order to sustain a situation of relative equality, the state intervened: by protecting small entrepreneurs, by the inheritance law, by the system of progressive taxes on incomes, by public assistance, it revitalized small business ownership, while economic growth tended to destroy it. Above all, it was a question of preventing the monopoly of wealth and the creation of a dependent proletariat.

Toward the end of the winter of year II, when the Revolution was undergoing a severe crisis, the efforts of the revolutionary government were far from bearing fruit. Had the confiscation of the possessions of Church and émigrés allowed the distribution of even a bit of ground to landless peasants? Would the abolition of corporations allow jour-neymen to set themselves up on their own?

This system of small independent producers implied the parceling out of land and the division of property; it had no appreciation of the need for social co-operation and the pooling of the means of production. The sans-culottes did not understand that when the small-enterprise regime reached a certain point in its develop-ment it would generate the agents of its own destruction. Individual and widely distributed production would per-force be transformed into highly concentrated production, and the small establishments of a mass of independent producers would be supplanted by large ownership and a capitalist minority. Business enterprise based on wage earners would replace business enterprise based on indi-vidual labor.

The sans-culottes argued over insoluble contradictions. Hostile to big shots and the rich, they were bound to the bourgeoisie either because they were already business own-ers, or because they aspired to become so. They demanded the taxation of and restrictions on property; but at the same time, bent on economic freedom so dear to the capitalist bourgeois, they demanded the independence of the shop-owning class, of the artisans and of the small rural landowner. These contradictions reflect the social composition of the sans-culottes, who, since they did not constitute a class, could not establish a coherent economic and social program. Partisans of a system of production based on individual work, the majority of the artisans were condemned to decline as the capitalist organization ad-vanced; only a minority would succeed during the upsurge of industrial capitalism.

The more progressive Montagnards, particularly the followers of Robespierre, whose social ideas were almost identical to those of the sans-culottes, were beset with the same contradictions: they, too, were victims. Hence we come to understand the irreducible antagonism which can exist between the aspirations of a social group and the objective conditions of historical necessity. This was the outline of the tragic conflict which, after the winter of the year ii, would bring about the defeat of the egalitarian republic which the sans-culottes desired, a defeat brought about by the exigencies of the bourgeois revolution.

III

THE POLITICAL INCLINATIONS
OF THE PARISIAN SANS-CULOTTES

*Although the militant sans-culottes were unable to devise
an original and efficacious social program, they brought
into play in the political arena a series of coherent ideas
which caused them to appear to be the most advanced
group of the Revolution. By interpreting popular sovereignty in its fullest meaning, the autonomy and the
permanence of the sections as being the right to make
laws, to have control over and to be able to dismiss elected
officers, they tended toward the practice of direct government and the inauguration of a popular democracy.
However, was it possible to reconcile bourgeois ideas on democracy and the exigencies of the revolutionary government with the political tendencies of the sans-culottes?*

1. POPULAR SOVEREIGNTY

Sovereignty resides in the people. This principle lies at
the root of every aspect of the political behavior of the
popular militants; sovereignty being for them not an ab-
straction, but the concrete reality of the people united in
sectional assemblies and exercising all of their rights.

Popular sovereignty is "an indefeasible right, an alien-
able right, a right that cannot be delegated"; on November
3, 1792 (12 Brumaire, year I), the *Cité* section concluded
that "every man who assumes to have sovereignty will be
regarded as a tyrant, usurper of public liberty and worthy

of death." On March 13, 1793 (22 Ventôse, year 1), a citizen declared before the general assembly of the *Panthéon-Français* section: "We are threatened with a dictatorship," whereupon the entire assembly rose and swore to "kill every dictator, protector, tribune, triumvir, every governor, under whatever style, who may attempt to destroy the sovereignty of the people." Doubtless this concern over protecting popular sovereignty explains Marat's lack of success on several occasions in nominating a dictator or tribune of the people, and the accusation made against Hébert and others, bound to lose them friends among the people, for having considered creating a "supreme judge."

The indefeasible and inalienable character of popular sovereignty was considered *a fact* by the sans-culottes when they infiltrated the sectional assemblies en masse after July 1792. Thus the distinction between active and non-active citizens. "An address made in the *Théâtre-Français* section on July 30, 1792, declared that a particular class of citizens does not have the authority to assign itself the exclusive right of saving the fatherland." The speaker therefore called upon those citizens "known in aristocratic terms as passive citizens" to fulfill their obligations to the National Guard, to debate in the general assemblies, in short to share "in the sovereignty which belongs to the section." Expressing a similar view, Hanriot declared more straightforwardly, speaking on the parade ground of the *Finistère* section on May 31: "For a long time, the rich made the laws, it is about time the poor made some laws themselves and that equality should reign between the rich and the poor."

The exercising of popular sovereignty would not be curbed: the sans-culottes intended to enjoy it in all its totality and in every area.

And first in the area of legislation: laws were valid only if they were made or sanctioned by the people. When on May 10, 1791, the Constituent Assembly, in denying the sovereignty of the group in the name of individual rights, forbade collective petitions and attempted to restrict debates in communal assemblies to "topics dealing only with municipal affairs," the Fraternal Society of the Two Sexes sitting at the Jacobins meeting hall protested against this restriction: "It deprives the communes, that is to say, the sovereign people, from exercising their basic public right, that is to deprive them of their right to exist." Sovereignty resides in groups of assembled citizens, one cannot forbid them to meet, or deprive them of the right to throw out laws they disapprove of. Every law was arbitrary, if they had not participated in drawing it up. This principle resulted in the practice of direct government, particularly during periods of crisis; these were in fact the occasions when the sans-culottes demanded their rights in totality. An address of the *Théâtre-Français* section on July 30, 1792, announced that when a nation has been declared to be threatened, "the people naturally find themselves more concerned with their sovereign rights." Furthermore, this address posited "the need to allow each département to make local laws while the fatherland was threatened." This freedom-loving tendency contradicted the exigencies of a collective national movement. According to a pamphlet published during the summer of 1792, in times of crisis, the people would not be content with electing representatives and delegating them their powers; the sovereign people's assemblies must be allowed to meet during the term of the National Convention. "While the country is in danger, the sovereign people must be at their posts, at the head of their armies, in charge of the affairs of the state; they must be everywhere."

In exceptional situations, the sans-culottes effectively exercised legislative power, such as during uprisings, or when the Constitution was accepted. On July 14, 1793 (25 Messidor, year I), numbers of sections appeared at the bar of the Convention to indicate their acceptance of the Constitutional Act; pressured by these sections, the Assembly decreed that the speakers remain in the hall, "because it is not as if they were here as petitioners but as members of the sovereign people." Similarly, on September 4, 1793

(19 Fructidor, year 1), the chamber of the General Council of the Commune was invaded: the people sat with their magistrates and held discussions with them. If the *Moniteur* simply noted that "friendly discussions were held between the people and their magistrates," the *Journal de la Montagne*, which went into detail, was more accurate: "Since the audience chamber was full, and the people found themselves mingling with their magistrates, they set to talking with them." Leclerc stated unequivocally in *L'Ami du Peuple*, August 21, 1793: "My sovereign lord, tend to your own affairs; representatives of the sovereign, descend from your high places; they belong to the people; take your seats on the benches of the amphitheater."

The establishment of the revolutionary government does not seem to have reduced the number and nature of these claims, at least until Germinal, year II. If we are to believe the denunciations of the year III, statements concerning popular rights to legislative powers were not at all unusual. In the *Marchés* section, "when a decree annoyed the conspirators [a moderate was speaking here], they used to say we are the sovereign power, only we have the right to make laws, and as a result, we are not required to enforce those which do not suit us." In the *Contrat-Social* section, Guiraut, a member of the revolutionary committee, was not in the least frightened to declare from the tribunal during the summer of 1793: "The time has come when the sections must rise and present themselves en masse before the Convention, that they tell it to make laws for the people, and above all laws which suit them; they should give them [the Convention] three months, and warn them that if by the end of this time, laws have not been passed, we will force them through at the point of a sword." Balestier, another commissar, stated, "The Convention is composed only of men paid to make laws which we ask them for, and if the decrees are unsatisfactory, they should not be discussed or put into effect."

From the principle of popular sovereignty confusedly asserted by the sans-culottes, to the theory of direct gov-

ernment, we can discern a fundamental demand of a legislative nature which the militants persistently asked for:
approval of laws by the people.

Rousseau had already proclaimed that since sovereignty
could not be alienated and since laws were the result of
the general will, "every law which the people themselves
have not ratified is null and void." In the *Bouche de fer*,
Nicolas de Bonneville explored these same principles. On
May 30, 1791, the Cordeliers declared that the nation
could be held responsible only for laws which it had con-
sented to and demanded, that the Constitution would not
be final until it had been ratified by the people; if the
primary assemblies were deprived of the right to criticize
the laws and make known their desires, the aristocracy of
representatives would succeed the landed aristocracy.

During the crisis of the summer of 1792, when the
sans-culottes invaded politics and when the August 10
uprising showed popular sovereignty in action, these principles were vociferously acclaimed. On August 9, the
general assembly of the *Marché-des-Innocents* section, outlining the *main points* of a national convention, demanded
that "its decrees on the establishment of a constitution
and of such permanent laws as those regarding marriage,
inheritance, judicial precedents," should not be enforce-
able before they had been accepted by the local assemblies. On August 27, the *Bondy* section reserved the right
to accept or reject the Constitution declared by the Convention. On September 9, speaking before the electoral
assembly of the Paris département, a representative of the
Halles section proposed that the decrees of the Convention could become law only after they had received the
sanction of the people in the local assemblies. On September 18, the general assembly of the *Halle-au-Blé* section
delegated to the deputies nominated to the Convention
"the powers necessary to propose to the French every kind
of law and every mode of government," and reminded
them that sovereignty resided in the people alone. On the
same day, the *Poissonnière* section adopted a petition
demanding that the Constitution be ratified by the peo-

ple. On September 29, the *Cité* section, considering "that it was impossible to have a Constitution without the free consent of the people," declared itself in favor of the abolition of royalty by the Convention, and of the latter's proclamation of the unity and indivisibility of the Republic; it demanded that even before concerning itself with constitutional laws, the Convention must "inform the local assemblies of the manner in which its decrees had been sanctioned." The right to ratify was asserted not only with respect to the Constitution but to all laws. On November 2, 1792 (11 Brumaire, year I), the general assembly of the *Piques* section adopted another project "on the means of sanctioning laws"; since sovereignty was inalienable, "we alone should establish our laws; their [the representatives'] only task is to suggest them to us." The laws were to be submitted to the people in the local assemblies and not to a ratifying assembly composed of delegates.

The sans-culottes did not limit their activity to theoretical assertion of rights. They used those declarations to justify their occasional opposition to decrees of the Convention and to legitimize violations of the law to serve their political interests. On December 16, 1792 (27 Frimaire, year I), the Convention, in spite of Montagnard objections, banished all the members of the Bourbon family, a measure which gave rise to considerable disturbance in the Paris sections. On the nineteenth, in the *Sans-Culottes* section, Hanriot declared that the decree constituted an attack on liberty; the general assembly insisted "that a body of men who formed a society had the right to condone or refute whatever it wanted"; as a consequence, it demanded that the decree of December 16 be subject to the sanction of the people. On July 5, 1793 (Messidor, year I), in the *Mont-Blanc* section, the president of the general assembly invoked the law to close the session at ten o'clock, whereupon Auvray, commander of a battalion, objected, "There is no such law, because the law on the books was not sanctioned by the people." If we are to believe a denunciation made on 29 Ventôse, year III, against the revolutionary committee of the *Bonnet-*

Rouge section, the commissars were in the habit of declaring "that the National Convention had passed a decree in favor of the detained, and supported by the president, they would not accept it simply because the committee had not approved it." In the *Amis-de-la-Patrie* section, Cailleux was denounced on 2 Brumaire, year III, for having said that "he had a right to question a law."

Popular ideas of sovereignty did not accept a division of powers: the people were sovereign legislators as well as sovereign judges. On May 16, 1793 (26 Floréal, year I), speaking before the General Council of the Commune, Leclerc declared, "Justice is always to be found in the midst of the people." Sans-culotte Bouland declared on several occasions, after August 10, during meetings of the *Finistère* general assembly, that "in these times of crisis, we don't need tribunals, the people are sovereign, it is proper for them to judge and execute the guilty." Was it not true that justice had always been, since the beginning of time, one of the fundamental attributes of sovereignty? When applied to the system of sectional democracy, sovereignty quite simply becomes the prerogative of the people, who will seize it if the need arises. The tribunals that sat during the September days received their powers from the people, who had not abdicated their sovereignty by delegating this power; if the people made a demand, the tribunals deferred. Thus the *Fontaine-de-Grenelle*, *Sans-Culottes* and *Quatre-Nations* sections demanded that they be under their jurisdiction: the Abbaye and Force tribunals complied. These tribunals, created by the people, were also composed of the people. One of the commissars of the General Council of the Commune declared before the Legislative Assembly on the night of September 2–3: "Having taken their revenge, the people also rendered justice."

The popular execution of justice, an attribute of sovereignty, particularly marked the crisis of September 1792. There was little opposition: it was a question of legitimizing the uprising of August 10 and overcoming the threat to the nation. In the meantime, in every critical situation the same demands were made. In March 1793, during the raising of 300,000 men, Pouxlandry, soon to be a revolutionary commissar, demanded, before the general assembly of the *Bonne-Nouvelle* section, that there be a renewal of the *September activities*, that the people must condemn all those deputies who had voted for an appeal during the trial of the king. In Prairial, year III, cobbler Duval insisted on the creation of a people's tribunal in order to save the Republic.

Lastly, there was one fundamental aspect of popular sovereignty which the sans-culottes consistently demanded and which, between July 1789 and Prairial, year III, gave rise to irreversible consequences: the power of weapons. The sovereign people must perforce be armed.

A pamphlet published as an address to the electoral college in August 1792 listed as the *pillars* of freedom: the permanence of the sections, the freedom of the press, "the free arming of every single citizen." When the sans-culottes entered sectional general assemblies in July 1792, they also forced their way into the ranks of the National Guard. The pike became the symbol of the armed sovereign people and of the new order; it was lauded, it became the *holy pike*, and ended by becoming the symbol of the sans-culottes themselves. Their political advancement can be measured in terms of their arms; their disarmament signaled the end of their influence. Since guns were, of course, more efficient than pikes, the sans-culottes were always demanding them, as when they protested the move to take away the cannons belonging to the sections, to transfer them to the armed forces, during the autumn of 1792. On November 4, the *Champs-Elysées* assembly acted on a decree issued by the *Bonne-Nouvelle* section: the assembly will never consent "that its cannons, which are its property, won on July 14, leave it except as arms of the section." On November 6, the *Cité* section adopted the same measure: the cannons were its property, only the general assembly can authorize the company of gunners to leave their posts in the section. In December 1792, an address of the *Quinze-Vingts* section reminded the Convention that only citizens had the right to be armed in the city of Paris; the ministers could not summon troops there. June 2, 1793 (13 Prairial, year I), marks the date of the general arming of the sans-culottes, as well as their political victory. On that day, the *Réunion* section, like all the more avant-garde sections, disarmed the aristocrats and the moderates, "in order to give weapons to those really worthy of fighting for freedom." The disarming of the sans-culottes in the year III was not only a precautionary measure. It symbolized political reaction to the sans-culottes, and also generally meant their exclusion from the general assembly. One of the first measures demanded by the insurgents in Prairial was the restitution of arms to citizens who had been deprived of them; Duroy had proposed this measure and it was to be one of the major charges leveled against him. The people armed and resuming their fundamental rights by insurrection: this was the extreme application of the principle of popular sovereignty that was rejected by the Thermidorians.

Popular ideas about sovereignty and its possibilities had in themselves a revolutionary content; backed by the force of the armed sections, this was demonstrated throughout the course of the Revolution, particularly during the summer of 1792. A year later, however, the aspirations and political behavior of the sans-culottes clashed with the exigencies of the revolutionary government: an exceedingly serious problem which, more than any social question, was at the heart of the crisis which was finally to bring about the downfall of the revolutionary government and the popular movement.

The popular idea of sovereignty was a decisive factor in the struggle against the monarchy. On July 31, 1792, the *Mauconseil* section made its celebrated declaration to resume its rights and no longer to recognize Louis XVI as King of the French; if it were to remain faithful to the nation, it must reject "the rest of its oath of allegiance as an abuse of its good faith." The principles of popular sovereignty and of sectional autonomy were thus carried to their logical outcome: the dissolution of the body politic. Accepting a report prepared by Vergniaud, the Legislative Assembly voided, on August 4, the *Mauconseil* decree: sovereignty belongs to all the people, not just to a small group. Thus two concepts of sovereignty confronted one another: there was but one recourse, that was to insurrection. The sections took the plunge.

After August 10, it was only a matter of time before sovereignty was concentrated within the Convention, then in the hands of its governing committees. The problem of August 1792 was less acute in the year ii, but not entirely resolved: how to reconcile the exigencies of popular sovereignty, as conceived by the sectional militants, and the needs of the revolutionary government, which was completely absorbed by the strategy of national defense.

The very term *popular sovereignty*, as it was used between 1792 and 1793, disappeared from the government's political vocabulary by the year ii; one seeks it in vain in Saint-Just's speech of October 19, 1793, on the need to declare the government a revolutionary government until peacetime, or in the constitutional decree of 14 Frimaire of this government, or in Robespierre's speech of 5 Nivôse on the principles of revolutionary government. The absence of the term is significant: after the decree of 14 Frimaire, the sections played no part at all in the revolutionary government. A decree dated 5 Brumaire had already suspended municipal elections; the elections were canceled; when replacing magistrates and civil servants, revolutionary national agents confined themselves to consulting the popular societies. Thus the sovereignty of the people was not concentrated "in the clubs, that is to say, in the party in power," as suggested by Albert Mathiez, but in the hands of the governmental machine. The sansculottes valued above all their electoral power, symbol of their sovereignty. They lost it in the year ii. The revolutionary committees were elected by the general assemblies in the spring of 1793, re-elected in September, purged in the autumn by the General Council of the Commune, and during the winter, came under the influence of the Public Safety Committee; during the spring of the year II, their members were nominated by the Public Safety Committee. It was the same for the General Council of the Commune. After Germinal and the execution of Hébert and Chaumette, the committee stripped the members of the council of their powers and nominated replacements without consulting the sections. On 16 Floréal, Payan, national agent for the Paris Commune, reminded the sections that "in a system of revolutionary government, there is no such thing as a local assembly; only general assemblies." This notified the sans-culottes that their sovereign rights had been transferred to the revolutionary government. Speaking before the tribunal of the society of the Amis-de-la-République in Germinal, cobbler Potel, commissar for the *Contrat-Social* section, declared that since it had a share in sovereign power, the society had the right to make laws; he was arrested. The failure to understand popular aspirations concerning sovereignty was largely responsible for the sans-culottes' dissatisfaction with the revolutionary government during the spring of the year II.

After Thermidor, the reactionaries realized the threat to bourgeois supremacy posed by notions of popular sovereignty, and denounced what they considered its abuse. The people had a concrete concept of sovereignty: that it resided in the sectional general assemblies. An abstract concept of sovereignty that conformed to the tendencies and interests of the bourgeoisie was substituted for these views, considered too simplistic. On 12 Vendémiaire, year III, Representative Lambert complained to the Public Safety Committee against the indiscriminate use that had been made of the words *sovereign people*: "True sovereignty belongs to the people alone, taken collectively; hence sovereignty is essentially one and indivisible, is but a purely metaphysical being, that is to say, the expression of the general will." For the sans-culottes sovereignty was made of flesh and blood, it was the people exerting their rights themselves, in the sectional assemblies. One can have no doubt about the persistence of this idea. On 1

Prairial, Jean Thevenin, a dry goods merchant from the *Arsenal* section, declared that the Convention no longer had the right to make laws, "that the only laws will be those made by the people themselves on that particular day." The sans-culottes stormed the Convention on precisely that day, 1 Prairial, and sat on the deputies' benches; one demonstrator cried out: "Get out of here; we are going to act as the Convention ourselves." The deputies had failed to complete their task, and the people were reasserting their sovereignty.

When the Convention began to fall apart, the moderate leaders, who had benefited from the Constitution of the year III, used the arguments of the sans-culottes themselves when protesting against the decree whereby two thirds of the deputies voted themselves back into office. On 20 Fructidor, year III, the *Fidélité* section declared, "When the sovereign people is assembled it cannot and should not recognize any superior authority, and therefore it alone can make laws and will accept none from others." An absurd statement on the part of citizens whose future status as inscribed electors negated the principle of popular sovereignty itself.

2. THE CONTROL AND RECALL OF ELECTED OFFICERS

The indefeasible and inalienable nature of popular sovereignty gave rise to deductions which were the levers for popular action: the censorship, the control and the recall of the elected.

Once again we must go back to Rousseau and the *Contrat-Social*. Rousseau had vehemently criticized representative government as it operated in England. "If the British people thinks it is free, it is making a terrible mistake; it is only free while electing a member of Parliament; as soon as these are elected, it is enslaved; it is nothing at all. . . . The deputies of the people therefore are not and cannot be their representatives; they are only their commissars"; the sans-culottes would have said that they were their agents. The deputies to the Convention, observed a citizen from the *Tuileries* section on September 22, 1792, "should not be called representatives of the people, but agents of the people." In *L'Ami du Peuple*, in the August 21, 1793 (Fructidor, year I), edition, Leclerc, in paraphrasing Rousseau, made it clear that the sans-culottes were confused in their thinking: "Above all remember that a people governed by representation is not free and should be chary of considering themselves represented . . . the public will cannot be represented . . . all your magistrates are only your agents." In the year II many sans-culottes, when writing to representatives, signed themselves *your equal in rights*.

In order to reconcile government by representation with the needs of a genuine democracy, the sans-culottes demanded the right to sanction laws; control of elected officers by the people was aimed at the same goal. During elections to the Convention, the Parisian sections were particularly insistent upon this right. Since elections in two stages multiplied, in respect to popular sovereignty, the disadvantages of representative government, many sections tried to remedy the situation by censuring the choices of the electoral assembly of the département of Paris and by exercising their right of control and recall of elected members.

When the Legislative Assembly banned all distinctions between active and passive citizens, but conserved the two-stage system of voting, direct universal suffrage was claimed by the more advanced sections. In his "Suggested Methods for the Permanent Establishment of Freedom and Equality," presented to the *Marseille* section, Lacroix denounced the two-stage voting system as being "immoral, destructive of the sovereignty of the people, inviting intrigue and the formation of cliques." On August 21, 1792, the *Quinze-Vingts* section adopted a petition initiated by the *Montreuil* section "to demand that there should be no electoral corps, that every kind of election be conducted in the primary assemblies." On August 27, the *Place Vendôme* section, urged on by Robespierre, accepted the two-stage system, but declared that "the people's elected officers must be nominated by the people directly, that is to say, in the primary assemblies"; in order to correct the disadvantages of indirect voting, the electors would vote by roll call in the presence of the people. On the same day, the *Bondy* section's primary assembly stated "that the sovereign people should grant no one the exercise of rights which cannot be delegated without ill consequence, and that representation is only genuine when it derives immediately from the represented." The General Council of the Commune granted these wishes on August 27 by issuing an order to the effect that the electors would vote by the roll call, in the presence of the people, and that the choice of the electoral assembly would be subject to veto by the various sections.

The censuring or purging of elected officers not only aimed at correcting the disadvantages of voting in the two-stage system; they were a manifestation of the indivisible nature of popular sovereignty. On August 27, the *Place Vendôme* section demanded that the deputies nominated by the electors be "subject to revision and examination by the sections or the primary assemblies, so that the majority could reject those unworthy of the confidence of the people." The *Bondy* section gave the electoral assembly only the right to nominate, "reserving for itself the right to recognize only those deputies which had been confirmed or approved by the majority of the primary assemblies of the département." On the same August 27, the General Council of the Commune took the same stand. On August 31, the *Maison-Commune* section decreed that in the future the electors were to do no more than present candidates for the office of deputy; the sections would either accept them or reject them. On September 1, the *Poissonnière* section, "being of the opinion that the sovereign people had the right to tell its elected representatives how to act according to its will," declared that the candidates for deputy would be discussed, approved or rejected by the primary assemblies. On September 9, the *Invalides* section finally decided that the members of the Convention named by the electors should be definitively admitted only after approval by the primary assemblies.

Public pressure was such that on September 12, the electoral assemblies decided to present to the sections the list of deputies elected to the Convention "in order to give the people the opportunity to reject the candidates, and also to rouse the sense of sovereignty in every member of the body politic."

The censuring of deputies, amending the two-stage voting system, was not enough to protect the principle of popular sovereignty. It was also essential that the elected officers fulfill the mandate they had received. Without formally reverting to the theory of absolute mandate, as asserted during the elections for the States General and as in the petitions in the Cahiers,[1] the Paris sections, during the elections to the Convention clearly stated the principle of control and recall of elected officers by the sovereign people; thus the disadvantages surrounding the representative system were, to a certain degree, mitigated.

On August 25, 1792, the general assembly of the *Marché-des-Innocents* section proposed that a national convention should be based on the notion that "the deputies could be forced to resign if their départements so desired" and that "public officials could be recalled by their constituents, whom they will be obliged to consult." On the same day, in order to publicize the right of the sections to recall their elected officers whenever they wished, the general assembly of the *Bonne-Nouvelle* section invited the Paris sections "to remind their delegates of their absolute right to take away their powers and to remind them of the objectives of their mission." On the ninth, during a meeting of the electoral assembly of the Paris département, an elector from the *Halles* section proposed "that it declare it a principle that the absolute sovereignty of the people was an inalienable right, that

[1] Ed. Note: Cahiers de doléances.

the people could recall their representatives whenever they deemed it necessary and in their interest." On the eighteenth, the assembly of the *Droits-de-l'Homme* section declared that it reserved the right to recall deputies "if, during the course of their meeting, they were suspect of incivism." On the same day, the *Poissonnière* section granted the deputies to the Convention the right to inscribe in the future Constitution the principle of the recall of elected officers "at the will of the local assemblies"; the general assembly of the *Réunion* section declared "that it expressly reserved the right to recall elected deputies in the event that, during their service, they commit an act which might render them suspect of incivism, or if they sought to introduce a government in France that was against freedom and equality."

The principle of control and recall of deputies was not expressed in the Paris sections in a merely abstract manner: during the events of the summer of 1792 it corresponded, as did that of the censuring of nominations to the electoral assemblies, to concrete tactical necessities. It was a question of guaranteeing the triumph of the progressive party. This principle was also invoked every time revolutionary policies were threatened. To cite a pamphlet published during the summer of 1792, the representatives were only agents, bearers of the orders of the citizens; they should therefore follow these orders strictly, not shirk them, and report to their constituents on everything that they had said, written or done during the exercise of their function as representatives. In the conflict which from the autumn of 1792 pitted the Girondins against the Montagnards, the more advanced sections claimed the right to censure elected officers and to insist on their rendering account of their activities, whereas the more moderate sections contested this claim.

During the campaign which began on November 11, 1792 (20 Brumaire, year 1), for the re-election of the Paris authorities, the *Panthéon-Français* section announced on December 2 that it reserved the right to scrutinize and, if necessary, reject newly elected citizens. Likewise,

on the eighteenth, the *Quatre-Vingt-Douze* section urged
the electoral assembly to remain faithful to its agreement
to submit its nominations to the approval of the sections;
elected officers also had to defend their qualifications. On
December 30, 1792, the *Champs-Elysées* section denounced "orders dictated by a Machiavellian and disrup-
tive attitude: they control the votes of the citizens by
threats of proscription and forget principle to the extent
that they want to influence, through the publicity of an
indiscreet promise, the representatives of an entire nation." It demanded *absolute* respect for the freedom of
representatives. Thus we can see the extent of the opposition between two concepts of representative government,
one popular, the other bourgeois.

The crisis grew more serious during March 1793 (Ventôse, year I), and the more avant-garde patriots demanded
that the right of the people to dismiss its representatives
be exercised against the *unholy faction*. On March 10,
during the first attempt to eliminate the Gironde, the
Cordeliers Club invited the Paris département, "an integral part of the sovereign," to exercise its sovereignty: that
the electoral courts of Paris be convoked to replace "those
members who were traitors to the causes of the people."
On the same day, the *Quatre-Nations* section demanded,
"as the supreme and only efficacious measure," the convocation of the sections to authorize the electoral assemblies of the département of Paris "to recall the unfaithful
representatives, who are unworthy of being legislators of
the public good," since they have betrayed their mandate
by voting in favor of "sparing the tyrant and for an appeal
to the people [on the execution of Louis XVI]."

When the Girondins opposed to the principle of recall
of elected representatives that of their inviolability, the
Tuileries section observed, on April 10, 1793 (Germinal,
year I), that "this inviolability, having been dreamt of
only under the monarchy," the deputies cannot benefit
from it under a republican government; "those who have
our mandate must render an account of their deeds to a
free people." The *Tuileries* section consequently demanded

the suppression of inviolability as being "an odious privilege, a perfidious cloak with which a corrupt representative could cover himself in order to betray with impunity the interests of the people." Citing these principles, the *Finistère* section, on May 12, announced that "it was displeased . . . about the misfortunes which negligence, incompetence or bad faith on the part of the Convention had caused us," and called upon the representatives "to explain categorically whether or not they could save the nation."

The theoretical justification for the events between May 31 and June 2, 1793, can be traced to this public conviction about the responsibility of elected officers and the right to recall them; since the Convention did not obey the injunctions of the sovereign people concerning representatives who were considered to have abused their mandate, the people resumed their sovereignty and forced the resignation of the Girondin deputies. On May 31, Lullier, public prosecutor of the département, called upon the Convention, in the name of the revolutionary authorities, to accede to the will of the people; the delegation and a crowd of citizens came and mingled "fraternally with the left members." On June 2, the spokesman for the delegation of revolutionary authorities declared that the citizens of Paris should "reclaim the rights that their elected representatives had so ignobly betrayed." The uprising was the final outcome of the principle of sovereignty.

Were the Montagnards, who since August 1792 had supported and clarified popular demands concerning sovereignty, once in power, going to make them law? On May 25, the *Unité* section, "bearing in mind that responsibility is the essence of a Republic," had demanded "that a five-man tribunal composed of members from the eighty-six départements should, during the elections for deputies, appraise the conduct of those of the previous session, and that those who had failed the mother country . . . be forever banned from any public office in the Republic." The members from Arras put the problem in all its urgency: on June 18, before the Convention, they declared that they had lost their confidence in five deputies from the Pas-de-Calais; the Assembly took no action on this matter. In response to these issues, Hérault de Séchelles, during discussions on a draft constitution, presented a section on June 24 entitled "Concerning the People's Censuring of Deputies and Its Privilege to Act against Oppression by Legislative Bodies"; it aroused considerable opposition; Couthon, in the name of the Public Safety Committee, had it rejected. Once again practical necessities forced him to forsake principle.

The increasing power of the Public Safety Committee, then the gradual establishment of the revolutionary government, did not completely silence sectional demands concerning these measures, which were supported by the popular press. In *L'Ami du Peuple* on August 21, 1793 (4 Fructidor, year I), Leclerc reminded the deputies that they were "being watched" by the people: "The people will support or condemn you, according to your actions." On August 4 (16 Thermidor), the *Amis-de-la-Patrie* section had asked the General Council of the Commune that the deputies be evaluated after every session and "that they be rewarded according to their deeds." On September 29 (8 Vendémiaire, year II), the *Halle-au-Blé* section solemnly declared, "Only the sovereign people has the right to investigate members, whose constitutional powers stem from them." In the beginning of the year II, the *Observatoire* section again reminded people of the fact that "the people's sovereignty necessarily includes the right to recall unfaithful representatives and all officeholders unworthy of its confidence."

In the meantime, this control by the people strengthened the authority of the representatives to whom they did accord their confidence: certain Montagnards realized this and, during the crisis of the summer of 1793, considered it necessary to justify their actions to their sections. Thus Collot d'Herbois, representative of the *Lepeletier* section, on mission to the Oise and Aisne départements, writing from Senlis on September 4, explained his conduct and listed his decrees, which the assembly discussed and approved. This kind of communication gave the sections control over their elected officers, and allowed the representatives to contribute to the molding of public opinion.

Once the revolutionary government was finally established by decree on 14 Frimaire, and the authority of the Public Safety Committee unquestioned, statements on the principles of popular sovereignty were heard no longer. Concerned above all with centralization and efficiency, the government committees no longer tolerated even the slightest reminder of the people's right to control and dismiss its elected officers. These principles took second place to the exigencies of the policy of public safety.

The sans-culottes were not content with claiming, in the name of their sovereign rights, control over legislators; they also wanted to watch over the executive and its agents. As long as the conflict between the Girondins and Montagnards lasted, until the moderates were removed from office, the principle was clearly stated and the right loudly demanded. Even the establishment of the revolutionary government failed to silence the sans-culottes.

On December 14, 1792 (13 Frimaire, year I), the *Bon-Conseil* section, referring to defective equipment being manufactured for the volunteers, stated that "the actions of the executive powers of all the ministries must be supervised relentlessly"; it invited the other sections in the name of public safety and freedom "to form a committee to watch over ministerial operations." The *Quatre-Nations* section supported the resolution on December 17 (16 Frimaire), but the *Gardes-Françaises* section, where the moderates were dominant, denounced on January 11, 1793 (21 Nivôse, year I), "any organization which might tend to weaken the individual responsibility of the ministries."

Popular surveillance over ministerial power also extended to the military, even to the conduct of combat operations. The *Bon-Conseil* section, where feeling for the rights of the people seems to have been peculiarly keen, summoned Santerre, commander-in-chief of the Paris National Guard, to appear before its general assembly in order to settle a problem about military service; he appeared on February 10, 1793 (22 Pluviôse, year I), arguing that "he did not appear before the sections as often as he would like for fear of giving the appearance of being a lackey." In March 1793, deciding that "traitorous activity cannot be prevented unless we watch for it more carefully," the *Lombards* section proposed the creation of a permanent commission which would send certain of its members to the Vendée, in order to keep a watchful eye on "all the generals' operations, army maneuvers and troop morale"; after examining their reports, the commission would make the necessary "denunciations, offering advice, clarifications." Although this proposition does not seem to have been followed up, the *Gardes-Françaises* section on June 17, 1793 (29 Prairial, year I), did not hesitate to send two commissars to Tours: they were to give an account of the position of the army, its successes, its defeats, to consort with the captains of companies from the section and watch over the conduct of officers and soldiers; they "must remind officers and the rank and file who might have strayed, of their duties, and this with every means of brotherly persuasion." The mission was no mere matter of form. The powers of the two *Gardes-Françaises* commissars were validated on June 25 (7 Messidor) at Tours by the Côtes-de-la-Rochelle representatives attached to the army. On September 4 (17 Fructidor), at the general headquarters of the battalion at Saumur, the chief of staff gave a pass (allow the bearer access to anything he might wish to see) to François Lemaître, commissar from the *Gardes-Françaises* section in Paris, deputy to the Vendée army; on September 21, General Bournet renewed Lemaître's powers at Saumur.

Needless to say, administrative employees were closely watched by the people. The sections' right to censure officials was asserted many times between the summer of 1792 and the winter of the year II. They demanded both the sovereign's prerogative and immediate response; the purged should make way for good sans-culottes. The political aim of this demand was also clearly stated. On December 14, 1792 (23 Frimaire, year I), the *Bon-Conseil* section demanded a copy of the list of employees in all the Paris administrations, "in order to expose its agents to public censure and to bring about reforms dictated by circumstances, and also to replace those whose ideas were contrary to the present government system with good heads of families and other patriots who, by having sacrificed everything for the Republic, are without work or bread." The *Quatre-Vingt-Douze* section made the same demand on December 18.

After June 2, the exercise of sectional power strengthened the conviction among sans-culottes that officials should depend upon the people and upon the people alone. If we are to believe a denunciation made in the year III, "Many citizens believed and perhaps still believe that the right to nominate officials also gave them the right to dismiss them." The *Amis-de-la-Patrie* section elected a certain Bailly commissar of monopolies and wanted to dismiss him for a lack of firmness. On August 23, 1793 (6 Fructidor, year I), the General Council of the Commune debated the question of whether a commissar could be recalled by the section that had nominated him, and ended by concluding to the contrary: "If the sections were to be allowed to change their minds in this manner, there would be no more stability in the Republic." The *Amis-de-la-Patrie* section nevertheless dismissed Bailly. The matter was brought before the Convention on September 1 (14 Fructidor), which agreed that the choosing of commissars lay solely in the hands of the sections.

In this field, too, and at this time, the principle mattered less to the revolutionary authorities than who applied it: it was good when the sans-culottes claimed it, and became evil in the hands of the moderates. When the moderate sections attempted to gain control of the Paris food supplies and insisted on the opening of the shops, they invoked "the inalienable right to watch over the operations [of the people's representatives], or to make them account for their activities, when they are finished," as did the *Beaurepaire* section on July 28; to oppose this measure "would be a blow to national sovereignty, a distortion of the desires, the rights of constituents." When the Convention dissolved the sections' committee of food supplies on August 25, the *Indivisibilité* section protested on the twenty-ninth, citing its inalienable right" to receive reports from its commissars on every administrative measure enacted by its representatives, to make inquiries into every aspect of their administration"; this decree therefore attacked the sovereignty of the people. The moderates turned the principles of the sans-culottes against the government committees.

During the autumn of 1793, when it was a question of putting an end to the threat from the moderates and of placing the revolutionary government on a solid basis, the control over, and censure of, elected officers were claimed with greatest vigor. After August 28, the *Arcis* section demanded the creation of a commission charged with investigating the civism of all employees, this commission to be under the authority of the sections. On September 29, the *Halle-au-Blé* section declared the purges made by the département *null and void:* "Only the sovereign people have the authority to scrutinize the conduct of officers of bodies they themselves established." At about the same time, the *Observatoire* section stated that the sovereign power of the people necessarily involved the right to recall not only unfaithful representatives, but "also all public officials unworthy of confidence"; since this principle "was tacitly violated by the legal impossibility of its being enforced," the section demanded that the Convention "come up with a method of recalling any public official who does not fulfill his duties."

When the moderate threat was averted, the censuring of civil servants, as of elected officers, was no longer in the hands of general assemblies and popular societies. The decree of 14 Frimaire, which established the revolutionary government, entrusted purges to the Public Safety Committee and to its representatives on mission to the départements. The sections lost all rights of control or dismissal: stability and centralization prevailed over the people's observance of democratic principles. This development contributed to the alienation of the sans-culottes from the revolutionary government, particularly after Germinal. Their deeply felt feelings, now curbed, were very real. "Where shall we be," declared a citizen from the *Contrat-Social* section on 25 Pluviôse, "if we are not allowed close investigation of the conduct of those who lead us!" At about the same time, Citizeness Auxerre, employed in a workshop which made flour sacks in the Rue du Temple, declared "that the people were sovereign, that municipal employees and the authorities were merely agents"; she was denounced on 6 Ventôse by the committee of the *Amis-de-la-Patrie* section for counterrevolutionary proposals.

3. The Permanence and Autonomy of the Sections

The militant sans-culotte was perhaps more interested in local than in national policy. Hence the importance he attached to the grass-roots organizations in political life: city assemblies, and, even more important, sectional assemblies and popular societies. For the abstract notion of sovereignty put into practice through the intermediary of a national assembly, he substituted the concrete reality of the people gathered together in their sectional assemblies: there the sans-culotte was fully aware of his sovereign rights and the use he could make of them. Among the attributes of sovereignty, he gave first place to the permanence and autonomy of the sections.

Hence the sans-culottes of the year II began making demands similar to those of active citizens in the year 1790, but these demands had a new social content. The

Chaussée-d'Antin district had reminded citizens on March 18, 1790, "that patriotism and the permanence of the districts were at the root of French freedom"; the sections must retain "their inalienable right to assemble freely, either to rule their own districts, or to oppose municipal action, or for any just and reasonable cause." Fifty-three districts out of sixty adopted a resolution demanding the permanence "of assemblies meeting regularly each month"; on March 23, 1790, the mayor of Paris presented their wishes to the Constituent Assembly. On April 10, 1790, the districts made further demands, while the pamphlet campaign continued. One of these pamphlets, which was anonymous, pointed out that permanence meant the right of the citizens to assemble every month and "in the event that important matters required general assemblies," and to form permanent committees "for enforcing the regulations of the municipality and of the police." To a pamphlet objecting that the permanence of the sections would transform Paris into so many sovereign republics, and that to confer all administrative powers on the sections would mean the end of the Commune, another replied, supporting the *necessary inspection* by the sections of every aspect of public power and the advantages of permanence for the civic education of citizens.

From the very beginning of the year 1792, the progress of the democratic movement, then the general crisis which brought about the declaration of war, broke over the fragile barriers erected by the Constituent Assembly to restrict the sovereignty and autonomy of the sections. On February 2, 1792, the Fraternal Society of the Two Sexes, sitting in session with the Jacobins, demanded the permanence of the sections, not for the exercise of legislative, executive and administrative powers, which "a great society can exercise only through its delegates," but for that power of surveillance which every society of free men has the right to exercise directly"; no authority has the right to prevent a commune or section from assembling when and as often as it wants. The fraternal society brought forward the usual arguments: permanence would contribute to the civic education of the citizens, would do away with misunderstandings and would unite all the classes into "one single collective power."

Mounting problems during the spring of 1792 gave patriotic demands for permanence irresistible strength; to quote a petition prepared by the fraternal society, it alone could make provisions for the surveillance of "the agents of the Austrian Cabinet and the Coblentz Committee." On May 28, the *Théâtre-Français*, *Croix-Rouge* and *Fontaine-de-Grenelle* sections demanded that the Legislative Assembly issue a decree which would authorize "surveillance powers so necessary in these circumstances." The *Lombards* section made the same demand: "When the nation is in danger, every citizen should fly to its assistance; and how can they do this if they do not have a place where they can assemble promptly." On June 16, the *Croix-Rouge* section again demanded the *active* permanence of the sections: "In these sections, at all times, at every hour, your intrepid defenders will be standing ready and armed." Next day, the *Faubourg-Montmartre* section "in view of the dangers that threatened the country everywhere" and in order to prevent "terrible mishaps," adopted the same resolution. On June 28, the *Montreuil* section decided on the basic wording of an address "in favor of the permanence of the forty-eight sections of Paris, with the right to discuss anything to do with public safety." On July 2, a delegation of citizens of Paris again demanded the permanence of the sections.

On July 11, the proclamation declaring the nation in danger entailed the permanence of constituted authorities; but the sections were not included in this measure, having neither established authority nor special functions. During the course of July, however, the permanence of the sections was finally established; they met daily and were open to all citizens. On July 3, the *Postes* section determined that its meetings be public. On the twenty-fourth, it adopted the ideas of a petition presented to the Legislative Assembly on the means of averting threats to the nation: foremost, the permanence of the sections. On the same day it decided to meet three times a week, "until the National Assembly orders otherwise." On July 24, the Legislative Assembly finally yielded and decreed the permanence of the sections. Circumstances had forced a measure which the members of both the Constituent and the Legislative Assemblies had persistently refused to adopt during the two previous years.

From then on, permanence was one of the cornerstones of the popular political system, and of the direct government which the militants, in their confused manner, were attempting to inaugurate. During periods of crisis, it proved to be an excellent instrument for action. It was also jealously protected. In early September 1792, an elector from the *Thermes-de-Julien* section, during an appeal to the electoral corps, considered it one of the "four pillars of freedom." On November 16, 1792 (Brumaire, year 1), the general assembly of the *Butte-des-Moulins* section decided to meet only three times a week, but stressed that it was not renouncing its permanence.

In the struggle between the Girondins and the Montagnards, permanence offered the sans-culottes decisive leverage. The Girondins also began to demand its suppression early in 1793. On January 6, Richaud demanded its suppression; Salles exploited the notion that permanence was a *revolutionary* instrument, which could not be extended without theatening public safety. Marat, on the other hand, insisted that this would compromise public security, and demanded that permanence continue as long as the nation was threatened. Robespierre spoke along similar lines. The debate was resumed in May, when the crisis grew worse. On May 20, the *Poissonnière* section proposed that the meetings be no longer permanent, "bearing in mind the small number of citizens who attend." The assembly took pains to reject this notion, which it considered dangerous; "only after four days of discussion can we concern ourselves with dissolving the permanence of the assembly." On May 24 the Commission of Twelve decided that the general assemblies should be closed every evening at ten: an indirect measure which destroyed the advantages of permanence, as it was practiced by the sans-culottes. The more avant-garde sections paid no attention to this decree: on May 28, the *Marchés* section declared that it would not obey it; at the suggestion of Hébert, the *Bonne-Nouvelle* section decided to hold private meetings after ten o'clock "to take care of its interests."

Permanence was also a double-edged sword. Although the sans-culottes crowded the general assemblies during periods of crisis, they tended to desert them when the danger was over. Their opponents therefore had only to be more diligent for the majority to be reversed. There were many instances of this in the Parisian sections after June 2; the moderates, defeated in general policies aimed at taking revenge in the sectional assemblies, which they invaded. Desperate struggles ensued, a true masked civil war; in certain, the sans-culottes did not seize power until the summer or the beginning of the autumn of 1793. In large cities such as Lyons and Marseilles, the permanence of sections was an instrument of counterrevolution. Realist that he was, it was Marat who pointed out the danger of the situation. On June 21, in a letter to the Convention, he demanded the suppression of permanence, the cause of disaster in many large cities, "because the rich, the intriguers and men of ill will move around in crowds to the sections, establishing themselves as masters there, issuing the most liberticide orders, whereas journalists, workers, artisans, shopkeepers, small farmers, in a word, the mass of poor people forced to work for their living, cannot participate in order to check the criminal inclinations of the enemies of freedom."

The argument was taken up again by Danton and contributed to the voting of the decree of September 9, 1793 (24 Fructidor, year 1), which reduced the sessions of general assemblies to two days a week. Whatever the merits of this decision, the suppression of permanence was a blow to the popular political system. It played a role in the evolution of the revolutionary government, which tended to control the popular movement and to bind it into the cadres of the nascent Jacobin dictatorship. Famous moderates, such as Nicoleau, former president of the Paris département, applauded the decree. In a memoir justifying his stand, he declared that the Convention had prevented serious disturbances "by suppressing this disastrous permanence which gave intriguers so many opportunities to mislead the people; that the assemblies were few in number and that the more enlightened patriots were forced to stand apart in order to attend to business or fulfill their public duties." Nicoleau was using the argument of Marat and Danton: their conclusions were the same.

If granting the forty-sous payment caused trouble among the sans-culottes and divided the sections, the suppression of permanence gave rise to unanimous opposition: the sans-culottes reversed the decree of September 9 by forming sectional societies. Nevertheless, throughout the year II they continued to demand more frequent sessions. The communal authorities obstinately continued to refuse to concede, and the Robespierrist Commune, more so than its predecessor, imposed a strict application of the law.

The sans-culottes were the more insistent in their claim for retaining permanence as they were convinced that the section was not only an organ for supervising general policies, the source of national representation and the means of control over it, but was also an autonomous body performing its own administrative functions; the section is a sovereign power, its affairs are the concern of its general assembly alone. In 1790, when the new law concerning municipal organization was being drawn up, a certain Boileux de Beaulieu demanded that each section or district be organized as a municipality, be reponsible for its police, administration and the apportionment and collection of contributions; so that the Commune [the city as a whole] could make "no ruling, concerning either administrative functions or the police, until they had proposed the motion in each section or district, so that it could be discussed and decreed, and that new administrative or regulatory laws could be promulgated or executed only when they had a plurality in the various sections or districts."

The inscribed citizens [paying sufficient taxes to qualify as voters] of 1790 and the popular militants of the year II had similar views on this subject. The fear of being deprived of absolute autonomy pushed the *Sans-Culottes* section to demand on March 3, 1793 (12 Ventôse, year I), the transfer of registry offices to the sections. The *Cité* section supported this motion, and, on May 4, challenged the claim of Santerre, commander-in-chief of the Paris National Guard, to the right to pick his aides-de-camp, adjutants and assistants of every rank in the newly recruited battalions, on the pretext that "the volunteers should not risk being sacrificed to their leader's incompetence." Santerre's claim was an attack on the freedom of the sections; the *Cité* section would tolerate as company leaders only those officers it had nominated. Having opposed the election of Raffet as commandant of the Paris National Guard, the *Unité* section declared, on June 26, 1793 (8 Messidor, year I), that it would not obey his orders if he were elected. In order to guarantee the smooth running of sectional services, certain general assemblies levied a tax on their constituents in the year II, despite the law which forbade them from imposing direct or indirect taxes. In Pluviôse, one section decided "that a tax of ten or fifteen sols should be levied on each person in the section once or twice every ten days in order to defray the many expenses of each section." On 16 Pluviôse, the Commune General Council had to remind the sections that none of them had the right to demand a contribution, "considering that only the sovereign people has the right to vote on, and to agree to, taxes and that a section is not allowed to impose its own tax."

Sectional autonomy was most vociferously demanded when it came to the police. Already by February 4, 1791, the *Théâtre-Français* section declared that the police de-

partment was run in an unconstitutional manner, dangerous to freedom; the police must be divided among the
forty-eight sections. On September 12, 1792, the *Mirabeau*
section stated that "it is a natural right . . . that each
individual found guilty be provisionally placed in the safe-
keeping of the section he lives in." The section is the
foremost *natural tribunal*; in its own territory, it alone
must be entrusted with making arrests and issuing search
warrants. Sections were so sensitive in this area that, on
September 8, 1792, the *Quinze-Vingts* section stated that
"it was not proper for the Commune to enter a section
officially without a previous ordinance and unless its officers, whatever the circumstance, produce [documents
showing] the powers entrusted to them." On December
24, the *Louvre* section solemnly declared that it reserved
the right to police its own territory. The *Contrat-Social*
section maintained, on May 11, 1793 (Floréal, year I),
that a section has no reason to account for the activities
of the police under its jurisdiction. By applying this principle, those police commissars who, although nominated
by the general assemblies, were placed under the control
of the Commune, must be subordinate to sectional committees; otherwise we shall "return to this terrible police
regime so justifiably abhorred." At the height of the crisis
of March 1793, on the twenty-seventh, Marat announced
to the Jacobins: "Each section has sovereign powers within
its walls." These principles were considered incompatible
with the exigencies of the revolutionary government.

The importance which the sans-culottes attributed to
the permanence and autonomy of the sections was shown
after 9 Thermidor by their persistent demands for more
frequent meetings, and also by their recourse to permanence during the attempted uprisings of Prairial in the
year III.
    On the other hand, the reactionaires imposed increasing
restrictions on the holding of assemblies, in order eventually to do away with them. On 9 Thermidor the

Convention forbade the sections from meeting without authorization from its committees. On 4 Fructidor, it reduced the meetings of general assemblies to every ten days, while at the same time doing away with the forty-sous payment; Thuriot, who had proposed permanence on July 25, 1792, stressed the inconvenience of the vast number of sectional meetings.

The sans-culottes protested in vain. On 28 Fructidor, François Paris, grease monkey from the *Piques* section, was arrested for having said "that the sectional assemblies had already been reduced to meeting every ten days, and that in a few days they will be abolished . . . that the assemblies were the strength of the Republic." On 30 Fructidor, the *Gravilliers* section invited the Convention "to consider the need of the people to learn, to discuss their interests, that three meetings of the assembly each month would not satisfy their patriotic fervor and their civic duties, and to decree that Paris sections could assemble as they had before." On the same day the *Montreuil* section adopted a similar resolution, which the *Montagne, Tuileries* and *Popincourt* sections also adopted on 10 Vendémiaire.

During the spring of the year III, it was considered dangerous to allow the assemblies to meet every ten days: they served as a rallying point for the sans-culottes. On 10 Ventôse, the *République* section, composed of a large number of "workers, carters and others," proposed that the sans-culottes be forbidden from holding meetings between six and ten in the evening, changing the time to the period from eleven in the morning to three in the afternoon; then "we shall no longer have to fear terrorist activity." On 8 Germinal, one of the first measures taken by the Convention for putting an end to the troubles was to change the hour of the meeting of general assemblies to between one and four o'clock in the afternoon: thus the sans-culottes would be unable to attend. The rebellious sections declared that they would sit in session until the conclusion of business; on the evening of 13 Germinal, the citizens of the *Popincourt* section met together, *armed,*

and declared their adherence to a city order which had
been issued during a "permanent" session; they invited
"their brothers from other sections to use the same tactic
to find the means of saving the nation and to inform each
other of those measures which they considered most likely
to produce this result." On 10 Floréal the *Montreuil* section decided to hold a session for as long as was necessary
to discuss foodstuffs. On 1 Prairial, among the demands
made by a mass of people who had invaded the Convention, was the permanence of the sections. After the voting
on a few decrees by a small number of members present,
Romme declared: "It is not enough to issue decrees that
are beneficient, we must also guarantee the means of en-
acting them"; he then proposed the convocation of the
sections and their permanence.

This was the last assault. On 4 Prairial, the Convention
decreed that women would be no longer admitted to sectional assemblies, to which they had been admitted since
the summer of 1792, and in which they had often participated duing the summer of 1793. The general assemblies in the meantime continued to hold their monthly
sessions. On 24 Thermidor, referring to a petition from
the *Bonne-Nouvelle* section, an obscure deputy expressed
astonishment that the Paris sections were still holding
meetings. On the next day, Boissy d'Anglas made the remark that it was useless to propose any new measures,
bearing in mind the small amount of time left before the
Constitution was drawn up: the latter would contain
specific rules on the subject. When the sectional assemblies took part in royalist agitation during Vendémiaire in
the year IV, Merlin de Douai proposed the immediate
application of Article 353 of the Constitution of the year
III, which suppressed them; the establishment of the constitutional government, set for 5 Brumaire, was ahead of
time on this issue.

Thus disappeared the sectional assemblies, which had
given the sans-culottes a forum for their political action,
and whose permanence, in their eyes, was a symbol of the
principle of popular sovereignty itself.

4. Insurrection

The ultimate recourse of the sovereign people lies in insurrection. The Constituent Assembly had not written this right into the Declaration of August 1789. However, "resistance to oppression" was one of the inalienable rights. The Convention confirmed this right in Article 35 of the Declaration of June 1793 as much to legitimize the August 10 and May 31 events as to protect the people from oppression.

In this article, the sans-culottes did not see a theoretical and formal confirmation of their sovereignty. Imbued with ideas about their rights, confusedly practicing methods of direct government, they naturally were moved to reclaim their sovereign rights when they considered that these rights had been betrayed by their representatives. There were increased instances of popular assertions of the right to rebel during every period of crisis until the year III. On 1 Prairial, year III, Duval, a cobbler from the *Arsenal* section, summoned Boissy d'Anglas, who presided over the Convention, to recognize that insurrection was one of the sacred duties, that these words had been inscribed in the Declaration of Rights. This after having read the insurgents' petition from the Convention rostrum.

Insurrection, however, has various connotations, depending upon the circumstances. Insurrection, as conceived by the sans-culottes, did not necessarily mean armed uprising. On October 6, 1792 (16 Vendémiaire, year I), the *Gravilliers* general assembly declared that the sovereignty of the people was misunderstood by the Convention, which asserted a "ridiculous and limitless power over the sections of Paris." The *Gravilliers* assembly said, "Let us rise for the last time, and let us hold our ground until we prove to our representatives and to the men of '89 that those who participated in the events of August 10

and of September 3 did so with a pride and strength which
belongs to sovereignty alone, in order to redirect them
toward their duties and make them remember our rights
which they have had the imprudence to ignore." The
Théâtre-Français section declared itself in a state of insurrection on December 27, 1792 (7 Nivôse, year I), until
"France shall be purged of its tyrants"; by this expression,
they meant "a continual state of useful defiance, of activity, of surveillance, of patriotic concern, a state which
every good republican should be in until freedom be established on firm ground." The *Unité* section understood
insurrection in this sense, when, on May 27, 1793 (8
Prairial, year I), it refused to surrender its registers to the
Commission of Twelve and moved to the next order of
business, justifying its actions "as being sanctioned by the
right to resist oppression." The same went for Hu, justice
of the peace and president of the *Panthéon-Français* section. On 25 Frimaire, year II, a citizen invoked the decree
of the fourteenth, containing an article which banned all
central committees or gatherings; he left the office, declaring that this law should be stricken off the books; "that
if it was not struck off the books, the people must rise
en masse and must have the courage to go before the Convention, say it has gone astray, and have this law abolished." When the Cordeliers declared themselves to be in
insurrection on 11 Ventôse, the intention was to start a
mass demonstration rather than an armed action. Finally,
in the year III, the military commission outlined its plan
for peaceful insurrection; Brutus Magnier was astonished
at the insulting pairing of these two words, and replied
that a peaceful insurrection consisted of "the majestic
movement of a people which says to its elected representatives, do this because I want you to do it." Insurrection,
therefore, for the sans-culottes meant the resistance of the
people, their refusal to obey laws which they did not accept, their reassertion of their sovereign rights, their
insistence on their elected representatives rendering an account of their activities and fulfilling the decisions of the
people; at this point, insurrection was a mass demonstra-

tion which expressed both the unanimity and majesty of the people.

Peaceful demonstrations are not always effective; the insurgents enforced their will through the implicit threat of their strength and of the possible recourse to violence, as much as by rallying around their rights. On May 1, 1793 (11 Floréal, year I), a delegation from the Faubourg Saint-Antoine sections, after having proposed measures concerning public safety before the Convention, offered a real ultimatum: "If you do not accept these measures, we shall declare ourselves, we who wish to save the nation, to be in a state of insurrection: 10,000 men have gathered outside the doors of the hall." Again, in May, the Faubourg Saint-Marcel sections announced to the representatives that the people were always alert to safeguard their rights, so much so that "the slightest provocation will be enough to cause them to rise en masse, that you are surrounded by the people, that the people demand an account of your activities, since you have been entrusted with an honorable mandate." In some instances, the threat was more explicit. On the evening of 9–10 Thermidor, a sans-culotte in the *Quinze-Vingts* section stated that in the event of "the procurement agents [he does not use the term *representative* or even *proxy*] not fulfilling their duties, the people have the right to rise and dismiss them."

Armed insurrection was an extreme manifestation of popular sovereignty. It began with drumbeat and tocsin indicating that the people were once again demanding their rights and were going to impose their will by force of arms. A certain Pitton, a steel polisher from the *Poissonnière* section, declared during the course of the uprising on 12 Germinal, year III, "that the sovereign people had the right to issue a call to arms and to open the assemblies." On August 10, an embroiderer by the name of Cardas, from the *Lombards* section, who had been a police administrator in the year II, declared that "since the people had risen, they should recognize no other law but that of sovereign right." During the night of 9–10 Thermidor, Lécrivain, formerly a member of the Public

Safety Committee of the Paris département, head clerk of the Revolutionary Tribunal, declared "that there was no need to obey the orders of the committees of the Convention, that when the tocsin sounded, the Convention no longer counted." On account of its emotional impact, of the memories of the great days of July 14, August 10 and May 31, when the people came forth in all the majesty of their sovereign power, insurrection assumed an aspect of exaltation for many a sans-culotte. The atmosphere surrounding those days was unforgettable. The closing of the city gates, the call to arms, the beating of drums, the tocsin, with all the attendant excitement, contributed to mass exaltation and also to the feeling among these simple, humble men of participating in an action which made them forget their misery, and whereby they made their mark on the destiny of the nation. During the night of 9–10 Thermidor, a certain Pellecat from the *Quinze-Vingts* section said to a young soldier in the National Guard: "You're new to revolution and you don't know what it's like when a commune beats the call to arms and rings the tocsin!"

Having by insurrection resumed their sovereign rights, the people are all-powerful: they can make laws, dispense justice, perform every function of the executive. They alone are in command as soon as they are in insurrection. In the *Indivisibilité* section, a humble sans-culotte [he could not read], a commissar by the name of Marchant, declared on 1 Prairial, year III: "Authority does not exist any more, the people have revolted, we no longer need orders, since the people are in command." On the second, a certain Lallemand, a worker in gauze from the *Mont-Blanc* section, refused to obey the injunctions of the authorities: "I no longer recognize the Convention, I am in revolt." Again on the second, Louis Vian, a bailiff attached to the local tribunal, came before the civil committee of the *Finistère* section and told it that "it no longer counted, that the sovereign people had regained their rights." During the rising of September 1792, the people took control of the administration of justice, as an essential aspect of their sovereignty. Having by insurrection demonstrated that they were totally sovereign, the people, when they had laid down their arms, once again delegated their sovereignty to representatives, who once again had their confidence. In an address dated May 31, 1793, the *Sans-Culottes* section declared: "If our section, in the precious moment when the people are in revolt, comes to speak to you again, it is in hope that by surrendering its arms again and allowing you to exercise its sovereign powers, you will use them for the good of the people."

A document of the year III describes the mechanics of insurrection, such as they were conceived by the sans-culottes. On 11 Floréal, a large crowd of men and women in the *Bonnet-de-la-Liberté* section in vain lay siege to the empty bakeries, and toward five in the evening marched on the headquarters of the civil committee; they arrested its members "in the name of the sovereign people and of the law." A sans-culotte called upon the drummer of the section: "Go fetch your drum so that we can sound the tocsin and declare the section to be in insurrection." Another cried out: "When the people are in insurrection, when they have unfaithful representatives, they must indict them, judge them and punish them on the spot." Whereupon the insurgents named four commissars to examine the conduct of the elected authorities of the section. Were they satisfied with this action whereby they once again expressed confidence in new representatives and assigned them their sovereign power? Numbers of sans-culottes in fact immediately retired; the insurrection was over as far as they were concerned. Toward midnight, the armed force led by four representatives had little difficulty in dispersing those left behind and in freeing the beleaguered civil committee.

This gives us a good idea of the strength as well as the weakness of the popular understanding of sovereignty and insurrection. It was not enough to announce an uprising in the name of sovereign rights: it still had to be organized. It was not enough to invest the people's confidence in new representatives: it was still necessary to keep in line by force of arms. The events of August 10 and May 31 are proof of this; conversely, the events of Prairial were an even more tragic confirmation.

Thus we see the limitations of sans-culotte political maturity; the predominant influence of the bourgeoisie on the course of the Revolution is also illuminated. The sans-culottes furnished the mass of manpower necessary for the assault; the bourgeoisie, or at least that small percentage of the bourgeoisie which saw safety for the Revolution achieved by alliance with the people, prepared and organized the great revolutionary events, such as those of August 10 and May 31, and exploited their outcomes. Were these days of great popular enthusiasm days of bourgeois revolution after all?

Could it be otherwise? The sans-culottes' impulse to rebellion in Ventôse, year II, and their attempts in Germinal and Prairial, year III, were accompanied by tragic defeats; it was as if the sans-culottes, isolated and forced to act alone, were doomed to impotence. True, there was a basic contradiction between popular action and the objective needs of the bourgeois revolution. This contradiction created tremendous tensions in the political arena between the sans-culottes, who took their sovereign rights literally, and bourgeois democracy, which stated that the power of the sovereign people could be exercised only in naming representatives, then through them as intermediary.

On March 13, 1793 (24 Ventôse, year I), Vergniaud, in the name of the Girondins, speaking against abuse of the word *sovereignty* by the anarchists, stated: "They have almost toppled the Republic by making each section believe that sovereignty was its own domain."

Popular ideas concerning sovereignty provided the Montagnard bourgeoisie with their justification for the uprisings of August 10 and May 31. These principles did strike them as being incompatible with the smooth running of the revolutionary government and a sound policy of national defense: a contradiction which, considering the objective conditions of the time, could be resolved only by forcing the Paris sections to obedience. But this would have meant quenching the enthusiasm of the popular movement which had brought the revolutionary government to power and which alone sustained it. Thus the crisis grew worse.

IV

POPULAR POLITICS IN ACTION

The sans-culottes could not fail to cause anxiety to the bourgeoisie, as much on account of their attitude as of their behavior and their political activity, and thereby to rouse the opposition of the revolutionary government, which was above all concerned with stability and efficiency.

Two fundamental principles guided the political activity of the sans-culottes, for whom violence constituted the ultimate recourse: publicity,[1] the people's protector, which in the year II constituted the corollary of revolutionary surveillance; unity, which, based on a unanimous sense of purpose, allowed them to achieve concerted action, thereby pointing the way to victory. Hence a certain number of practices characteristic of popular political behavior were contrary to those of the bourgeoisie. Conceived of, and manifested during the heat of action, they contributed to the progress of the Revolution and to strengthening the dictatorship of the committees. But were they compatible with the needs of the latter, as they were with the fundamental attitude of the former?

[1] Translator's note: The eighteenth-century meaning of the word, "the quality of being public; the condition or fact of being open to public observation or knowledge" (Oxford English Dictionary).

1. Publicity, "The People's Protector"

On 25 Ventôse, in the year II, the *Fontaine-de-Grenelle* section wrote to the popular society of Auxerre that the "patriot had no privacy, he relates everything to the common good: his income, his pain, he shares everything with his brothers, and herein lies the source of the publicity characteristic of fraternal, that is, republican government."

Publicity stemmed from the sans-culotte notion of social relations. This attitude had a marked effect on the political behavior of patriots; they did not have to hide their opinions or their actions, as long as they had the public good in mind. Political life was a public affair, observed by the sovereign people; the administrative bodies and general assemblies debated in public sessions, the elected officers voted out loud under the watchful eye of the tribunes. One was secretive only if one had bad intentions; denunciation became a civic duty. Publicity was indeed the *safeguard of the people*: this precept, put into action during every period of crisis between 1792 and 1794, provided the sans-culottes with a powerful revolutionary weapon.

On February 22, 1792, more than two hundred citizens of Paris explained to the Legislative Assembly "how essential it was that administrative sessions be public, so that the people should know who is not working or watching out for their interests, and beware of those who had received their confidence only to further their own ambitions or indulge in their own whimsey." When war was declared, publicity appeared to be a still more indispensable means of revolutionary surveillance. On July 1, in order to force the administrative cadres "to be more mature in their debates and to speed up their business," and so that the people could exercise their right "to watch

over the conduct of their administrators," the Legislative
Assembly decreed the opening of sessions of administrative bodies. Under popular pressure, this practice was soon
extended to every aspect of political life. In the year II,
it was tantamount to revolutionary surveillance. On March
13, 1792, a citizen from the *Postes* section demanded that
the general assemblies be opened to the public; the
authorities agreed to do so, with the result that passive
citizens [who lacked the property needed to qualify as
voters] were granted access to the assembly. But on July
3, the general assembly of *Postes* recognized "that it is
important that every citizen should be able to witness the
debates"; its sessions would be open to the public. On
July 20, the *Roule* section made the same decision and, at
about the same time, so did all the others. The sans-
culottes invaded the general assemblies and were not content to play the role of spectator. Platforms were erected
in the assembly halls, which were crowded every night
with women and children and citizens from other sections.
Henceforth the section deliberated in the presence of the
people.

Were open sessions sufficient safeguard? The people
still had to watch over the most important political activities, elections and votes: in order to eliminate their opponents, the patriots insisted upon roll-call voting by
acclamation.

The practice of roll-call voting was inaugurated on August 10, 1792. On the seventeenth, when two municipal
officers read to the *Théâtre-Français* assembly the law
creating a special criminal tribunal, the assembly announced that, "considering the urgent need to organize
this tribunal speedily," it would name its representative
by acclamation. During the Convention elections, the roll-
call vote was imposed for all business at hand. This
brought pressure on the electors to weigh their choices
and thus, to a certain extent, modified the two-stage system of election, considered both dangerous to popular
sovereignty and conducive to intrigue. Encouraged by
Robespierre, the *Place-Vendôme* section decided, on Au-

gust 27, 1792, that in order to avoid the inconveniences of the two-stage election, the electors would vote by roll call in the presence of the public; in order to assure the effectiveness of this last precautionary measure, the elections were to be held in the Jacobins' assembly hall. On the same day, the *Bondy* section decided that all elections would be conducted by roll-call vote and that the electoral assembly must surround itself with the largest number of citizens possible "in order to witness the decisions of each elector," the only measure capable of "doing away with intrigues and forcing the electors not to abuse their powers." The General Assembly of the Commune granted these wishes on the same day: voting would be by roll call, and the sessions would be held in the presence of the people; since the bishop's palace did not have a hall large enough for the public, the electoral assembly should meet at the Jacobin headquarters. The electoral assembly complied with this order.

The question of voting procedure came up again in October of 1792, on the occasion of the nomination of the mayor of Paris and the municipal officers; the same question of revolutionary surveillance brought the majority of the sections to use the same procedure. When the electoral laws voted by the Convention on October 19, 1792 (28 Vendémiaire, year 1), required the secret ballot, the *Mirabeau* section demanded roll-call voting "to avoid the dangers of secrecy." More prudent, the *Champs-Elysées* section was content to assert the sovereignty of the primary assemblies, without prejudicing their decision; on October 3, it posited the principle that the exercise of voting rights would not be tampered with unless the order issued from the primary assemblies themselves, "since this is the only right which cannot and should never be delegated"; they were therefore free to decide which method of voting they would use. In the meantime, on the same day, the *Arsenal*, *Bon-Conseil* and *Butte-des-Moulins* sections announced that they were against the secret ballot and for the roll-call *viva voce* vote, which method was also adopted by the *Marais* section. The *Gravilliers* section was more circumspect. On October 7, it protested the law, but asserted that in the future, elections would be conducted by roll call; thus no one could be influenced by "party politics." The *Piques* section adopted a similar method, and, on October 9, declared that the secret ballot "was not conducive to freedom."

The crisis grew more serious during March 1793, when the sans-culottes once again insisted on roll-call voting as a means of successfully opposing the moderates. The system was soon deemed suspect of failing to reflect the unanimity which should imbue the sans-culottes; therefore, during the summer of 1793, the system of voting by acclamation spread. Even more than roll-call voting, acclamation, or the rising vote, forced the hesitant to make up their minds and eliminated all forms of opposition. It was soon to be the only revolutionary voting method.

In March 1793, when the Paris sections, which first spontaneously, and then backed by the law of March 21, named their revolutionary committees, the elections were generally conducted by roll call, often by rising vote; for example, the *Contrat-Social* section's elections of March 29. These choices were subsequently ruled illegal, and, during the repression of year III, were one of the complaints most frequently made against former commissars. In May and June, during the bitter struggle between the sans-culottes and the moderates for domination of the general assemblies, the voting system was contested by the rival factions. "No secret ballots, or else the clique will have it," said a sans-culotte from the *Mail* section on May 21. During the elections for commander-in-chief of the Paris National Guard, the sans-culottes, in their desire to elect Hanriot, imposed roll-call voting in the sections they dominated; the moderates, who supported Raffet, wanted the secret ballot. The *Lepeletier* section, led by the moderates, complied with the law; but the sans-culottes voted by roll call. Thus cannoneer La Merlière declared: "I don't give a damn, I'm voting for Hanriot." When they could not dominate, the sans-culottes resorted to compromise. Thus on June 27, a citizen in the *Unité* section reported on the resolution whereby the assembly had adopted the secret vote; the ballots were to be signed by the voters, otherwise they would be considered void. Thus the principle of publicity was maintained.

During the summer of 1793, as the sans-culottes won increasing political influence, the roll-call vote spread. The measure was adopted on 7 August by the Hommes-Libres society of the *Pont-Neuf* section; it was "the free men's ballot"; on September 4, the general assembly followed suit, urged on by public opinion. In Brumaire, the last moderate sections or societies were sans-culottized: on the twenty-seventh, the *Lepeletier* popular society decided that it would vote by roll call on all nominations. Those moderates who persisted in wanting to use the secret ballot were arrested on suspicion. Thus, early in Brumaire, citizen Bourdon from the *Bonne-Nouvelle* section was arrested for voting on the nominations in a low voice. Louis Maillet, a copperplate engraver from the *Panthéon-Français* section, was arrested on 12 Frimaire "for being vehemently opposed to the patriots' desire to vote by roll call in the general assemblies." Toward the beginning of the year II, the secret ballot disappeared from sectional politics as no longer considered constitutional.

Masters of the general assemblies, the sans-culottes forced a procedure which better corresponded to their revolutionary temperaments and to their ardent quest for unanimity: voting by acclamation. It was not something new—the sans-culottes had already used this method in moments of acute crisis. For example, on August 2, 1792, the general assembly of the *Postes* section elected its president by acclamation and rejected a demand for balloting. After September 1793, voting by acclamation was general. At about this time, the general assembly of the *Beaure-paire* section, "not wanting to waste time in a ballot election," got in the habit of electing its president by vote of acclamation, "which they also intended to do when the president of the committee received orders which he had to tell them about, and on which a prompt decision was needed." Urgency was not the only motivation for voting by acclamation; it was also a means of disposing of opposition, a manifestation of the revolutionary unity so dear to the sans-culottes. This system survived until the spring of the year II, along with the standing vote, less often used, but just as efficient. Although the general assembly of the *Butte-des-Moulins* section decided, on 20 Brumaire, to proceed "in a revolutionary manner by rising vote," on 25 Frimaire it re-elected its staff "in a revolutionary manner by acclamation." This method was usually used in the *Invalides* section, and by the popular society of the *Poissonnière* section. Finally, under public pressure, voting by acclamation was adopted by the General Assembly of the Commune. On 2 Ventôse, its president, Lubin, asked to be replaced. Immediately, nearly all the members of the Council shouted "Lubin! Lubin!" and the tribunes took up the cry as well: "Lubin! Lubin!" Lubin pointed out that such a nomination was invalid. "We have consulted the laws of the provisional government and we have discovered that the General Council has the right to elect and dismiss its president whenever it wishes, and in *whatever manner* it wishes." Should they name tellers, and proceed to a ballot? "It would waste so much time." Lubin was proclaimed duly elected.

At this time, voting by ballot had almost disappeared: it did not survive the Ventôse crisis and the condemnation of the Cordeliers. When the Jacobin dictatorship was in power, bourgeois procedures were used: voting by acclamation or by roll call was formally abolished for nominations in the general assembly by Payan, national agent for the purged Commune. The sections had to obey. But the sans-culottes, rather than use a method of voting which they considered favorable to their opponents, deserted the general assemblies. On 30 Messidor, during the election of two clothing commissars, a discussion took place in the general assembly of the *Invalides* section: were they to vote by acclamation or by secret ballot? "When instructions were issued saying that the said commissars were to be chosen by ballot, many citizens who did not wish to take part in the discussion left the as-

sembly hall." The return to the secret ballot was one of
the measures which marked the reaction that set in in
the spring of the year II; it was partially responsible for
the sans-culottes' dissatisfaction with the revolutionary
government.

The Thermidorian reactionaries retained the Robespierrist Commune's policy concerning this matter. Furthermore, in Prairial, year III, they sought out those who
had commended the roll call or standing vote or vote by
acclamation, since they had benefited from them. The
last mention of the use of this system was in the *Indivisibilité* section. When its primary assembly met, on the
first intersalary day of the year III, a certain Berger said
that the only way to vote was by roll call; he was thrown
out of the assembly—an almost unanimous decision—"for
being a notorious Terrorist."

By opening sessions of administrative bodies to the
public, by banning of the secret ballot, political life became a public affair: all citizens were called upon to survey the actions, the words, even the intentions of both
their friends and their enemies. But they must not keep
silent in matters which concerned public safety. Thus denunciation became an extreme application of the principle of publicity; for the sans-culottes, it was a question
of civic duty.

In public places, during demonstrations, the *watchful
eye,* one of the most common emblems of revolutionary
symbolism, reminded the citizens to be vigilant. Denunciation often figured among the commitments of the republican oath. Denunciations were often made during sessions of the general assemblies and the popular societies.
The law itself urged the people to denounce suspects.
After the decree of September 16, 1791, was promulgated,
civic denunciation was obligatory on the part of anyone
who witnessed suspicious behavior. At the suggestion of
the Jacobins, on 26 Ventôse, year II, the General Council
of the Commune urged every good citizen to be more
watchful than ever and to denounce the enemies of the
nation.

The sans-culottes were not content with denunciations, they also justified them. In his "Essay on Political Denunciation," read before the society of the *Guillaume-Tell* section on July 25, 1793 (Thermidor, year I), Etienne Barry defined it as an act whereby "without being forced to sign, if one does not wish to, and without responsibility, one reveals public scandals to the elected authorities." Under the ancien régime, the denunciator was considered contemptible, "because under a despotic government, what is known as public order is nothing short of a means of protecting and extending despotism." Since the Revolution, "far from being a moral crime, political denunciation has become a virtue and a duty"; its aim is to protect man's every right. What better weapon against *noble* or *bourgeois* aristocrats? The example of Marat offers proof enough. And Barry concluded: "Denunciation is the protector of freedom in a people's republic." According to a sans-culotte from the *Chalier* section, speaking on 27 Floréal, year II, denunciation, like publicity, is the *protector of the sovereign people*; it should be considered "as important as probity or honor." Those who do not speak up when they should are bad citizens, those who denounce others are worthy of reward. There was no need to have been witness to the event in order to make a denunciation: "It will be up to the juries and ministers of justice, traditional defenders of the accused, to evaluate your declarations."

Thus, in the year II, denunciation was a manifestation of revolutionary vigilance. Deemed justified by its aims, it lost all its odious connotations for the sans-culottes; it was a civic duty. On September 25, 1793 (4 Vendémiaire, year II), Marrans, a wigmaker, informed the revolutionary committee of the *Chalier* section "that he was on the track of one and even possibly several counter-revolutionary societies, to which he would try to gain admission, in order to denounce them; that he would do everything he could in order not to be suspected of being a traitor." In the same section, a militant by the name of Montain-Lambin, as a member of the charity committee, helped a citizeness whom he, on the other hand, denounced "as entertaining ideas contrary to the precepts of the Revolution." In the *Muséum* section, Chassant, a former priest attached to the Church of Saint-Germain-l'Auxerrois, considered that it was the duty of children to denounce their parents if they insisted on their practicing the Catholic faith.

When in the year III, the sans-culottes were charged as denouncers, far from defending themselves, they were astonished at the complaint. In the *Thermes-de-Julien* section, a launderer, Landru, was arrested on 9 Prairial for having denounced a certain Duhamel for his royalist sympathies; he defended himself by saying "he thought he was supposed to denounce people." Michel de Bonne-Nouvelle, the painter, was arrested on 5 Prairial for the same reason. "Is it therefore a crime," he wrote in a petition to the Public Safety Committee, "to have exposed and denounced facts that were true and useful to public safety? Will disorder, anarchy and confusion reach such a point that *civic denunciations* will be likened to those dictated by vested interests, vengeance or cupidity?" He had denounced people, but not out of hatred, or out of vested interests, or as an act of vengeance. "Nothing short of love of my country guided me in my denunciations. If the majority of citizens were virtuous enough to denounce all the enemies of the nation, we, the nation, would be saved." Further: carpenter Gentil, former commissar in the *Contrat-Social* section, was sentenced to death on 5 Prairial, year III. "Why did I denounce several people in this section?—Because I thought they had acted contrary to the interests of the nation."

2. UNITY AS A GUARANTEE OF VICTORY

The principle of publicity showed, in its extreme consequences, the ardent desire for unanimity which animated the sans-culotte: he related himself wholly to the mass movement; he could not conceive of isolating himself from it; conformity of sentiments, of mind and of votes struck him as being not only desirable, but necessary. Unity, therefore, was to be one of the driving powers of their political activity, an almost mystical concept. It wasn't only a question of embodying a sense of the national unity asserted during the night of August 4, proclaimed by the Constitution of 1791, then by the Convention, and solemnly celebrated on August 10, 1793 (Thermidor, year 1). In the hands of the sans-culottes, unity became a political weapon, a guarantee and means of victory; they wanted complete union between political organizations, and even more so, between the various social classes bent on the ruin of the aristocracy. Correspondence and fraternization were the means of achieving unity; the brotherly kiss was its symbol; the oath gave it a religious value.

The need to unite all the revolutionary forces was first felt on the sectional level. "The more the nation is in danger, the more the citizens should unite," declared the *Beaubourg* section on September 6, 1792; this section issued a "proclamation of brotherhood," and abandoned the *insignificant* name of *Beaubourg* in favor of *Réunion*: so that there be no differentiation between citizens, and so that the entire section be composed "of a single family all of whose members are in perfect union." A kiss of peace followed the oath.

The sans-culottes were intent upon involving all citizens in political life, unable to conceive of anyone being either indifferent or neutral. Many were the calls to unity, but they were far from convincing those whose interests the Revolution had injured. If they could not persuade, the sans-culottes were severe; masters of the sections, they turned against those who, indifferent to the dangers confronting the nation, were waiting out the storm. During the autumn of 1793, indifference, casualness and egotism became motives for suspicion: there could be only one party in the Republic. The ardent quest for unity strengthened the Terror.

The calls for increased attendance at the meetings of

the general assemblies, accompanied by threats against indifference, increased during the early part of 1793, when the crisis mobilized the militants and increased their ranks. On December 13, 1792 the *Arsenal* section had urged citizens to attend meetings more frequently. They brought up the subject again on January 2, 1793, stating bitterly that the more conscientious were the least well off; "they are the workers . . . they are those who in times of difficulty are the first to expose themselves to danger." Conversely, "wealthy citizens of all classes," some indifferent, others "devoting all their time to their business or to other useful speculations, are almost entirely preoccupied with taking care of their fortunes." Only a minority frequented the assemblies therefore. The *Gardes-Françaises* section supported a resolution of the *Arsenal* section which ordered voters to sign their names in a register; thus they would be able to differentiate "citizens who fulfilled the sacred duties imposed upon them by the interests of the nation, from those who for various reasons are not involved."

Exhortations and threats were of little use. On April 1, the *Bondy* section launched a new appeal to the *uninvolved*. It was in vain. On April 10, the *Bondy* section's *Last Appeal to the Uninvolved* warned of sanctions. Those who missed three successive sessions of the general assembly would be declared bad citizens: the names of the *uninvolved* were to be sent to the sectional committee, which would refuse to honor their evidence for the issuing of certificates of civism and passports. The uninvolved person was already considered an inferior citizen, and soon was to be suspect. Furthermore, the *Bondy* section labeled despicable "every property-owning or land-owning citizen, or every person known to have sufficient independent means who had no public position or refused one when elected to it." Since elected sectional officers were not yet paid, the sans-culottes did not seek out these positions; if the "haves" rejected them, they were accused of incivism.

The frequency of these calls to action emphasized their

futility. The political ideas and behavior of the sans-culottes were too widely opposed to those of the bour-geoisie; lack of involvement was not the real reason for the well-to-do citizens deserting the general assemblies, but rather their distaste for associating with the working class and being compelled to participate in their political behavior. Toward the end of May, the *Molière-et-Lafontaine* section again invited them "fraternally [to] come and share in its work, to offer their talents, which every individual owes to his country." On June 5, the *Théâtre-Français* assembly decided, as a symbol of redis-covered unity, to destroy "every form of distinction be-tween citizens" and to refuse "to be labeled either left or right." Every appeal, like every advance, was made in vain.

Unable to interest the uninvolved or to integrate them into the revolutionary nation, when the sans-culottes be-came masters of the sections, they turned against the in-different: during September 1793, absence of involvement was call for suspicion, a situation which lasted until Ther-midor. The law of September 17 made no mention of indifference as being among the characteristics of those people reputed to be suspect. Going further, the General Council of the Commune rescinded an order it had issued on the nineteenth of the first month, and insisted that an "indifference clause" be inserted; thus every person who had done nothing against freedom, but who had still done nothing for it, became suspect.

The revolutionary committees had in the meantime outstripped the Commune in terms of power. The law on suspects had barely been passed when the uninvolved and uncommitted began to be arrested. On September 18, 1793 (Fructidor, year 1), in the *Muséum* section, a certain Blondel, a former valet, was arrested; he was suspect "be-cause of his lack of involvement and of his ambivalence." On September 21, in the *Invalides* section, François Lagrange, who had a private income, was arrested "be-cause he was a man who lived among us without partici-pating in helping others and is consequently considered to be uninvolved." A former notary, Arnault, from the *Bondy* section, was arrested on October 2: "If nothing else, he is an egotist, and an uninvolved one at that"; he is never to be seen in the section; he can only be an enemy of the Revolution since he has never taken part in it. On October 5, in the *Indivisibilité* section, one Voutray, a former paymaster, was considered suspect for "never having offered his services to the nation"; he further prejudiced his case when, upon being arrested, he declared "he was neither democrat, royalist nor republican, but that he was quietly sitting it out." Bluteau, a writer from the *Arcis* section, was arrested on 2 Brumaire: he had never taken up arms during the Revolution. Bossu, a silk merchant from the *Bon-Conseil* section, "never showed himself a friend of the Revolution"; he was remiss in offering his services, having done so rarely. He was arrested on 28 Brumaire, and on the same day and in the same section, François Boucher, a dealer in pearls, was also arrested: "He has never been involved and belongs to no party."

Although less frequent after Frimaire, when the revolutionary government was finally established, arrests for indifference or lack of enthusiasm nevertheless continued to be made, attesting to the permanence of sans-culotte activism. André Angard, an appraiser from the *Bon-Conseil* section, was arrested on 18 Nivôse for being uninvolved. Another uninvolved person was Lachapelle, a bachelor with a private income from the *Contrat-Social* section: "He devotes his entire time to the pursuit of pleasure, the Revolution is of little concern to him." Arrested on 6 Germinal, "today he must give us an account of his political conduct since 1789." Again, on 23 Floréal, the revolutionary committee of this same section gave orders for the arrest of Brasseur, a clockmaker: "His lack of involvement is known to us; he has never mounted guard, has refused to serve, and has done nothing for the Revolution."

The sans-culottes considered that education and talent compounded the offense of apathy: another revealing characteristic of their political behavior, of their faith in education and their belief that knowledge could only further the sense of civic duty. On 15 Brumaire, the revolutionary committee of the *Montagne* section decided to arrest Jean-

Charles Choderlos, formerly an employee of the East
India Company, a *very enlightened man:* "It grieves us
[wrote the commissars] to have to remind you that a large
number of these educated men, such as Choderlos, have
not used all the means at their disposal to fight the enemies
of the Republic, who are powerful in our section; in short,
to see them friendly with every party, while the sans-
culottes, who can barely read and write, energetically up-
hold true principles and have no other interests but the
nation's." Berthel, a notary from the *Amis-de-la-Patrie* section, was "notorious for being enlightened and remaining
neutral toward the Revolution." He was arrested on 25
Brumaire. "Although he is an eloquent and talented man,"
Civet, clerk in the National Treasury, residing in the
Faubourg-du-Nord section, "has never defended the rights
of the people." He was arrested on 4 Frimaire. On 25
Ventôse, the revolutionary committee of the *Montagne*
section again issued orders for the arrest of the writer
Laharpe: he had rendered services to the cause of freedom;
"yet he is to be reproached for one thing, that is, not attending the assembly of his section to support the sans-
culottes, to use his talents to develop the great principles
of nature, in order to crush the still powerful aristocracy."

The class characteristics of this attack against indifference are clearly defined: lawyers, businessmen, men of
independent means . . . the *uninvolved* all belonged to
the comfortable, even to the wealthy class. The vexation
of the sans-culottes at their refusal to rally to the Revolution is only the more indicative of their own desire for
unity and their lack of class consciousness; the uninvolved
were arrested less for their station in life than for their
political behavior. Did the sans-culottes believe that one
could affect the other? It would appear not. Their quest
for unity beyond class barriers emphasizes the utopian
aspect of their social and political aspirations.

Unity was necessary not only at the sectional level but
also among popular organizations; the success of their actions depended upon it. To co-ordinate the popular move-

ment, to mold the sections and the clubs into one uniform body of opinion—these were constant concerns of
the sans-culottes, and of all subsequent revolutionary
leaders. Collective petitions, and correspondence between
sectional organizations were methods that were successful
for quite some time.

The right to petition had been unanimously granted
to all citizens; if it was not stated explicitly in the Declaration of 1789, that of 1793 proclaimed it in Article 32.
But how was this right to be interpreted? Again, two concepts confronted one another: that of the individualist
bourgeoisie and that of the group-oriented sans-culottes.
One thought petitions should be signed individually; the
other, by groups. On April 6, 1791, the *Moniteur* put the
difference clearly: "Every petition is an individual act on
the part of citizens who consent to sign it. It is absolutely
contrary to the principle of freedom, contrary to all principle to draft a petition supported by a plurality of votes,
to call such a document a petition presented by a section,
or a petition presented by a commune, unless all the citizens of the section or the commune were present at a
meeting, and unanimously voted 'aye.' They would also
all have to sign the petition." On May 10, 1791, the Constituent Assembly banned collective petitions. Although
on the following August 9 it put the right to petitions
among the *fundamental provisions guaranteed by the Constitution,* it declared that petitions must be signed individually. Nevertheless, the practice of petitioning in the name
of groups continued; it harmonized with popular attitudes;
it served the interests of the Revolution. On February 4,
1792, the recorder of the Legislative Committee raised
a veritable fury on the benches and among the Left in
the Assembly by proposing that all collective petitions be
rejected. The sans-culottes' participation in the affairs of
their sectional assemblies, and their increasing political
activity finally established this practice during the summer
of 1792; how could it have been otherwise, when many
sans-culottes could not even sign their names?

The debate concerning the right to petition was taken

up again during the course of the conflict between the Gironde and the Montagnards. On April 15, 1793 (25 Germinal, year I), when the commissars of the Paris sections presented themselves before the Convention to demand the dismissal of twenty-two of its members, the Assembly decreed that they should sign their petition individually. They had to do so: the president ordered an usher to collect their signatures. This moved the *Gravilliers* section to protest, on April 18; it defended the right to present collective petitions by alluding to the threat confronting the nation and the need for unity: "In these moments of stress, rather than seek to divide the citizens, we all need and have interest in closing our ranks to form an impregnable rampart"; ever since the nation was threatened, the sections had always implemented their right to present collective petitions; to abolish them would mean holding back the Revolution. Furthermore, individual acceptance of a petition was "immoral and suggested on purpose to break the fraternal unity existing between good citizens . . . [that procedure] is not appropriate to our system of government, which calls upon every citizen, without distinction, to fulfill his civic duties; the majority and the soundest of our citizens would be stricken silent because they do not know how to write and so are deprived of ever making their desires known."

Despite the Gironde, however, the sections continued to present collective petitions. They were the rule after June 2, throughout the course of the year II, and even after 9 Thermidor. They disappeared at the same time as the popular movement, after the events of Prairial. The Constitution of the year III recognized the right of petition, but specified that "[petitions] should be individual, and no associations may present them as a body." With the sans-culottes stripped of their powers, there was a return to the individualistic and bourgeois concept of the right to petition.

The collective petition would scarcely be the effective weapon for "unity, concerted action" which the *Lombards* section deemed necessary for the well-being of the Revolution on March 27, 1791, unless the sections kept in touch with each other. Communications, letters giving each other accounts of their debates and demands would, in fact, achieve unity of action. Generally, contact was established by commissars, an extremely slow process; when all the sections had been alerted, it was often too late to take action. To be effective, communication had to be fast. On March 27, 1791, the *Lombards* section proposed the organization of a central office of communications where commissars would inform one another of their respective sections' resolutions and discuss them. In February 1792, the *Sainte-Geneviève* section also tried in vain to organize a communications office or joint committee.

Under pressure from events, on July 27, 1792, the Commune opened a central communications bureau for the sections, a mere information center, where there was no debating, but which did allow the rapid co-ordination of popular action. With the same purpose, on August 11, 1792, the *Théâtre-Français* section named "two civic couriers, authorized to deliver messages wherever necessary . . . in order to give or gather all the details, explanations and instructions which could affect the nation and report them to the section." The Commune's central communications office did not survive the summer of 1792. On February 10, 1793, the *Quatre-Vingt-Douze* section complained of the time wasted by communication through commissars. On the other hand, the moderates were busy destroying the system: on May 24, 1793 (5 Prairial, year I), the Commission of Twelve passed a decree controlling it; on the 25th, the *Arcis* section, controlled by the moderates, demanded that "every form of communication" be forbidden to the popular societies. On July 4, ascertaining that sectional unity had been a factor in their victory, the *Halle-au-Blé* section proposed the creation of a central committee of delegates from revolutionary committees to maintain continuous communication between the sections: "This would be the only means of preventing betrayal." On 1 Frimaire, year II, the *Halle-au-Blé* section again went before the General Assembly of the Commune, pointing out the need for a sectional central committee "for the speedy promulgation of their orders." All these attempts failed, sabotaged by the ill will of the Commune; composed of representatives from the sections, the General Assembly was, after, the actual link between sections. A central committee for communication would have constituted a rival authority.

During the height of revolutionary crises, for reasons stressed by the *Lombards* section in March 1791, the communications system proved to be inadequate. Insurrectionary committees, like those acting on August 10 and May 31, could not move until the last moment, when the sections delegated their sovereign powers. In order to prepare for the supreme moment and lacking any official central organ, the sans-culottes perfected the communications system: they invented *fraternization*.

For the sans-culottes, unity obviously implied fraternity; the words are to be found most frequently linked in documents dated 1793 and the year II. *Fraternity* meant not only bonds of friendship between citizens, but also implied equality. Correspondence was only an administrative process. Fraternization had an emotional content and took on a mystical aura. Its origins can be traced back to the federations of 1790. Here one finds the same ardent declaration of unity. But the federations embraced all classes of the nation; their manifestos were solemn statements rather than calls to combat. Fraternization united only those who were attracted to the sans-culottes; it was concerned with immediate action; it was a weapon against the moderates. Communication between the sections employed commissars with certain powers. The sans-culottes fraternized in bodies: if a section was threatened by moderates, the general assembly of the neighboring section would move in en masse; in the name of fraternity, the two assemblies became one, united by the mystical bond of the oath and of the fraternal kiss, and decisions were made collectively. Fraternization was a pact of mutual assistance, which, beyond sections and societies, united all sans-culottes.

Fraternization first appeared in March 1793. The Society of the Defenders of the Republic invited sections and popular societies to assemble on the seventeenth in the Place de la Réunion "in order to bind the union which should exist among patriots with a fraternal embrace." Fraternal demonstrations increased when the moderate threat was more acute. On April 21, 1793 (2 Floréal, year I), a large delegation from the *Lombards* section assembly turned up at the *Contrat-Social* session. Their spokesman denounced "the numerous intrigues, the anarchy and trouble caused by the royalist-dumourialiste party and the vicious internal division which they [sic] caused in the assemblies." The two sections should make a solemn declaration "to live and communicate fraternally in an intimate union, and to annihilate the aristocratic hydra." The members of the delegation and the assembly exchanged fraternal embraces. On April 23, the assembly of the *Contrat-Social* section, led by its officers, in turn visited the assembly of the *Lombards* section. The two sections formed one single assembly of *brothers and friends*, the two groups of officers mingled on the platform. The oath of unity and fraternity was repeated and a fraternal kiss closed the meeting. Henceforth the two sections were linked together in a quasi-religious pact. When on May 14, a delegation from the *Lombards* section informed the *Contrat-Social* section that "the aristocracy wants to exterminate the patriots," the president immediately suspended discussion and the entire assembly moved to the *Lombards* section to help the threatened sans-culottes.

Fraternization, like communication, tended to unite not only two neighboring sections, but also all the Paris sections. On April 26, 1793 (7 Floréal, year I), when a citizen told the *Contrat-Social* assembly that the *Gardes-Françaises* section was "in a sort of insurrection," it immediately decided that "the sans-culottes citizens" would send a delegation to that section "in order to restore peace, fraternity and cordiality." On the twenty-seventh, a similar order was issued: on the following day the *Contrat-Social* assembly, led by its officers, visited the *Gardes-Françaises* section "in order to fraternize with them and to promise them union, concord and assistance against all rowdies and men of ill will who are attempting to destroy the Republic." On April 28, the two united assemblies debated the measures to be taken. Finally, on the nineteenth, a delegation from the *Gardes-Françaises* section took an oath before the *Contrat-Social* assembly "to unite and fraternize in harmony." We shall fraternize "once a week, in each section alternatively."

The political importance of fraternization is stressed in the verbatim report of the *Contrat-Social* section for May 12, 1793 (22 Floréal, year 1); the *Bon-Conseil* and *Contrat-Social* sections met in a joint assembly and decided: "Wherever and in whatever locale one or more Paris sections meet together, these sections will form one single assembly and the debates will be open to everyone. This is a basic principle for all sans-culottes." Fraternization produced united action in avant-garde sections.

Toward the end of May, there was increased fraternization. When, on the eighteenth, the moderates gained control of the *Contrat-Social* section, "a delegation of more than two hundred" proposed "to fraternize with the sans-culottes of the *Contrat-Social* section twice a week, in order to distinguish the aristocrats from the sans-culottes." This delegation was joined by equally large delegations from the *Halle, Gravilliers,* and *Lombards* sections; the five sections decided to fraternize "with their sans-culottes brothers of other sections should they be threatened by the aristocracy"; first they would go to the rescue of the *Arsenal* and *Butte-des-Moulins* sections "in order to throw out the aristocrats." On the following day, there was further fraternizing in the *Contrat-Social* section with delegations from the *Droits-de-l'Homme, Marchés, Bon-Conseil* and *Gravilliers* sections: "They announced their intention of visiting a few sections where it was said the aristocracy was predominant."

A similar situation occurred on May 20 in the *Droits-de-l'Homme* section. The Amis-des-Droits-de-l'Homme society demanded that it be associated with the section under the banner of "war on the aristocracy, union against intrigue and tyranny." A very large delegation from the *Contrat-Social, Bon-Conseil, Unité, Lombards, Gravilliers* and *Marchés* sections arrived: "Expressions of patriotic and fraternal enthusiasm lasted for some time." Citizen Guiraud, president of the *Contrat-Social* section, took the floor: "We have come here to pledge our assistance to the *Droits-de-l'Homme* section in their struggle against the aristocracy; we are here to swear to fight with them unto death the enemies of holy equality, relentlessly to pursue the moderate monster . . . we are here to help you to unmask these hypocrites, unworthy of the glorious title of free men." The assembly then agreed to adopt the May 12 resolution, which formed a pact of unity, and as the charter of fraternity, "The united sections form only one assembly, their debates are open to all." A sans-culotte from the *Droits-de-l'Homme* section finally brought up the real reason for this session: he demanded reorganization of the revolutionary committee and headquarters, "which could be justifiably called the Committee of Moderantism." Guiraud, from the *Contrat-Social* section, took the chair of the new committee. He proceeded to reorganize the assembly and resorted to the vote by acclamation in order to get the people's approval of appointments and dismissals. The newly elected members took the oath in front of him, and the seven sections present were decreed responsible for decisions taken. Thus fraternization would "revitalize" the moderate sections. This demonstration of sans-culottes unity became the instrument of the class struggle against the moderates.

When moderantism in the Paris sections was crushed, fraternization disappeared from popular political practice. Nevertheless, the sans-culottes occasionally felt it necessary to state the need for unity with some solemnity. Thus on 6 and 10 Pluviôse, year II, the society of revolutionary sans-culottes and the committee of the *Chalier* section swore "union and close fraternity" and declared "eternal hatred of whoever dares or attempts to destroy our unity." During the spring of 1793, fraternization had been an effective weapon in the struggle against the moderates. In the absence of an organized party, or of a central organ which would have co-ordinated the political action of all popular forces, it enabled the sans-culottes to unite in specific situations and once again wakened class consciousness in them. When the sans-culottes were masters of the general assemblies, and the revolutionary government was established on firm ground, fraternization was only symbolic. In order to maintain united action between the sections, communication by commissars again appeared sufficient. This is revealing, both of the nature of the crisis of Ventôse, year II, and of the impotence of Cordelier leadership; in attempting to restore unity among the sans-culottes, they failed to use fraternization, or even communication, which had been one of the reasons for victory a year earlier.

On the contrary, in their last assault during the year III, the sans-culottes, with a sure instinct, once again returned to fraternization. On 10 Germinal, the *Guillaume-Tell* section re-established a system of communications; they relayed to other sections every stand they took on issues of public safety or of general interest; the passwords were *unity, fraternity*. On 12 Germinal, after having accepted a policy statement issued by the *Cité* section whereby it declared itself permanent, the sans-culottes of the *Popincourt* section informed their brothers of the *Arsenal, Maison-Commune, Arcis* and *l'Homme-Armé* sections of the results of their debate: "They would always be prepared to fraternize with the citizens of other sections." Popular politics presented a coherent program: fraternization and permanence were irrevocably linked. Since the general assemblies no longer met after the suppression of permanence, the *Popincourt* section was satisfied with sending commissars to alert the civil committees. Arrested on the Place de Grève, one of these commissars declared that he was on his way to the *Cité* section to "invite it to continue in the same opinion, that we are in a state of crisis." And another said that he was going "to invite the other sections to fraternize together, so that no one should disunite us and that we shall be all brothers together."

This *Popincourt* militant thus outlined the essential characteristics of sans-culottes political behavior. It was based on fraternity. That was not an abstract virtue, but rather the feeling, the sensation itself of unity among sans-culottes. The sans-culotte did not conceive of himself as an isolated individual: he thought and acted en masse.

3. VIOLENCE

The sans-culottes considered violence to be the ultimate recourse against those who refused to answer the call of unity. This stand was one of the characteristics of their political behavior. Popular violence had allowed the bourgeoisie to carry out its first attacks against the ancien régime; indeed, the struggle against the aristocracy would not have been possible without it. In 1793 and in the year II, the sans-culottes used that violence not solely against the aristocrats, but also against the moderates who were opposed to the establishment of an egalitarian republic.

Doubtless we should at times seek the biological roots of this recourse to violence, of this exaltation. Temperament offers some explanation. The reports of Prairial, year III, on the former Terrorists often mention their irascible, passionate nature and their tendency to fits of rage; "Their outbursts were usually the result of being in a position to make malicious remarks without thinking of the consequences." Their reactions were the stronger because the sans-culottes were often frustrated, poor, uneducated, inflamed by awareness of their misery.

In the year III the reactionaries indiscriminately labeled all Terrorists drinkers of blood. Although one must be careful not to generalize and take denunciations and police reports literally, one must nevertheless concede that, for certain individuals, violence did mean the spilling of blood. A certain Arbulot, a cloth shearer from the *Gardes-*

Françaises section, arrested on 9 Prairial, had the reputation for being a dangerous husband and neighbor, a hard and savage man; he was known to have delighted in the September massacres. Bunou, from the *Champs-Elysées* section, who was arrested on 5 Prairial, demanded in the year II that a guillotine be erected in the section, "and that he would act as executioner if there was none to be found." Lesur, from the *Luxembourg* section, was arrested on 6 Prairial for having made a similar suggestion: "that the guillotine was not working fast enough, that there should be more bloodletting in the prisons, that if the executioner was tired, he himself would climb the scaffold with a quarter loaf to soak up the blood." In the *Gardes-Françaises* a certain Jayet was arrested on 6 Prairial for having declared in the year II, "that he would like to see rivers of blood, up to the ankles." On leaving the general assembly of the *République* section, another declared: "The guillotine is hungry, it's ages since she had something to eat." Women shared this Terrorist exaltation. A certain Baudray, a lemonade vendor from the *Lepeletier* section, was arrested on 8 Prairial for having said "she would like to eat the heart of anyone opposed to the sans-culottes"; she intended to raise her children on the same principles: "You hear them talk of nothing but cutting, chopping off heads, not enough blood is flowing."

Nevertheless, temperament alone does not sufficiently explain the fact that the majority of the popular militants approved of if they did not exalt violence and the use of the guillotine. For many, brute force seemed the supreme recourse when a crisis had reached its paroxysm. These same men, who did not hesitate to make blood flow, were more often than not ordinarily quite calm, good sons, good husbands and good fathers. Cobbler Duval from the *Arsenal* section was condemned to death on 11 Prairial, year II, for his role during the uprising of the first; his neighbors testified that he was a good father, good husband, good citizen, a *man of probity*. The feeling that the nation was threatened, the belief in the aristocratic plot, the atmosphere of turbulent days, the tocsin and the issuing of arms made these men beside themselves and created in them something like a second nature. According to the civil committee of the *Faubourg-du-Nord* section, Josef Morlot, a house painter, arrested on 5 Prairial, year III, was a man with two distinct personalities. "One of these, guided by his natural bent, was gentle, honest and generous. He has all the social virtues, which he practices in private. The other, subjugated by present threats, manifests itself in the bloody colors of all the conjoined plagues in their utmost virulence."

This violence was not gratuitous. It had a political aim and a class content; it was a weapon which the sans-culottes were forced to use in their resistance to the aristocracy. A teacher by the name of Moussard employed by the Executive Commission of Public Instruction, was arrested on 5 Prairial, year III. "Yes, I was carried away," he wrote in his defense. "Who wasn't during the Revolution? . . . They say I am fanatical: yes; passion burns within my breast, I am intoxicated with the idea of liberty and I shall always rage against the enemies of my country."

The guillotine was popular because the sans-culottes saw in it an instrument whereby they could avenge the nation. Hence the expressions *national cleaver, national ax;* the guillotine was also known as the *scythe of equality.* Class hatred of the aristocracy was heightened by the belief in an aristocratic plot which since 1789 had been one of the fundamental reasons behind popular violence. Foreign war and civil war further strengthened the popular notion that the aristocracy would only be exterminated by the Terror and that the guillotine was necessary for consolidating the Republic. Becq, a clerk in the Navy Department, a good father, a good husband and well thought of, but extraordinarily impassioned according to the civil committee of the *Butte-des-Moulins,* turned his impassioned nature against priests and noblemen, whom he *usually* recommended for assassination. Jean-Baptiste Mallais, cobbler and revolutionary commissar of the *Temple* section, was the same: he did not heistate to use clubs when arguing with noblemen and priests considered enemies of the people; he spoke of arming the wives of patriots "so that they in turn can slit the throats of the wives of aristocrats." A certain Barrayer of the *Réunion* section declared, in the year II, "We must kill the wolf cub in the Temple"; otherwise, "one day he'll kill the people." Even more indicative of the political aims which the sans-culottes hoped to achieve through violence and through the Terror were the words recorded by the observer Perrière on 6 Ventôse, year II: "Is the guillotine working today?" asked a dandy. "Yes," replied an honest patriot, "there is always somebody betraying somebody or something."

During the year III violence became even more important for the sans-culottes. The Terror had also been an economic aspect of government; it had sanctioned the application of the "maximum," which had guaranteed the people their daily bread. Whereas the reaction coincided with the abolition of price-fixing and the worst shortages, certain among them came to identify the Terror with abundance, in the same way as they associated popular government with the Terror. Cobbler Clément from the *République* section was denounced on 2 Prairial for having declared "that the Republic cannot be built without blood flowing." In the *Brutus* section, a certain Denis was arrested on 5 Prairial; as far as he was concerned there was no such thing as "a good republican, unless some of his colleagues were guillotined." Mistress Chalandon from the *l'Homme-Armé* section declared, "Nothing will really work properly until permanent guillotines were erected at every street intersection in Paris." Carpenter Richer, from the *République* section, touched the heart of the matter when he said, on 1 Prairial: "There will be no bread unless we spill some blood; under the Terror we didn't go without."

Whatever specific aims the Parisian sans-culottes had in mind, the Terror and popular violence to a great extent swept away the remnants of feudalism and absolutism for the bourgeoisie. They nevertheless corresponded to a different form of behavior, in the same way as popular political practices, essentially characterized in 1793 and in the year II by voting by acclamation and by fraternity, expressed a concept of democracy that was fundamentally different from that of the bourgeoisie, even of the Jacobins.

Doubtless the revolutionary bourgeoisie, during the critical moments of its struggle against the aristocracy, also resorted to violence; they, too, made use of certain popular practices; for example, during the course of the Convention elections, in Paris, they used the roll-call vote. Events justified this departure from the usual concepts of liberal democracy, and also class interests. Once the revolutionary government was in power, neither these interests nor the events would allow these practices to continue. Although these practices were in accord with the popular temperament, they were incompatible with the behavior and political ideas of the bourgeoisie. They also threatened its sovereignty. Furthermore, they undermined the centralized organization of the government and the dictatorship of its committees. This contradiction further contributed to intensify the crisis.

V

THE POLITICAL ORGANIZATION
OF THE PARIS SANS-CULOTTES

The strength which the Paris sans-culottes placed at the disposal of the bourgeois revolution, like their demands, would have lost its effectiveness if it had not been organized. By taking advantage of the legal institutions created by the Constituent Assembly, but giving them a new content, by making use of the revolutionary institutions created by the Convention, and lastly by forging the sectional societies into a specifically popular force, the militant sans-culottes provided the revolutionary movement with an organization that was both flexible and effective. Between the spring and the autumn of 1793, it proved itself in the struggle against the moderates and greatly assisted the formation of the revolutionary government. Once the last-mentioned was stabilized, the duality and soon the incompatibility between governmental and popular powers became apparent.

The sections, guided by their committees, supported and manned by their societies, were to a great extent autonomous, and through a concerted action, showed themselves capable of imposing their will upon government committees and upon the Convention. An example of this would be September 5, 1793 (18 Fructidor, year I). With the attendant crisis, and particularly toward the beginning of that anxious spring of 1794, could it not be said that a new popular uprising threatened to topple the revolutionary government? From spring to autumn of the year II, problems of communication between the revolutionary government and sectional democracy increased with

*tragic intensity. Through its various organizations, the lat-
ter appears to have been an autonomous power at the
heart of the Revolution.*

1. THE SECTIONAL ASSEMBLIES

In view of the States General elections, the city of Paris
was divided into sixty districts by royal proclamation on
April 13, 1789. When the elections were over, these districts continued to meet and debate in permanent general
assemblies; the districts declared their intention of admin-
istering their own business and taking part in public affairs.
On August 30, a municipal decree gave the administration of each of them to a committee of between sixteen
and twenty-four members.

The Constituent Assembly, which had organized the
kingdom's municipalities by the decree of December 14,
1789, would not tolerate Paris having a particular form of
organization which favored autonomous tendencies. After
considerable discussion, it adopted the decree of May 21–
June 27, 1790, which constituted the municipal charter
of Paris. The sixty districts were replaced by forty-eight
sections. The previously tolerated districts were abolished;
the sections became electoral wards; they met to vote, and
disbanded as soon as the balloting was over. Although
the law restricted their freedom to meet, it did not suppress it; in certain situations, and if requested by more
than fifty citizens, the sections might meet for other purposes than balloting.

The assembly was the most important body in the section: it was the *sovereign power* in continuous presence.
Citizens met to vote in local assemblies; they debated in
the general assemblies.

The primary (local) assemblies, the sections' *raison
d'être*, met infrequently, although legislatively speaking
they were the most important; there were only fifty ses-

sions between November 11, 1791, and February 11, 1794. The abolition of the distinction between active and passive citizens decreed by the *Théâtre-Français* section on July 27, 1792, was immediately picked up by all the other Paris sections, and changed the nature of the assemblies: they really did become the fountainhead of popular sovereignty. By decreeing on August 10 that every citizen twenty-five years of age domiciled in Paris for more than one year was allowed to vote in the elections for justices of the peace, the Legislative Assembly was merely sanctioning a *fait accompli*; as it did the next day, when it decreed that "the classification of Frenchmen in terms of active and non-active citizens was abolished."

The law of May 21, 1790, stipulated the conditions under which the assemblies could meet; it did not prescribe the length or frequency of these sessions, their powers or their aims. Although in the beginning the general assemblies met infrequently (from December 4, 1790, to July 25, 1792, when they were formally established as permanent bodies, the *Postes* section held only fifty sessions), the sections were at least largely responsible for interpreting the law; they continued to take part in public affairs and in politics in general. The Constituent Assembly added a restrictive clause to the law by a decree dated May 18–22, 1791: the general assemblies could only be called to session to deal with matters of municipal administration; any other form of decision making would be considered unconstitutional, and therefore null and void. Sectional activity was therefore distinctly restricted; the sections became mere administrative subdivisions of the capital. The *Postes* section held only six meetings between May 30 and September 9, 1791.

The war and the threat to the nation brought about the revival of the permanence of the general assemblies, and gave them theoretically unlimited powers. Although permanence was suppressed on September 9, 1793—the forty-sous indemnity was established at the same time— the assemblies continued until the spring of the year II to concern themselves with general politics as well as local affairs.

The municipal law of 1790 was aimed essentially at the organization of primary assemblies; it did not specify the duties and functions of the general assemblies. It stipulated only that upon its formation, each assembly proceed to nominate a president and a secretary. The assemblies would remain in complete control of their own organization. For lack of documentation, it is impossible to discern the details of this law, in particular its sub-clauses. In 1793 and in the year II it appeared quite straightforward. The assembly was headed by a president, who was assisted by a committee, and a recording secretary, who took down the minutes. Tellers were responsible for counting votes, rising or roll-call; ushers maintained order in the assembly hall. The committee was generally renewed each month, usually by standing vote or by acclamation. There was little change in the personnel, a small number of militants sharing the places with each other; the presidents of certain general assemblies stayed in office throughout the year II.

The sessions began with the reading of the minutes, then the laws and decrees or resolutions of the Commune; this took time, and often delayed the opening of discussion on the agenda, which the president was generally supposed to draft with the consent of the committee. So sessions supposed to start at five o'clock and end at ten, in accordance with the law, often lasted much longer. In the *Montagne* section, they usually ended at eleven-thirty, which, according to the observer Hanriot, "meant that the worker would not get to his workshop on time next day." On 25 Ventôse, year II, a citizen vehemently demanded that the sessions begin at five o'clock, that the discussion start at six o'clock, so that the assembly could break up at ten o'clock. Generally, the sessions appear to have been disorderly, if not noisy, even then the sans-culottes were in absolute control. According to the observer Prévost, on 30 Pluviôse, when it was a question of debating important matters, many citizens talked at random or screamed deafeningly, making all discussion impossible; this was in the *République* section. In the *Chalier* section on 1 Ventôse, the president of the assembly drank a glass of wine in the chair, and some wanted to dismiss him: "This place is a wineshop now; it will soon be a tobacco shop as well." Others remarked that several citizens had done the same; after an hour's confusion, they merely returned to the order of business. The sites of the general assemblies did not exactly lend themselves to order. Churches and chapels that had become state property were not really suitable for meetings of this sort. The sections were forever demanding renovation or relocation. On 1 Germinal, year II, the *Montagne* section supported a petition sponsored by the *Bonne-Nouvelle* section which proposed that new assembly halls be erected in each section, to be paid for by the Republic: "Numbers of citizens entered the assembly halls through several doors, which wouldn't happen if there were a restricted enclosure."

In order to appreciate fully the role played by the general assemblies in the organization and political activity of the Parisian sans-culottes, we must ask a series of questions: How can one gauge the importance of the primary or general assemblies? What proportion of citizens received the forty-sous payment for attendance?

The loss of nearly all the minutes of the sections makes it impossible to draw up a chronological chart which would allow us to follow, along with other events, the attendance figures of the general assemblies, and to graph them. The recording secretaries also, more often than not, failed to note the number of people present, and were content with vague estimates. The information we have is scattered and fragmentary and generally only about elections. Only an approximation is possible; the figures take on all the worth they have if they are scanned in relation to the number of active citizens (the lists of these were compiled with care after 1790), or in relations to the whole number of citizens; several estimates of their number were made after August 10, 1792.

From the very beginning of the Revolution, except during the heights of crises or during the "great days," only a minority participated in sectional political life. Under the *censitaire* regime, only a small number of active citizens [qualified to vote by possessing property] participated in the general assemblies, even when they were transformed into primary assemblies for elections. The level of attendance appears to have been particularly low, varying according to section and period between four and nineteen. Doubtless in order to come closer to reality, we should bear in mind the social composition of the various sections, and the political pressure the sans-culottes exerted on the active citizens. In this respect, it is significant that for the three sections of *Faubourg-Montmartre*, *Fontaine-de-Grenelle* and *Louvre*, which together counted approximately 12,000 inhabitants, the general assemblies, between April and May of 1792, had a high attendance despite their active citizens being fewer. In the largest, the *Faubourg-Montmartre*, attendance was 18 per cent of the total number of active citizens, whereas the *Louvre* section, which was the wealthiest, had no more than 5 per cent attendance. Between April and July 1792, attendance at the *Fontaine-de-Grenelle* sectional assemblies stabilized at 7 per cent, while the *Louvre* general assembly appeared more aware of the worsening situation, its attendance rising from 5 per cent at the beginning of May to 19 per cent by the end of July; passive citizens swelled the numbers.

The presence of passive citizens in the sectional assemblies in July and August 1792 for a while swelled attendance. However, it quickly dropped again. The attendance graph of the assemblies in the *Contrat-Social* section, formerly the *Postes* section, is significant. The numbers rose between October and November 1792 and were at a level never achieved during the course of the censitaire period. However, the subject under discussion at the time was the election of the mayor of Paris. The numbers dropped when the business at hand was less interesting, from 330 voters on November 12, 1792 (21 Brumaire, year 1), to 151 on the twenty-eight for the election of a municipal official. The complication of electoral procedures and the large number of ballots tired citizens who until that time had been constant in attendance; the timid and the unconvinced withdrew when political battles intensified. On February 11, 1793 (22 Pluviôse, year 1), only 194 people voted in the election of Pache to the Paris mayoralty, even fewer, 123, when a mere municipal official was elected on January 18 (29 Nivôse); although the assembly's social composition had changed, active participation had, nevertheless, declined to the average level of the censitaire period. The October 25, 1792 (4 Brumaire, year 1), edition of the *Moniteur*, referring to an election which took place in the *Panthéon-Français* section, stressed this low level of participation in sectional affairs: "Each of the forty-eight sections is capable of mustering 4,000 voters . . . and yet 150, 100, even fewer citizens, attend meetings of general assemblies." The anonymous editor of the *Moniteur* does not mention an important fact: the change in the social composition of the general assemblies after August 10.

Faced with the tremendous influx of sans-culottes, numbers of formerly active citizens henceforth did not take part in any political activity. When the danger had passed, among the formerly passive citizens, only a minority continued to concern themselves with public affairs. The control of the assemblies had simply passed into other hands; the little information handed down to us by the minutes of the meetings leads us to believe that the entry of the sans-culottes into political life did not greatly change the number of active participants in the assemblies.

After June 2, sectional political life was confined to a particular social minority. The moderates were gradually eliminated. Only a minority among the sans-culottes frequented the assemblies; a still smaller fraction attended meetings of popular or sectional societies. On September 2, 1793 (15 Fructidor, year 1), for the election of four members to the revolutionary committee, only eighty-seven people were present at the meeting of the general assembly of the *Pont-Neuf* section; "a fair number of citizens" left the assembly hall when delegations arrived from other sections to *fraternize*. The general assemblies, nevertheless, were better attended during the censitaire period, even more than from August 10 to May 31, when the sans-culottes and the moderates clashed. Henceforth in complete control of the assemblies, the sans-culottes felt more at ease. Many considered constant attendance at the meetings to be a mark of civism; although the forty-sous indemnity did not attract all the workers, it did attract a certain number of the poorest.

According to the fragmentary documentation for the period between June 2 and 9 Thermidor, the sectional assemblies were particularly active during the second half of June 1793, on the occasion of the elections for the commander-in-chief of the Paris National Guard; the stakes were high in the struggle between the moderates and the sans-culottes. Interest in this election ran particularly high in the *Sans-Culottes* section, Hanriot's section (678 persons attended the meetings on June 19), and in Raffet's section, the *Butte-des-Moulins*. During the three ballots cast on June 16, 18 and 27, attendance rose from 780 to 824, then to 1,215. In the year II, the greatest increase in attendance was on 10 Ventôse, when 900 attended a session of the *Bon-Conseil* general assembly; this can be explained by the importance of a political debate which aroused passionate interest in the section: on that day Lullier was replying to Marchand's denunciation. Elections for military posts always drew larger crowds than elections for magistrates. On 15 Germinal, year II, only 100 citizens appeared in the general assembly of the *Brutus* section to vote for a new committee, whereas 430 made an appearance on 15 Floréal to name a new commandant for the section. The varied attendance at the assemblies in the *Montagne* section, formerly the *Butte-des-Moulins* section, from June 1793 to the year II, and at those in the *Invalides* section between Pluviôse and

Messidor is significant: the numbers swelled for the elections for military posts, only to decline again for the elections for civilian posts. Forced to serve in the National Guard, while at the same time considering military service a right, and not an obligation, the sans-culottes obviously attached considerable importance to the election of their officers.

The lack of documentation does not allow us to discern the dissatisfaction of the sans-culottes with the revolutionary government after Germinal and the executions of Hébert and Chaumette in terms of numbers attending the sessions of the general assemblies. The few facts gleaned here and there seem to indicate that the level of attendance was the same as before, higher for military elections, lower for the infrequent civilian elections still within the competence of the assemblies; elections were still popular. But what attracted people to the ordinary assemblies?

After Thermidor, the social composition of the general assemblies changed once again. The sans-culottes were gradually eliminated, and attendance declined. On 30 Frimaire, year III, only forty people attended the session of the *Unité* general assembly; in 1791 there were 2,653 active citizens in the section! On 20 Germinal, sixty-nine citizens participated in the elections for the welfare committee in the *Invalides* section; in the year II, this section had 2,440 voters. At the end of the year III, after a long period of time when there were no elections, the "respectable people," now no longer harassed by the sans-culottes, came in droves to attend the primary assemblies. But in order to appreciate fully this increased attendance, one must not forget the voting hours: in the *Arcis* section, the polls were open from seven in the morning to ten at night and polling went on for three days. The bourgeois reign was beginning.

What percentage of the popular minority who attended the general assemblies during the year II received the forty-sous indemnity? In other words, to what extent did the workers participate in sectional politics during the year II?

On September 5, 1793 (18 Fructidor, year I), Danton requested that the sessions of the general assemblies be reduced to two per week "so that all the sans-culottes can attend these meetings; each should receive an indemnity for the time he spends away from work discussing the issues of the day." As a result of this plea, the Convention decreed that *poor citizens* would have the right to an indemnity of forty sous for each session attended. On September 9, the decree of enactment was proposed by Barère. Article II stated, "Those citizens who have nothing to live on but their daily work can claim an indemnity of forty sous for each session attended." Article IV stated that commissars would be nominated by each section to determine "the eligibility of those citizens included in Article II," and to check their attendance in the general assemblies.

From the very beginning, a certain ambiguity burdened this important measure. Was it a question of indemnifying those workers who attended the general assemblies for their loss of wages? Danton clearly stated that this was so; but the declaration of principle concerning this measure on September 5 only mentions *poor citizens*. Was it therefore merely a means of assisting poor sans-culottes? Barère, who was the recording secretary at the meeting which passed the decree of September 9, would lead us to believe that this was so: he recalled the declaration of principle adopted four days previously "whereby every citizen who has no other source of income save his daily wages was entitled, *in case of need*, to an indemnity." The wording of Article IV is the same: the sectional commissars would have to certify the neediness of those who claimed the right to indemnity. Article II is quite clear on the matter: the indemnity will not be automatically given to those "who have no other source of income than their daily wage"; they alone could claim it. The enactment decree severely limited the measure proposed by Danton: it applies to the poor rather than the wage earners. This restrictive interpretation of the law caused further problems: the higher echelons of sans-culottes society and certain sectional groups considered the forty-sous indemnity degrading to its recipients. According to observer Perrière, speaking on 14 Ventôse, year II, the citizens of the *Sans-Culottes* section persistently refused the indemnity, "not wanting to be labeled forty-sous patriots."

The application of this ruling often revealed the same attitude. Article IV of the September 9 decree stated that the sections should nominate commissions to draw up the list of recipients and check their presence in the assemblies. On September 25, 1793 (4 Vendémiaire, year II), the assembly of the *Gravilliers* section adopted this ruling. The citizen "who had the right to an indemnity and claimed it" should obtain from his company captain "a certificate which would determine whether he really had nothing to live on but his daily wage." A committee of eight commissars would draw up the list and announce the recipients; if a citizen were refused the indemnity, he could appeal to the general assembly as a last resort. The recipients received a red card stamped by the indemnity committee: a discriminatory practice, if nothing else. The ruling specified in detail the "means of establishing uninterrupted presence" at a session: two commissars would check the identity as citizens entered the assembly hall; six hours later, the sessions starting at five o'clock, the list would be closed; an absence of more than half an hour would mean forfeiture of the indemnity. This ruling was adopted on September 25, after the elimination of Jacques Roux and his supporters. It was evidence of a latent hostility against those citizens who would soon be called the *"quarante sols"*. Existing documents do not allow us to determine the exact proportion of *"quarante sols"* in the *Gravilliers* section, and thereby to ascertain the commissars' interpretation of the law of September 9: would they favor wage earners (whose only source of income was their

daily wage, to use the wording of the decree) or only the
poor?

The application of the decree in fact gave rise to numbers of difficulties and gave the sectional authorities a pretext for multiple interpretations of the law, all of them
restrictive. On 20 Brumaire, the *Montagne* section decided that servants would be denied the benefits of the
indemnity; this was a flagrant violation of the decree. In
numbers of sections the authorities grudgingly applied the
law. Although the authorities in the *Bon-Conseil* section, in drawing up the list of recipients, were satisfied
with their oath, the indemnity had not yet been paid by
25 Frimaire in the *République* section; on that day several
citizens complained of not having been able to get a penny
out of the elected commissars "for the registering of good
sans-culottes who have been admitted to the general assembly"; further complaints were made on 8 and 9 Nivôse.
"In general," noted the police supervisor, "all those citizens
who have work in this section are despots who refuse to
pay up." According to the observer Pourvoyeur, writing on
17 Nivôse, the authorities of the *Lombards* section refused
to grant the indemnity accorded by law to poor citizens
because they did not approve of it. Discussion was opened
on 5 Ventôse in the *Réunion* section concerning the right
to indemnity; the assembly concluded that the law granted
the indemnity only "to the genuinely poor and not [to
workers] who earned good wages"; a commission was to
advise "on means of granting it only to those who were
genuinely in need." On 9 Ventôse, its revolutionary committee approved of this interpretation. In the *Maison-
Commune* section the ruling for the granting of the
indemnity was not passed until 30 Prairial. A twelve-
member commission would examine "the needs and morals
of the claimants," the general assembly would decide contested cases. The head of every family who had no other
source of income save his daily work would be registered,
provided he were a patriot. The commission "must take
into consideration the need to economize the Republic's
money and will examine the conduct, expenses and lack of

work of bachelor workers before registering them." This
introduced a moral and political bias into the September
9 decree and applied it in a discriminatory fashion.

Whatever the restrictions usually imposed by sectional
rulings, indemnities were the object of the severest criticism until Thermidor and contributed toward increased
social antagonism within the sans-culottes party. Although
workers were persistent in claiming the indemnity, going
as far as asking for additional assembly sessions, the "haves"
nevertheless considered them second-class citizens. When
the clothing commissars of the *Poissonnière* section were
excluded from the popular society on 17 Germinal, one of
them protested: "There were very few people at the meeting, all of them *"quarante sols"*, and therefore their ruling
is illegal." A significant, hostile attitude of a "have" toward
a simple worker which betrayed the persistence of the
former differentiation between active and passive citizens.

Claiming continual harassment caused by the payment
of the indemnity and its abuses, the "haves" demanded its
suppression, pointing to the expense involved. "Why give
the quarante sous every tenth day, when the workers did
not work on that day?" asked the observer Mercier on 1
Nivôse. On 14 Ventôse, Perrière observed that "people
who were apparently interested in banning from the assemblies this interesting group of people naturally friendly
to an entirely popular revolution were striving to deprive
these poor citizens of the minimal sum of money which
the Convention, always just and humane, wanted to offer
them in compensation for a portion of their precious
time." Thus the forty-sous indemnity lay at the heart of
the opposition between the popular revolution and the
bourgeois revolution. The Convention had adopted the
measure on September 9 less for humanitarian reasons
than for forcing the suppression of the permanence of the
sections. When it was a question of applying the measure,
the sectional authorities, who generally belonged to the
highest levels of the sans-culottes, imposed considerable
restrictions, if they had not already given evidence of distinct ill will when it came to making the payments. The

governmental authorities did not intervene until after Germinal, when the popular movement was being curtailed.

On 27 Floréal, abuses of the forty-sous indemnity were once again denounced by the *Indivisibilité* section before the General Council of the Commune, "so that greedy and uninvolved citizens cannot abuse a beneficent law." There observations were brought to the attention of the Public Safety Committee. The latter imposed a restrictive interpretation of the September 9 law: they would no longer indemnify workers for the time spent in assemblies away from their work, but only give assistance to the poor. In this area also, the concepts of the Jacobin dictatorship prevailed over those of the sans-culottes democracy. On 7 Messidor, by command of the Public Safety Committee, the Committee of Public Assistance sent a circular to the Paris sections "pertaining to the abuse on the part of several citizens of the right to attend the general assemblies of their sections, by receiving the forty sols granted to them with this object in mind, without having the right to this money, not being poor, without attending the meetings, or making only brief appearances to receive the indemnity." The circular insisted on the restrictive interpretation of the September 9 decree: the indemnity was only for *patriots in distress*, "a form of assistance which the nation offers only to poverty."

In applying the measures set forth in this circular, the sections proceeded to revise the list of recipients; numbers of sans-culottes were eliminated—another complaint they had against the revolutionary government. Unfortunately, the paucity of documentation does not allow us to discern the precise number of victims of this purge and, as a result, the importance of the objections it aroused. In the *République* section, a certain Rocherie was arrested on 5 Thermidor for having made a nuisance of himself in the general assembly; he protested having been struck off the list of recipients. The *Maison-Commune* assembly, which had adopted a very strict ruling on the matter on 30 Prairial, nominated twelve commissars on 10 Messidor for the enactment of the measures laid down in the circular of the seventh. Their report, prepared on 15 Thermidor, denounced the abuse "which would do nothing less than dissolve our happy Republic by expending, in the form of an indemnity, a portion of our nation's funds earmarked for the defenders of the nation, their indigent families and for poor republicans only." It concluded: "The Republic does not need paid partisans." The commission rejected the claims of 104 sans-culottes, retaining only ninety-one recipients; they were doubtless all of them impoverished.

Sans-culottes democracy had already been dealt its deathblow. On 4 Fructidor, Bourdon de l'Oise denounced "the fatal forty-sous decree," stressing that it was the *intermediary class* (meaning between the aristocracy and the sans-culottes, that is, the bourgeoisie) that had allowed the Convention to pass the measure during the night of 9–10 Thermidor. Cambon rose to speak against the abuses brought about by the indemnity. It was abolished.

Whatever the vicissitudes of this indemnity and the restrictions placed upon it by the application of the law of September 9, it is important to ascertain the number of indemnity recipients in each Paris section: in this way we can try to determine the influence of the workers in the political life of the sections. The documents, however, are too few and fragmentary. The law of 13 Frimaire, year III, obliged all the authorities and agents to render an account of their expenses since the beginning of the Revolution: in Paris, commissars were nominated for this purpose in each section. Unfortunately most of these account books have disappeared; only those of the *Théâtre-Français* and *Mont-Blanc* sections have been found. Supplemented by some other documents, these account books stress the small proportion of indemnity recipients in relation to the whole number of citizens.

In the *Temple* section, according to observer Béraud, on September 11 only fifty or so citizens turned up to pick up the forty sous—an astonishingly small number, bearing in mind that on June 6, 1791, the section numbered 1,662 active citizens, and 2,950 voters in the year II, and that 1,340 poor people were counted in Germinal, year II. The same proportions were widespread. Although 340 citizens received the indemnity in the *Arcis*' section on 5 Floréal, a relatively high number, only ninety-nine were registered on 25 Floréal in the *Indivisibilité* section. In the *Montagne* section, the lowest number of recipients was ninety-five, from October 3, 1793 (Vendémiaire, year II), to 20 Ventôse; in 1791 the section counted 2,395 active citizens, in the year II, 1,008 indigents on public assistance, and 5,031 voters. In the *Maison-Commune* section, the list of recipients before the 15 Thermidor revision included 195 names for 1,729 active citizens, 4,258 poor people receiving public assistance (a particularly high proportion), and 3,347 voters.

More interesting still are the accounts submitted by the commissars of the *l'Homme-Armé*, *Mont-Blanc* and *Théâtre-Français* sections, because they cover longer periods of time. In the *l'Homme-Armé* section, ninety-four citizens received the indemnity in Floréal, ninety-eight in Prairial, ninety in Messidor, eighty-seven in Thermidor, while the section numbered 1,784 active citizens, 358 poor people on public assistance and 10,841 inhabitants. In the *Mont-Blanc* section, the commissars distributed 8,352 livres between 1 Brumaire and 30 Thermidor; that is, there were an average of sixty-nine recipients for each session, for 856 active citizens and 1,031 welfare recipients. Between September 15, 1793, and 30 Thermidor, the *Théâtre-Français* section paid out 11,774 livres, that is, an average of eighty-four recipients for each session of the general assembly, for 1,736 active citizens, 846 indigents and 2,418 voters.

Finally, it is important to know the previous social situation of the sans-culottes who benefited from the forty-sous indemnity. The only mention of this point is to be found in the reports on the sums of money distributed by the commissars of the *Montagne* section during the 20 Ventôse session of the assembly. Out of 105 recipients, two were sick, nine jobless, twenty-six were low-salaried employees, six were manual workers or day laborers, fifty-one were artisans, probably journeymen. The number of those improverished by sickness or unemployment was barely one tenth of the total. But what was the situation of the low-salaried man and the day laborer? Doubtless miserable. The sans-culotte who had no other resources save his daily wage would only have the bare essentials; it is a question of knowing whether or not he was able to lift himself out of extreme poverty.

2. Sectional Committees and Their Officers

Attended during the year II by an ardent minority which was contemptuous of the forty-sous recipients, the general assemblies were theoretically the sovereign organs of the sections. They would have been impotent, however, if they had not had at their disposal administrative facilities to guarantee the continuity of their action.

According to law, the sections were not only electoral wards. They formed administrative subsections of the Paris Commune; in this capacity they had administrative facilities, officers and elected committees. Each section was headed by a committee specified by the law of May 21, 1790, which served as an intermediary between the municipality and the general assembly. This law also stated that in each section there would be a police commissar, to be assisted by a clerk-secretary. When the tribunals of the city of Paris were organized under the law of September 25–29, 1790, the sections were provided with a justice of the peace and a complement of assessors. Special committees were added to these essential bodies as the need arose: military committees, when the law of August 19–21, 1792, decreed the reorganization of the National Guard; revolutionary committees, as a result of the law of March 21, 1793 (Germinal, year I); welfare committees, voted into law on March 28, 1793; saltpeter commissions in

the year II; the spring of 1794 even saw the emergence
of agriculture committees. To what extent did these bodies
allow the sections to exercise a real autonomy? How far
were the popular militants able to exert any influence in
administrative matters and participate in political life during the year II?

After the passage of the law of May 21, 1790, the civil
committees both executed administrative orders and provided information for the municipality concerning the
affairs of their wards; they were the watchdogs and the
auxiliaries for the police commissars. Charged with supervising the enforcement of ordinances, rules or delibera-
tions, they also had to inform the municipal officers, the
general council, as well as the mayor and the Commune
attorney, or his equivalent, of all the explanation and advice that had been sought from them.

The Commune of August 10 suspended the civil committees founded earlier. On the fifteenth, it adopted a
new system: the elections of these committees would be
conducted by the assemblies. Consisting of sixteen members, who between them chose a president and a secretary,
to be changed every fifteen days, the civil committees were
once again invested with all the powers that they had had
previously. But once the sections were permanent, the
committees lost their importance and more or less came
under the control of the general assemblies, which were
jealous of their sovereign rights. On September 30, 1792
(9 Vendémiaire, year I), in the *République* section, and
on October 13 in the *Gravilliers* section, they issued a
series of regulations which would make them strictly dependent. The *Gravilliers* general assembly was of the
opinion that the civil committees could be recalled at
will: "They are agents of the assembly, they receive its
orders to execute them." The committees could make no
decisions about anything without referring to the assembly,
which alone had the right to decide; the committees could
issue no instructions, even provisional ones; "Their mis-

sion is to take charge of the administrative details of the police department." The ruling clearly stated how the registers and archives were to be kept. On every eighth day, the committee must account for its work to the assembly. Thus the sovereign rights of the people and sectional autonomy would be protected.

The civil committees, like all administrative bodies under sectional control, found themselves in a rather ambiguous situation. Elected by the assemblies, they were their representatives and agents. But as administrators, they were dependent upon the Commune, bound to obey its orders even if they were opposed by the general assemblies. The civil committees, overloaded with work, stuck protectively to their administrative tasks, and as a result avoided conflict with the assemblies; both in 1793 and in the year II, they rarely involved themselves in general politics; particularly on May 31. Also, on the same date, the revolutionary committees pushed them into the background; until 7 Fructidor, year II, they had only minimal functions to fulfill, except that in critical circumstances, such as on 9 Thermidor, civil and revolutionary committees deliberated together.

During the year II, the civil committees were generally occupied with food and welfare. The lines were never drawn between their functions and those of the welfare committee. Certain regulations point to the fact that the distribution of bread and meat was closely watched by the civil commissars, for example, those adopted by the *Maison-Commune* and *Mont-Blanc* sections on July 27 and September 17, 1793. Often, despite long hours, the commissars were overloaded with work: on 25 Ventôse, year II, an *Invalides* committee asked the general assembly to supply them with six assistant commissars.

The devotion of the civil commissars was all the more remarkable since until the spring of 1794, they were not paid at all. A municipal order dated January 18, 1791, had indeed granted each committee 1,200 livres per year, but this was for office expenses; this sum of money was considered inadequate and gave rise to numbers of claims for more. Once the sections sat uninterruptedly, this allocation was considered a joke. The Commune recognized this, and on April 2, 1793 (12 Germinal, year 1), granted 3,000 livres to each section so that they could pay off the debts which the committees had contracted since August 10. The sum allocated to each committee was increased to 1,500 livres a year on January 1; to 1,900, by order of the Commune, on April 25, 1793, "until such a time when permanence is abolished." The civil commissars could hardly have been satisfied with these arrangements, especially since the members of the revolutionary committees had, since September 5, 1793 (18 Fructidor, year 1), received three livres, five since November 8. The issue was important; its political significance was stressed by a member of the General Council on September 11. He demanded "that in the future, those sans-culottes employed on civil committees must be indemnified and salaried. Without that measure [he said], since man cannot live on the air he breathes, the right to these jobs would be reserved for people who wear wigs, former lawyers, notaries and clerks, who are, to say the least, suspect of incivism." Now that the sans-culottes controlled the general assemblies, these, too, began to make demands. Taking their cue from the *Observatoire* section, on 22 Brumaire, twenty-six sections demanded before the Convention that civil commissars receive the same indemnity as revolutionary commissars; "Would you like to see only rich people and merchants on these committees, would you like the virtuous poor to be excluded from them?" Since the sections were not unanimous in this matter, the Convention felt it had the right to reject the petitions. When the *Observatoire* section made a second assault on 10 Pluviôse, the *Montagne* section interrupted the proceedings with its own petition: "The true sans-culotte, if he devotes himself to public affairs, will always find support from his brothers among the good citizens." The *Montagne* section, formerly the *Butte-des-Moulins* section, was among those with the smallest proportion of lower-class people. On 6 Floréal, however, the Convention yielded and granted civil commissars an indemnity of three livres a day, for "the time they are forced to give to public business."

The measure was too late, and in spite of its being retroactive, could not change the social composition of the civil committees. At that time, the majority of the commissars had been nominated during either August or September 1792; what sans-culotte could have managed to survive since then without a salary? This explains why the members of civil committees were drawn from the upper levels of the petite bourgeoisie—retired shopkeepers and artisans, men with small incomes, and members of the liberal professions. Of all the sectional organizations, the civil committees were the least lower-class.

The civil committees developed in the same fashion as all autonomous sectional institutions. At first, agents of their fellow citizens, the status of the commissars changed as the revolutionary government increased its control by creating a cadre of low-grade officials, soon to be nominated by committees, finally salaried by the municipality: a change, at first unperceived, which was speeded up during the spring of 1794 and which was completed after the fall of the revolutionary government. Although the law of 7 Fructidor, year II, which reduced the revolutionary committees to twelve, restored the civil committees to their previous elevated status, and although they even received new powers, the Convention decreed on 28 Vendémiaire, year III, that there would be only twelve commissars for each section, three of them to be replaced every three months by the Legislative Committee. Thus, with their powers curbed, the civil committees survived for another year: they were disbanded by law on 19 Vendémiaire, year IV. The remnants of sectional autonomy disappeared.

During the censitaire period municipal organizations made the police commissar and the justice of the peace the two chief officials of the section, besides the civil committee. These offices still existed in the year II; but here again the revolutionary government, increasing its control, changed the nature of these institutions.

According to the municipal law of May 21, 1790, each section nominated a police commissar; his term of office was two years, and he might be re-elected. He also had the right to speak during the sessions of the civil committee. He had important powers: with the signature of one of the members of the civil committee, he might imprison persons arrested in *flagrante delicto*. Under his command a recording secretary, like himself elected for two years and eligible for re-election, took down the minutes of the sessions of the civil committee, wrote the verbatim reports, sent out messages, and was in charge of the committee registers and of those of the commissariat. Suspended by the August 10 Commune, reinstated under the decree of September 19, 1792, the police commissars saw their powers confirmed. The jobs became more available to the people; an annual salary of 3,000 livres, 1,800 for the recording secretaries, meant that the sans-culottes could afford to take the job. Nevertheless, during the autumn of 1793, their importance declined: police commissars became subordinate to the revolutionary committees.

Justices of the peace and their assessors were established in the Paris sections by the law of August 25–September 29, 1790, when the Paris law courts were organized. Their jurisdiction extended to cases involving personal affairs and property up to the value of fifty livres and appeals to the value of 100 livres. They also dealt with damage suits, actions for possession (of land), repairs to buildings, the paying of salaries and the fulfilling of contracts between masters and their employees, respectively, and, finally, injury suits and illegal activities for which the parties concerned were not criminally charged. Elected for two years and eligible for re-election, it was on their account that the Legislative Assembly banned on August 10, 1792, the distinctions between active citizens and passive citizens. On August 15, the Commune changed the system for their election: henceforth, the sectional committees would consist of eighteen members, and of the two candidates who received the most votes, the first would be justice of the peace, and the second, recording secretary. Once the sixteen commissars had been nominated, the six candidates with the most votes would be the assessors.

A justice of the peace received a yearly salary of 2,400 livres, to which was added a fee for time spent affixing, acknowledging and breaking the seals. His recording secretary received only 800 livres, and then a percentage of the attendance fees. Despite the salary, the post of justice of the peace in the year 1793 continued restricted to a small circle—the upper echelons of the petite bourgeoisie. A certain knowledge of legal procedure was necessary, which was not the case among genuine sans-culottes. Justices of the peace were usually recruited among those members of the legal profession during the ancien régime who had espoused the cause of the people. When the revolutionary government was finally in power, the sections were no longer allowed to choose justices of the peace and their recording secretaries: this function was assigned to the General Council of the Commune by the decrees of 8 Nivôse and 23 Floréal, year II.

Even more than by setting up civil institutions, the sections demonstrated their autonomy by creating armed forces in each section; all the ranks in these were opened to the sans-culottes in the year II.

In 1789, the bourgeois National Guard spontaneously modeled its organization on the districts, dividing itself into sixty battalions; the decree of September 12–23, 1791, upheld this division, provided that, for obvious reasons, only active citizens had the right to serve. The law of May 21, 1790, which created the sections, abolished the system of the formation of battalions according to district; the sections consistently protested this anomaly, a perfidious arrangement according to the *Croix-Rouge* section (May 9, 1792) that would deprive the sections of the free disposition of their armed forces. The system did not survive August 10, 1792. Indeed, on the thirteenth, the General Council authorized the sections to form their citizens into companies; the distinction between active and passive citizens had been abolished; everyone could carry arms. Hence the law of August 19–21 legalized this organization and slightly changed it. The Paris National Guard was divided into forty-eight armed sections, with the number of companies in each section being proportional to its population. Heading each armed section was a commander-in-chief, his chief officer, an adjutant and a flag-bearer. A company consisted of 126 men. Each section had one or more artillery companies. Every citizen in each armed section participated in the elections of commander-in-chief, officers and subordinates. The sections named their commander-in-chief for a three-month term, which could be extended to a year.

Thus the sections became masters of their armed forces. They took special care in electing their officers, assuming the right to dismiss them. In order to co-ordinate all matters concerning the various companies, they created military committees, or *war* committees, which could, if necessary, be converted into disciplinary bodies. For example, the *Théâtre-Français* section elected a military committee on August 10 and formed a disciplinary council in 1793. The pattern was followed by the war committee of the *Lombards* section, which was composed of twenty-eight members, elected by the general assembly; they pooled the money contributions collected by the captains, distributed to the volunteers the assistance until this time granted only to their parents, wives and children, corresponded with the administrative council of the battalion at the front, and dealt with arming, clothing and equipping it. All was under the command of the sectional general assemblies. Through their war committees or their military committees, the sections were in constant touch with the men at the front, both encouraging them and watching over them. Thus, the Army and the nation were always in close touch with each other; vide the numerous addresses to the armies which were voted by the sections, and the commissars they sent to the theaters of operations. For example, the commissar of the *Halle-au-Blé* section was, on May 14, 1793 (24 Floréal, year I), charged with accompanying the volunteers of the section to the Vendée and with maintaining an active correspondence with the general assembly. The disciplinary councils, slightly modified military committees, were composed of men of every rank. They had special instructions to enforce the regulations concerning military service drawn up by the various general assemblies: another demonstration of sectional autonomy. Among the sections acting in this way were *Marais* (November 5, 1792 [14 Brumaire, year I]), *Panthéon-Français* (29 Pluviôse, year II) and *Popincourt* (10 Germinal).

Sectional control of military affairs might have been dangerous for the central authority; after 9 Thermidor, the government committees understood this, and on the nineteenth placed the commander-in-chief and the second-in-command of the Paris National Guard under the direct control of the Convention and its committees of Public Safety and General Security. The National Guard was reorganized on several occasions during the year III; each time its autonomous character was curtailed and government control increased. On 13 Frimaire, the Convention decided that in order to be elected, an officer candidate must know how to read and write: this eliminated numbers of uneducated sans-culottes from the lower ranks. After the uprisings of Germinal, the law of 28 Germinal banned any form of correspondence between battalions and sections, and placed the National Guard under the control of the military committees of the Convention. The sections nevertheless kept their cannons, to which they were so attached; after the events of Prairial, on the twentieth, they had to give them up. Finally on 15 Vendémiaire, year IV, the National Guard was placed under the control of the commander-in-chief of the Army of the

Interior. It was all over. The sectional control over armed forces could not survive the popular regime of the year II.

Of all the popular institutions founded during the Revolution, and which developed in its rhythm, the revolutionary committees symbolized if not sectional autonomy then at least popular power.

After August 10, 1792, certain sections, either in imitation or at the instigation of the Commune and its committees of surveillance, organized general committees of revolutionary surveillance which anticipated those created by law on March 21, 1793 (1 Germinal, year I). Among these was the *Théâtre-Français* section, which acted on August 11, 1792. On the twenty-first the *Postes* section elected a twelve-member committee. The *Amis-de-la-Patrie* section nominated a committee of fourteen members. In accordance with the Commune's instructions, these committees were given particular orders to check and watch out for suspects.

In March 1793, the perilous state of the nation forced the creation of new committees. On the thirteenth, the *Croix-Rouge* general assembly organized a revolutionary committee of seven members, charged with processing denunciations and making house visits to those denounced. The Committee of General Security created after August 10 was disbanded; the new committee was no longer dependent upon the Commune; it was autonomous. On the previous day, the *Théâtre-Français* section had authorized its vigilance committee to issue orders for the arrest of citizens whom it considered "suspect of harboring antirevolutionary ideas." The Convention thus legitimized an institution which tended to spread; the law of March 21, 1793, stated that every commune or the sections in each commune should form committees of twelve members. But their powers were singularly limited: the law gave them only the right to maintain surveillance over strangers.

The new committees soon saw their powers increased. From the end of March or the beginning of April, amidst scenes of violence, more often than not manned by tried sans-culottes, these committees soon constituted a fighting force against the moderates. After April 1, 1793 (Germinal, year 1), the general assembly of the *Panthéon-Français* section *provisionally* granted its revolutionary committee "unlimited powers necessary to provide efficiently for the safety of the nation and the general security of its citizens." On March 30, the *Luxembourg* section asked the Commune for clearer explanations about the functions of the committees; the Commune replied with its circular of April 4, in an attempt to co-ordinate their action; at the same time it elaborated on the original recommendations. Not only were they to concern themselves with the surveillance of strangers, but also to deal with the distribution of *civic cards*, to examine the papers of military personnel and to imprison them in the event of their papers not being in order; they were to arrest anyone not wearing the revolutionary cockade. This was a major departure from the laws of March 21.

The law of September 17, 1793, legalized powers which the committees had in fact already arrogated to themselves: they were charged with drawing up the list of suspects, issuing arrest warrants against those suspects, and fixing the seals to their documents. The Commune's broad interpretation of suspicious activity gave further powers to the committees; already freed from control by the general assemblies, and gradually escaping from that of the Commune, they now sought to control every aspect of sectional life. Running contrary to the popular tendency toward autonomy, they became efficient agents of revolutionary centralization.

The indemnity allocated to the commissars was one of the means whereby the government committees reorganized the institution and finally placed it under their own control. Although the secretary's costs were paid for, the commissar's services were unpaid during the first months. On April 27, 1793 (8 Floréal, year 1), delegates from each section met in the *Contrat-Social* section to demand an indemnity; they considered the measure indispensable for the proper functioning of the committees and for democratizing their recruitment. The demand was not met until after June 2: on July 12, the Public Safety Committee of the Paris département granted a salary of three livres to the revolutionary commissars. On August 7, the Public Safety Committee placed 30,000 livres at the disposal of the mayor of Paris for this purpose. On September 5, the Convention made the measure law. On 18 Brumaire, year II, the indemnity was increased to five livres a day. Payment of revolutionary commissars transformed the job. Until now they had been elected by the general assemblies, and seemed to be agents of the sections, acting independently of administrative authorities. Now they became salaried officials, responsible to the Commune; on September 5, at the same time that the Convention gave the commissars the three-livre payment, it ordered them to submit to an investigation by the General Council—which was authorized to dismiss and replace them if necessary. The passing of the law concerning suspects, September 17, increased this subordination by modifying it: henceforth, the committees would be in direct contact with the General Security Committee, thus avoiding the watchful eye of the Commune. Pache stressed the inconveniences of this measure in a circular distributed among the committees on 27 Brumaire, year II; although they were directly responsible to the General Security Committee on the arrest of suspects, it might, however, be useful if the Commune were informed of their other activities. The municipal authorities tried to reassert an influence which escaped them; Chaumette called a meeting of all the members of the committees for 14 Frimaire. The attempt was foiled.

On 6 Pluviôse, year II, the *Finistère* section's committee dispatched one of its members to the Public Safety Committee to find out the procedure involved in replacing a commissar who resigned. The committee consulted the Committee of Public Safety, which did not reply. The *Finistère* committee then consulted this latter: the nominations should not be entrusted to the general assemblies, which were often dominated by revolutionary Tartuffes, but to the better-informed committees; while the Commune should retain a right of veto. The result was a joint nomination; on 22 Pluviôse the *Piques* committee indeed demanded that their choice of two new commissars be confirmed. Very rapidly, however, the nominations escaped from the control of the revolutionary committees and into the hands of the governmental authorities. The Public Safety Committee made no decision in Pluviôse, so as not to encroach on the activities of the Committee of General Security. The Ventôse crisis forced the measure through: on 9 Germinal, the two committees met jointly and named a committee for the *Marat* section. In Prairial, the Committee of Public Safety took over the nomination of commissars, an action which created considerable discord between the two government committees, while the general assemblies consistently protested against this violation of their sovereign rights.

The revolutionary committees, which had been one of the cornerstones of the Jacobin dictatorship, did not survive 9 Thermidor; the law of 7 Fructidor, year II, replaced them with twelve sectional vigilance committees, each with four sections under its jurisdiction; the Committee of General Security was charged with forming new committees, which were to remain under its direct control. The literacy required of committeemen definitely barred the humblest sans-culottes.

On account of their membership, the revolutionary committees, especially after the purge conducted by the General Assembly of the Commune, had been the most democratic of the sectional institutions. The civil committees, whose members were unpaid until 6 Floréal, year II, were recruited from among the more prosperous level of the sans-culottes; the revolutionary committees, whose members were on salary as of July 1793, and whose role had been essentially political, were usually composed of declared sans-culottes, in more modest circumstances, and often poor. These saw in their offices not only a means of devoting themselves to the Republic, but often an opportunity to earn a better living and to climb the social ladder.

The sectional institutions, civil and military, were founded early in the Revolution. These institutions were first designed on censitaire principles, accepting the distinction between propertied active citizens and non-propertied passive citizens. Before long, they underwent changes, first influenced by the desire for local autonomy, characteristic of the beneficiaries of the censitaire regime themselves, then affected by the masses, who insisted on their sovereign rights. Thus the sectional institutions developed at the same pace as the Revolution, tending toward an increasingly pronounced autonomy and taking on an increasingly popular character. They were undeniably successful in their revolutionary activity against state institutions and the various agencies of the central power. Neither the events of August 10 nor of August 31 would have been possible without the organization and the forces which the sections placed at the disposal of insurrectional committees. Born of the Revolution, the sectional institutions assisted its advances and were strengthened by these same advances. They soon grew rigid and finally fell into the hands of the revolutionary government, which they themselves had helped bring to power.

A double contradiction undermined their authority and brought about their eventual downfall. How was one to reconcile the popular aspiration to local autonomy with the increasing strength of the central power and the exigencies of the Jacobin dictatorship? Furthermore, once the threat of counterrevolution had been eliminated, how was one to make acceptable to the bourgeoisie those institutions which demonstrated the revolutionary enthusiasm of the sans-culottes, and which retained an undeniably popular character? After 9 Thermidor, the sectional institutions disappeared, swept away by the reactionary movement; but their real deathblow was dealt once the revolutionary government had been stabilized.

3. From Popular Societies to Sectional Societies

With the suppression of the permanence of the general assemblies, and the sectional committees soon under administrative control, the militant sans-culottes, concerned for the autonomy of their organizations, and dissatisfied with the control of the revolutionary government, adapted an old institution to their needs; they transformed the popular societies into sectional societies or created new ones. Since 1791, the Paris popular societies had played a prominent role in the progress of the Revolution. During the year II, the sectional societies appear as the foundation of the popular movement: through them, the militant sans-culottes directed sectional politics, administered the committees and gave impetus to the municipal and government authorities.

Whereas the moderates intended to restrict the societies to playing a purely educational role, the patriots from the very beginning gave them a political purpose. During the great debate which was begun in the Constituent Assembly during September 1791, at the end of which all political activity was forbidden them, Brissot and Robespierre joined to fight these limitations. Brissot considered that the popular societies should have three aims: "To discuss which laws to make, to clarify the laws that are made, and to keep a watchful eye on all public officials." Robespierre thought that they should safeguard the nation's rights. Marat, however, with his acute understanding of political necessity, outlined on February 7, 1791, in *L'Ami du Peuple*, the role that the sectional societies were to play after the year II: the popular clubs would not be satisfied with the simple role of educators; the patriots of each section should use them as a forum to discuss the orders submitted to the general assemblies; thus "the members of the clubs could offer their respective sectional assemblies a considered opinion, and the best citizens would no longer be swayed by the chatter of word-mongers"; the popular societies would, furthermore, keep a watchful eye on public officials and also government agencies.

Although on August 10, 1792, the oldest of the fraternal societies, which met at the library of Jacobins' Saint-Honoré Club, still considered their mission to be one of instruction, the patriotic society of the *Pont-Neuf* section transformed itself into a control and vigilance agency on June 6, 1792; events themselves led the societies toward taking an active part in politics. The crisis of the spring of 1793 was decisive in this respect. According to a declaration made on April 18, the popular and patriotic society of the *Mail* section would not be content "with stamping out intrigue, attacking people of ill will, unveiling artfulness, fostering civic zeal, revitalizing failing patriotism"; it would "be relentless in its fight against royalism, fanaticism, the moderates, the followers of Roland, the worst of all"; its members would be active and indefatigable missionaries; its crusade, that of freedom. The role of the societies in the struggle against the moderates and against federalism was such that on July 25, 1793 (7 Thermidor, year I), the Convention adopted a punitive decree aimed at curtailing their activity. On August 22, the Jacobins, in denouncing the Nancy municipality for having tried attempts to dissolve that city's society, demanded the death sentence "for those who might attempt to destroy these centers of patriotism."

As long as the nation was threatened, the government committees deliberately used support from the popular societies in order to consolidate the revolutionary regime and to sustain the war effort. On 23 Brumaire, year II, the Public Safety Committee asked the Paris societies to draw up a list "of the best candidates for every public office." Although the fundamental law dated 14 Frimaire did not define the role of the societies in the revolutionary government, and although it forbade them to send commissars or to form any central committee or congress, the Committee of Public Safety nevertheless considered it useful to specify their role in its circular dated 16 Pluviôse:

vigilance and surveillance, but also collaboration with the authorities empowered with filling posts. The popular societies should be auxiliaries of the agents charged with purging and reorganizing the duly constituted authorities.

Whatever the importance of this role, it nevertheless fell considerably short of that which the popular societies had played. The circular dated 16 Nivôse was part of the considered attempt of the government committees to discipline the popular movement, and to reduce it to a secondary role. In fact, throughout the winter of the year II, the societies, and more particularly the sectional societies, far from being satisfied with this secondary role, were the basic organs of political life.

From the autumn to the spring of the year II, an enormous net closed around the capital. Whether or not the popular societies were founded as a result of the oppression of the permanence of the general assemblies, they did, for the most part, tend to become sectional societies.

So far as one can determine the precise date of their foundation, two societies created in 1790 and three in 1791 appear to have met in session regularly until the year II. The same was true of eight societies founded in 1792, four prior to August 10, and three later on. Between January and September of the 1793 crisis, seven popular societies were founded. Twenty-six were founded to reverse the law abolishing the permanence of general assemblies, and appear as sectional societies from the beginning. In certain sections, two rival societies functioned for a while; for example, in the Contrat-Social section there were the older Amis-de-la-Patrie society and the sectional society created on September 26, 1793 (5 Vendémiaire, year II). In the Gravilliers section were the Amis-de-la-Liberté-de-l'Egalité-et-de-l'Humanité, which met in the Rue du Verte-Bois, and the sectional society. The old societies, supported by the authorities and by the Jacobins, prevailed over the sectional societies, which were forced to dissolve; hence the struggle between the patriots of '89 and those of '93, known as the new batch, a struggle the social background of which is well known. In the

Réunion and *Unité* sections, the sectional societies seemed to have absorbed the older but less firmly established fraternal societies; the Rue Saint-Avoye society merged with that of the *Réunion;* doubtless the fraternal society of the *Unité* society joined its sectional society.

Apart from these societies, all of which, old or newly founded, were at the center of sectional political activity, several long-established societies managed to operate during the year II without becoming sectional organizations. Among these were the society of the Amis-des-Droits-de-l'Homme-Ennemis-du-Despotisme in the *Montreuil* section, founded in 1791, and that of the Défenseurs-des-Droits-de-l'Homme-et-du-Citoyen in the *Maison-Commune* section. Besides the venerable Fraternal Society of the Two Sexes, which met at the Jacobin Club, one may mention a few more of the important ones: the Hommes-du-14-Juillet, formerly the *Gardes-Françaises;* the Défenseurs-de-la-République-Une-et-Indivisible, which met at the Café Chrétien, in what was formerly known as the Place des Italiens; the Hommes-Révolutionnaires-du-Dix-Août, who met in the Rue Saint-Denis at the former convent of the Filles-Dieu; the Evêché Electoral Club and the Popular and Republican Society of the Arts. These societies were generally frequented by militants who, under different titles and in various circumstances, had played an important role in the Revolution: on July 14, on August 10, on May 31. Thus, on account of their membership, in the year II, the popular societies often appeared to be the principal organizers of revolutionary action. The same was true, but on a higher level, of the Cordeliers Club. Although the sans-culottes, the women in particular, were a faithful audience at Jacobin meetings, they had no influence there. The sectional militants felt more at ease in their own societies; from the autumn of 1793 to the spring of the year II, they sustained the popular movement.

Imitating the Jacobins, the popular societies formulated statements outlining their aims, conditions for admission to membership, and the procedure and rules of order governing their sessions. In 1790–91, the older societies adopted similar regulations. These were a source of inspiration to the societies founded during the spring of 1792. In 1793, these societies changed their regulations to conform with the political situation, modifying declarations of principle, the wording of oaths and requirements for membership. During the autumn or the beginning of winter of the year II, the sectional societies finally adopted rules, which were often imitations of those of the older societies.

The regulations began with detailed descriptions of the aims of the society. The regulations of the *Luxembourg* society were revised on February 19, 1793 (1 Ventôse, year I); the society decided to enter into "frequent communication with citizens whose information and patriotism would be increased and energized by joining together." In a discussion on the role of societies, one of its members, who was concerned with differentiating them from general assemblies, called them schools of republicanism and morality. On August 28, 1793 (11 Fructidor, year I), the Hommes-Libres society of the *Pont-Neuf* section announced its intention of paying particular attention to the education of its members: each session would be devoted to reading and discussing matters of public interest, to lectures on the Constitution, the rights of man, on their duties and on the laws. In its plans of organization dated October 4, the fraternal society of the *Amis-de-la-Patrie* section stressed vigilance rather than instruction. "We must all keep watch over the government agents of the Republic," not only its functionaries, but also its suppliers, those *leeches on the state.* The Amis-de-la-République society of the *Piques* section was concerned with education; in its rules of October 19, it states its aims as "the study and knowledge of the laws, discussion of all matters relative to the public interest, defense of the oppressed, surveillance of traitors, denunciation of the machinations of the enemy, correspondence with all true friends of liberty and equality." Latest in point of time, the Germinal, year II, rules of the Rue de Montreuil society placed among its members' duties not only instruction and surveillance, but also mutual aid. The Belleville society outlined its aims quite simply: "The surveillance of those who govern us, public instruction, the propagation of morality and patriotism." And the popular society of Sceaux: "to survey the constituted authorities, the real means of preventing them going astray; to inform our brothers of their rights; to offer protection to the oppressed, to go to their assistance."

As for statements of purpose, the rules set the conditions for admission to membership; generally, it was enough to be able to prove one's civism and patriotism during the great events of the Revolution. The patriotic society of the *Luxembourg* section admitted "every citizen who is answering a call to patriotism and who is considered worthy of belonging to this association on account of his patriotic sentiment." The republican society of the *Marchés* section admitted every *patriotic* citizen of the section; that of the *Amis-de-la-Patrie*, "every citizen and citizeness who is recognized as being a good patriot and a real republican"; that of the Amis-de-la-République, in the *Piques* section, would merely be composed of patriots. According to the rules of the *Halle-au-Blé* society, which copied that of the *Gardes-Françaises* society, membership was open only "to those who could prove consistent and recognized patriotic fervor and personal service." To become a member of the Vertus-Républicaines society in the *Observatoire* section, it sufficed to be a *good French citizen*. For that of the *Montreuil* section, to have "the qualities required to be a good republican"; there was no explanation of what these qualities might be. The society of the Amis-des-Droits-de-l'Homme, in the same section, required its members to be "decent men," "without respect to anything but virtue and morality."

The candidates were usually presented by members of the society who acted as their sponsors; the list was drawn up by a membership committee; the votes were cast in public session, and in certain societies, three times. In the

Poissonnière society, the names of the candidates were posted for eight days on the door of the assembly hall. The age requirement, when indicated, was set at sixteen. Once admitted, the new member was sworn in. The *Marchés* society considered that these precautions were still insufficient: it sent the list of new members to the revolutionary committee, "to purge the list of those members of the society whose patriotism and values might be suspect." In order to protect the societies from lapses in civism, most of them had rules which provided for periodical purges; for example, in the *Luxembourg* society, "at the end of every quarter there will be a civic inspection." Strict rules regarding membership did not in fact suffice to maintain a reputation for patriotism among the popular societies, and even more so among the sectional societies. They were the butt of criticism and underhanded attacks from the Jacobins, and they retaliated with purges. This sort of activity increased during the winter of the year ii, when the revolutionary government had reason to fear that the societies might serve as a support to the popular movement. The Jacobins refused to associate themselves with the sectional societies, being bent on discrediting them; they conducted purges of their own in order to prove their civism. Thus on 22 Pluviôse, year ii, the society of the *Piques* section adopted a rule for purging its membership. The work had been done by a commission of twenty members, named on 14 Nivôse; the proposal was submitted to the revolutionary committee, and it was approved; one can see how, since the autumn, the societies had retreated, while the revolutionary government was strengthening its position.

Usually, a candidate accepted for membership had to pay a subscription. This modest amount did not exclude even the poorest sans-culottes. The Hommes-Libres society of the *Pont-Neuf* section asked for four livres; on September 1, 1793 (14 Fructidor, year i), a speaker observed, "We must lower the price of admission, if we are to allow all true sans-culottes to join, increasing the society's membership. The society can but gain by admitting the purest among our citizens." On September 18, the entrance fees were fixed at three livres, quarterly subscription at thirty sous. The *Amis-de-la-Patrie* society asked for a maximum of three livres, a minimum of thirty sous, without indicating how often; poor citizens were exempted. In the *Unité* society, the subscription was fixed at three livres for the first quarter, at two for the following quarters. The *Halle-au-Blé* society asked two livres upon receipt of the membership card, and the subscription of one livre every quarter. On September 17, 1793, the *Lepeletier* society asked for an entry fee of 100 sous; but "if a good sansculotte candidate could give only 100 sols, he would be no less welcome." The same was true of the *Poissonnière* section, whose subscription fee was forty sous: it admitted sans-culottes unable to contribute upon the recommendation of its committee. The members of the *Maison-Commune* society paid ten sous every month, those of the *République* society, twenty-five sous every quarter. As for the republican club of the *l'Homme-Armé* section, it rejected any form of monetary condition and "welcomed all the patriots of the section, whatever their means"; there was a collection box to receive members' contributions. These differing fees reflect the social composition of the sections; subscriptions were generally higher for the older societies than for the sectional societies.

The rules also provided for the organization of a committee. Generally speaking, the committee would consist of a president, a vice-president, one or two secretaries, sometimes three or four, who held office for one month and were eligible for re-election, a treasurer, and an archivist, who was usually a permanent member. The entrances were manned by inspectors; ushers maintained order in the assembly hall. Other committees or commissions assisted the committee in running the society: a nominating committee, an administrative committee, a correspondence committee, varying with each society. The Amis-de-la-République society had a welfare committee; the *Halle-au-Blé* society, a committee of surveillance to receive the denunciations.

The older societies usually met twice a week. Those created in 1793 appear, like the general assemblies, to have sat in permanent session, at least after June 2; they were organizations formed to fight against the moderates. An example would be the *Butte-des-Moulins* society. When permanent sessions of the general assemblies were forbidden, the sectional societies created to evade the law held meetings on days when the assemblies were not sitting, that is, every day except the fifth and the tenth; among them were the *Marchés* society, the *Amis-de-la-Patrie* society and the *Maison-Commune* society. A sectional militant had little leisure. Certain societies, among them the *Unité*, *Halle-au-Blé* and Vertus-Républicaines, limited their sessions to four every ten days, on the second, fourth, seventh and ninth days. Others, among them the republican society in the *Poissonnière* section, and the Amis-de-la-République society in the *Piques* section, were content with three sessions, on the second, fourth and seventh days out of every ten. The older societies, usually affiliated with the Jacobins, took into consideration the sessions of the mother society and only met twice or three times every ten days.

Although the doors were open to members at five o'clock in the evening, the sessions did not start until six; at seven during the summer. The committee sat wearing red caps behind a long table, on a platform; a slightly higher platform was reserved for the speakers. Busts of the martyrs of liberty dominated the committee, usually that of Brutus or of Liberty herself. The tricolor flag, the red cap, the society's pennant and republican emblems or symbols adorned the walls. Since the sessions were open to the public, a waist-high wooden barrier divided the room in two; often benches were provided for the auditors, women on one side, men on the other.

The session started with the reading of the minutes and of correspondence. Then the names of the candidates seeking admission to the society were announced, and the appropriate commission made its comments. Then came the various reports. The *République* sectional society started the actual order of business at seven o'clock. Between eight and nine o'clock, the *Journal du Soir* and the *Bulletin de la Convention* were read. In the Vertus-Républicaines society, *Observatoire* section, sessions started at seven o'clock with the reading of the minutes, dispatches and of the *Bulletin des Lois;* at eight o'clock they passed on to the *important order of business.* The same was true of the Rue de Montreuil society. Between eight o'clock and nine, the *Poissonnière* society arranged for "readings in morals and patriotic works." The Amis-de-la-République society in the *Piques* section set aside a session every ten days "for reading patriotic speeches, which are of importance to everyone."

The speakers addressed their remarks to the audience, wearing their red caps; the rules, often unobserved, forbade either interpolation or interruption. In the *Amis-de-la-Patrie* society, "any member who attacks or insults another member" shall be called to order. The patriotic society of the *Luxembourg* section proscribed "all set speeches, compliments and votes of thanks." Its members, as in all societies, were supposed to use "republican language commonly called *tutoiement* [use of the familiar second person singular form]." These speakers did not all have the gift of gab. According to the rules of the *République* sectional society, "if the speaker wanders or becomes tired, the audience has the right to rise"; if seven people stood up, the president would consult the society. Voting was *viva voce*, by show of hands, or by standing vote. Sometimes nominations were posted; if this were so, then they had to be signed. The secret ballot was something foreign to the sans-culotte; he always interpreted it as being part of an intrigue or a manipulation of some kind. Despite the rules, despite the ushers who watched for disorderly conduct, sessions were often noisy, and sometimes disorganized. Arguments and accusations frequently occurred. But the sans-culottes were all members of the same movement; sessions, more often than not, ended with applause and the fraternal kiss. Both the members of the societies and of the public were highly sensitive, and were easily swayed by speakers. These speeches gave rise to tremendous enthusiasm and republican hysterics. The whole meeting would rise and repeat their oath to live as free men, or to die fighting. A member would start "a song sung to the tune of the popular *Carmagnole*," the *universal choir* joined in, and then they all attacked the *Marseillaise*. These were moments of intense emotion, of patriotic fervor, when the humblest members of society offered praise, and celebrated the cults of Liberty and the Republic.

In the same way that the general assemblies had extended their power through correspondence, the popular societies wished to increase their strength through *affiliation*.

In a speech delivered on September 29, 1791, Robespierre defined affiliation as "the relationship between one legitimate society and another whereby they can better communicate with each other on matters of public interest." Affiliation necessarily resulted in correspondence. This double action tended to enclose the political cadres within a vast net; the power of the societies increased considerably. "How do we go about forming this necessary and intimate union?" This question was posed in a circular distributed by the Belleville popular society in the year II. "Brothers and friends, we shall achieve this by defining our rights, our duties, and by being vigilant and working together. . . . To achieve these goals, every citizen of the land must join together in patriotic societies; these societies must correspond frequently with each other, and with a central society or parent society, which will dispatch and receive constantly these shafts of light and of life which will enlighten, animate and energize patriotic fervor." The network of societies linked together through affiliation almost formed the skeleton of a party.

The right of affiliation and correspondence gave rise to lively controversy. The Constituent Assembly discussed the matter on September 29, 1791, but, although it forbade collective petitions, it did not dare take action against the right to affiliate. The debate resumed again in lively sessions during the spring of 1792, when the network of groups affiliated with the Jacobins appeared to be an effective instrument of revolutionary activity. In an anonymous pamphlet, "a friend of the Constitution" declared that "the clubs should be isolated, independent from each other and should have no contact with each other." In 1793, the affiliation of, and correspondence between, Paris popular societies were one of the reasons for the success of the popular offensive against the moderates. "Cut the ties between popular societies," declared a Girondin speaker. "And we are telling him, leave those healthy ties alone," retorted a delegation from the *Arsenal* section. "It is these ties which unite us; they alone will guarantee the safety" of the future Constitution.

The older societies already affiliated with the Jacobins and the societies created during the spring of 1793 asked for, or renewed, their affiliation after June 2. Thus, on the sixteenth, the *l'Homme-Armé* society requested affiliation with the Jacobins; on September 13, the Hommes-Libres society of the *Révolutionnaire* section, already affiliated with the Cordeliers and with the fraternal society, was affiliated with the Jacobins. The founding of sectional societies was to cause problems with the affiliation and correspondence network. The impulse for the older societies to affiliate with each other and with the Jacobins obviously stemmed from the parent society. The sectional societies, whose members were usually recruited among the lower orders and only locally, formed ties with one another; they generally did not seek affiliation with the Jacobins; they tended to form an autonomous movement. Hence, after the autumn of 1793, the animosity of the Jacobins and the government agencies, and, soon after, the general offensive of which the popular societies were the object. The sectional societies tried to improve their position by asking for affiliation; this was usually refused; they were more discredited than ever. The sectional societies were dissolved during the spring of the year II;

affiliation and correspondence favored only the Jacobins; they became no more than a means of centralizing the government.

When the revolutionary government toppled, the reactionaires saw the danger in affiliation. On 24 Fructidor, year II, Durand de Maillane brought to the attention of the Convention the *threat to freedom* posed by the affiliation of popular societies with the Jacobins. On 5 Vendémiaire, year III, a decree was passed which forbade the societies "all forms of affiliation, assembly, federation or correspondence."

During periods of crisis, affiliation and correspondence were considered inefficient means of guaranteeing the unified action of societies: the more clear-sighted militants tried to create an organization which would co-ordinate and direct them. This attempt to create a central committee of popular societies ran into the same obstacles as the central committee of correspondence once planned by the general assemblies. The initiative was taken by the Fraternal Society of the Two Sexes, which met at the Jacobin Club; "seeing a threat to the nation, and persuaded that the popular societies had members who were capable of saving it," the society, on August 24, 1793 (Fructidor, year I), invited others to send delegates to assist in the formation of a central committee. The fraternal society doubtless ran into opposition, particularly from the Jacobins: the meeting, originally to have taken place in the Hall of Fraternity, once known as the Saint-Honoré Jacobin Club, was eventually shifted to the Evêché. By-laws for the central committee were not adopted until October 20, 1793 (29 Vendémiaire, year II). The committee stemmed directly from the various Paris societies, each having sent two delegates. Its purpose was to conduct a continuous correspondence with all the popular societies of the Republic, to serve as a central meeting place, and to bring up for discussion by the societies those issues debated by the central committee or brought to its attention by other societies, and which the central committee considered of greatest consequence to the Republic. On

12 Brumaire, year II, the General Assembly of the Commune set about forming a central committee, which made its presence evident the eighteenth, presenting a petition "with the aim of rooting out the abuse of fanaticism, and error." The new committee took on the leadership of the popular movement.

This action aroused immediate protests from the Electoral Club, otherwise known as the Central Club of the Paris département, which met at the Evêché; it had been reorganized since September 21, 1793, and claimed the same role; on 27 Brumaire, it went before the General Assembly and denounced the central committee of the popular societies, whose activities it considered all the more suspicious because its sessions had been held behind closed doors. The matter was referred to the police. Confronted with that threat, the central committee was forced to dissolve. Besides, the Jacobins' assault against the sectional societies was not long delayed. Article 17, Section III, of the decree of 14 Frimaire banned all forms of joint central committee sessions established by the popular societies. In the organization of the revolutionary government there was no place for an *opinion-making body* other than the Jacobin parent society.

The societies were in fact not satisfied with their appointed role of education and vigilance. As a result of a series of subtle maneuvers, they assumed the power of the sections' general assemblies, and often controlled sectional officials: a popular power which to a certain extent encroached on that of the governmental system, and which doubtless weakened the latter's cohesiveness.

Education always played an important role during sessions; this function dominated during the spring of the year II, when the societies became dependent upon Jacobin and government authorities. Sessions generally began with the reading of patriotic newspapers, of speeches made before the Convention or the Jacobins, of decrees and laws, militants making civic or moral speeches, or children reciting from the Constitution or the Declaration of Rights. The *République* sectional society began each session with the reading of the *Journal du Soir*, the *Bulletin de la Convention*, the Commune's decrees and the National Guard order of the day. On 27 Pluviôse, a seven-year-old recited the Declaration of Rights from the rostrum. On 4 Ventôse, they heard a discourse on the planting of a tree of liberty. On 7 Ventôse, an eight-year-old girl recited a speech on the death of Chalier; on 22 Ventôse, Saint-Just's report on people who had been imprisoned received unanimous applause; Robespierre's already dated report on the principles of revolutionary government was read on 17 Germinal, that of Saint-Just on the arrest of Danton on 22 Germinal; on 7 Floréal, the society heard Saint-Just's report on the Police Department, on 22 Floréal, that of Robespierre on religious and moral ideals. Other societies had similar programs. The Lepeletier society held special sessions for children, who came to the platform and recited the Declaration of Rights, the Constitution or some appropriate oration.

Vigilance, in the largest sense of the word, also played an important part in the sessions. During the great purge of the autumn of 1793, the government authorities naturally turned to the popular societies. On September 13, they were asked to forward to the Public Safety Committee "the list of all untrustworthy agents known for their incivism"; on October 9, to keep a watch over the administration of military food and clothing suppliers; on October 15, to pass on information about administrative action relative to émigrés and their property. The societies were not slow in responding: on September 5, the Hommes-Libres society had decided to investigate every candidate for public office. A member of the Lepeletier society was given the task of seeking out information concerning posts about to become vacant and the candidates named to fill them. Department heads, in turn, acquired the habit of consulting the societies before declaring their choice of candidate. Thus, in Brumaire, year II, the registrar general's office asked the *Droits-de-l'Homme* sectional society if it considered a certain Jean Liard worthy of a post in its office; "The time has come when patriots should be everywhere, the best means of keeping the aristocracy out." Issuing certificates of civism, more often than not in the jurisdiction of the societies, was an effective means of controlling officials; on 2 Brumaire, the Hommes-Libres society ordered that every person employed by the administration who lived in the *Révolutionnaire* section would be obliged to renew his certificates of civism every month.

As a result of their vigilance activities, the societies inevitably came to control, then to run, sectional political life. According to the society of the *Poissonnière* section, popular societies were to be found only in *purged sections*. They tended therefore to assume the work of the general assemblies. Their authority increased when the sections were forbidden to meet in continuous session; sectional societies had been created to evade the law and to reform under a different name the assemblies forbidden to meet on certain days. Sure of their permanence, in many sections, the societies became the real power in the sections and reduced assemblies to mere registry offices.

On September 15, 1793 (29 Fructidor, year 1), a citizen proposed to the *Champs-Elysées* assembly "that on days when the law does not allow discussions, republican sansculottes should meet as a popular society which will maintain perpetual vigilance"; its essential task should be the preparation of "all matters to be discussed by the general assembly." On September 21, the society of the *Brutus* section asked the president and secretary of the assembly to inform them, before the session, "of those matters which they considered deserved attention and needed to be discussed ahead of time." A few days later, the society decided that it had the right to propose any measure it wanted adopted by the assembly. These same notions inspired the creation of the society of the *Maison-Commune* section. "The lapse of time between one session and another gives intriguers the opportunity to unite and interrupt the smooth running of general assemblies." The society would maintain continuous vigilance. "Since there is a restriction on the length of time the general assemblies can meet in session, it is important, in order to deal with everything at hand, to prepare the material to be discussed"; therefore, one of the aims of the society would be to *speed up the work* of the assembly. On 24 Brumaire, the *Réunion* sectional society declared quite simply, "Its main concern would be essentially to thrash out the issues prior to their being brought before the Convention."

These procedures, and the aura of conspiracy which occasionally surrounded them, accounted for the hostility which the sectional societies roused during the autumn of 1793 among the moderates, who accused them of forming a clique. The main charge leveled at the societies in the year III was their having usurped the right of the general assemblies. On 20 and 30 Pluviôse, the *Fontaine-de-Grenelle* society was reprimanded for being restricted to a narrow circle and for having monopolized nominations for civil and military posts, and for having assumed "every sovereign right that by law is reserved for the people gathered together in primary, communal or sectional assemblies." The assembly issued no orders, or certificates of civism, welfare or even residence without receiving instructions to do so from members of the society, whose previous knowledge and consent were necessary.

The reprimand was hardly unjust. For, during several months, between autumn 1793 and spring of the following year, power was concentrated in the societies, not in the assemblies, and more often than not, not even in the sectional authorities; in many sections, the general assemblies were content to ratify their decisions. On 15 Brumaire, year II, the *Invalides* assembly authorized its sectional society to deal with a petition about food supplies from the *Maison-Commune* section, "and either to endorse it or refuse endorsement, in its name." On the same day, the *Droits-de-l'Homme* section declared that it recognized only the cult of *Reason;* it charged the society with informing the General Council of the Commune of its decision. The *Montagne* section received a circular from the Public Safety Committee requesting the names of citizens fit to hold all sorts of offices; on 30 Brumaire, it charged the society with its administration. On the same day, the revolutionary committee of the *Observatoire* section, "desirous of putting a stop to all complaints and rumors concerning the disarming of citizens, which had been necessary to crush the aristocrats," ordered that disarmed citizens must address themselves to the society, whose judgment would be final. The assemblies, who had excluded the moderates and any opposition from membership, surrendered of their own accord: the *Beaurepaire* section on 10 Brumaire ceded its meeting place to the Sans-Culottes Révolutionnaires of May 31, waiving its rights on those days when it was not in session, "bearing in mind the important work done by the popular society."

The societies were even more interested in nominations for office than in the debates of the general assemblies. During the autumn of 1793, they censured and purged the sectional officers, a role assigned to them by government authorities. Censure, according to a denunciation made by the moderates in the year III against the *Brutus* society, is "the means of defeating and persecuting patriots." On October 20, 1793 (Vendémiaire, year II), this society censured the members of the revolutionary committee, the justice of the peace, his recording secretary, the police commissioner and the monopolies commissar. The societies were not satisfied with merely censuring public officials, but also intervened in the elections. To charges of acting in a "tyrannical manner, influencing the general assembly in matters of elections," and submitting lists of previously discussed candidates, the fraternal society of the *Panthéon-Français* section replied, on August 25, 1793 (Fructidor, year I), that it had never denied discussing candidates"; "we count it praiseworthy to have subjected candidates to a second scrutiny, and to have our choice always nominated." On 17 Brumaire, the *Lepeletier*, formerly *Bibliothèque*, popular society chose three commissars for forced loans; it invited its members to attend the session of the general assembly to participate in this election. The *Beaurepaire* assembly, on 5 Nivôse agreed to the society's candidate, Citizen Ricordon, becoming a member of the civil committee. The *Poisson-nière* society was regularly involved with filling vacant posts: on 19 Nivôse, it drew up the list of candidates for election to the civil committee, to be presented to the assembly on the following day; on 22 Nivôse, it chose a monopolies commissar; on 24 Nivôse, it chose the remaining candidates for the revolutionary committee; on 7 Ventôse, it chose a recording secretary; and on 14 Ventôse, it drew up the list of members for the welfare committee, who were nominated by the assembly on the following day. When the saltpeter commission of the *Brutus* section needed more commissars, it addressed the society on 28 Pluviôse, and the society nominated them. On 4 Ventôse, the *Lepeletier* society chose four of its members to sit on the assembly committee, which was to be renewed on the following day.

Finally, the societies denied the general assemblies, and often the revolutionary committees, the right to distribute certificates of civism. More often than not, the assemblies and the committees yielded, although they did demand that applicants should get their visas from them. On September 11, 1793 (25 Fructidor, year 1), the society of the *Beaurepaire* section proposed to the Commune General Council that requests for certificates of civism henceforth be transferred to their jurisdiction, for censorship purposes. The assembly eventually granted these powers: on 5 Germinal, it decided that certificates of civism would be distributed by a twelve-member commission to be chosen by the society. In the *Brutus* section, certificates could only be granted with the consent of six militant members of the society. Thus, already the source of nominations, as well as addresses and petitions emanating from the general assemblies, the societies eventually controlled every aspect of sectional political life: citizens to whom they had denied certificates of civism had no further legal recourse.

In order to make an accurate appraisal of the role played by the popular societies, we must ascertain the size of their membership and their social composition. Again, it is hardly worth being concerned with the nominal membership of a society: the extent of their involvement is what counts. The strength of the societies lay in their militants rather than their membership. Research is difficult in this field; very few documents have survived, because the archives of the societies were either poorly kept or, as a precautionary measure, were destroyed after Thermidor.

The membership of the societies seems to have varied, but within narrow limits, according to period or section. A delegation to the Jacobin Club declared on July 14, 1793 (Messidor, year I), the *l'Homme-Armé* society comprised "two hundred sans-culottes devoted to the Montagne interest." At about the same time, two thousand men of this section were fit to bear arms: therefore approximately one tenth of those eligible were members of the society. When the older *Lepeletier* society was reorganized and purged during September 1793, it retained only thirty-seven of its members, and swelled to eighty-nine members after its purge during Ventôse. In July 1793, the section's armed forces counted 3,231 men; only one or two out of every hundred, therefore, belonged to the popular society from the autumn of 1793 to the following spring. The Amis-de-l'Egalité society in the *Réunion* section set about purging its members between September 23, 1793 (2 Vendémiaire, year II), and 7 Frimaire, year II. The society's membership eventually stood at 148, the section numbering 4,378 voters, that is, three or four citizens in a hundred were members. On 23 Nivôse, year II, the republican society of the *Unité* section had a membership of 280, there being approximately 4,000 citizens in the section, or 9 per cent. According to the clerk of its commission on purges, there were four hundred members of the society in the *Piques* section in Pluviôse, year II, where 3,538 security passes had been issued; here the percentage of members rose to 11 per cent. After its purge on 22 Ventôse, year II, the republican society of the *Mont-Blanc* section had 112 members; in the previous

July the section's armed forces numbered 2,378 men: approximately four members for every hundred citizens. At the time of its dissolution on 30 Germinal, the society of the *Brutus* section counted a membership of 208, out of 2,670 voters in the section, or approximately 7 per cent. The proportion of society members to total number of citizens in each section rarely therefore appears to rise above 10 per cent.

In examining the progress of a single society, insofar as the documents allow, one sees that membership swelled for a while during the spring of 1793, then had a tendency to decline during the course of the winter of the year II, as the revolutionary government asserted its power. In June 1792, the Hommes-Libres society of the *Pont-Neuf* section counted forty-four members, four of whom had not paid their dues. Although it is impossible to ascertain the precise date, the membership did rise to seventy-two during the summer: the bourgeois beneficiaries of the June days opened their membership to sans-culottes. The conflict between Girondins and Montagnards, between moderates and sans-culottes, gave rise to several resignations: toward the end of the winter of 1793, the society had sixty-nine members. The membership rose again after June 2, a period of intense political activity during which sans-culottes and moderates fought for control of the sectional organs, general assemblies and popular societies; by early August, the membership of the Hommes-Libres society reached one hundred. Their number rose again after the triumph of the sans-culottes, either because these latter came into the organizations or because the moderates joined the popular societies as a precautionary measure. After the purge of 2 Frimaire, year II, the membership stood at eighty-five, seventeen members having been purged and twenty-two having been asked to resign for being "unknowns," or for having signed "unpatriotic" petitions. The decline of sectional political life, the discrediting of the societies in early spring, and the fear that seized numbers of militants ultimately brought about the final decline in society membership:

on 14 Prairial, the day the Hommes-Libres society was dissolved, its membership was only fifty-three. The *République* sectional society underwent a similar decline in membership after Germinal, although the figures were different. Founded on 5 Nivôse, year II, by sixty-two members, it had 264 by 2 Ventôse; a severe purge conducted between 22 Germinal and 17 Floréal reduced the membership to 154.

Although membership varied, the social composition of the societies appears to have been the same, with a distinct tendency toward democratization during the year II. Founded to educate the people, and, more particularly, those passive citizens denied the right to vote, from the very outset, their membership was drawn from citizens of modest circumstances, "local fruit and vegetable merchants," according to an article in the *Chronique de Paris* published on November 2, 1790; "water carriers and other good people," according to the June 25, 1792, edition of *Babillard*. However, at the outset of the Revolution, shopkeepers and master artisans seem to have predominated. After August 10, their membership was mostly composed of tradespeople, artisans or shopkeepers. Journeymen, workers, "little" people were not members of these societies, and did not play a role in them until the autumn of 1793. Throughout their existence, however, their membership included the liberal professions, but these were people of modest means, artists, employees, officials, not to mention numbers of displaced aristocrats or merchants. The social composition of the societies varied from section to section. For some time, the membership of the patriotic society of the *Bibliothèque* section was distinctly bourgeois. At first, the active citizens, who alone attended special sessions or discussed the affairs of the section among themselves, had certain privileges; passive citizens played only a minor role. These distinctions disappeared at the beginning of the summer of 1792. Active citizens of long standing nevertheless played the predominant role for almost a year. By the autumn of 1793, the sans-culottes were masters of the societies; once again, it is important to distinguish the older societies, enlisting the patriots of '89, and the more popular sectional societies, where the "new batch" of patriots met together, the patriots of '92, or even of '93, as they were called by their opponents. Police observers often mention the large numbers of workers who attended sessions of the sectional societies during the year II. On 11 Ventôse, Bacon mentions that considerable numbers of men in the sleeveless vests worn by workers and masons were attending sessions of the *Arcis* society; however, did they belong to the society, or were they members of the general public? On 20 Germinal, the *Maison-Commune* society declared that its membership consisted of citizens without fortune. On 24 Pluviôse, year III, the membership of the Rue du Vert-Bois society of the *Gravilliers* section was denounced for being "almost entirely composed of workers and uneducated men who were easily led astray." For lack of sufficient documentation, it is difficult to determine the precise social composition of the popular societies, since the few membership lists that have survived generally do not mention occupation.

In June 1792, out of fifteen members of the Hommes-Libres society of the *Pont-Neuf* section whose occupations were recorded, one finds, except for one Paris bourgeois, mostly artisans or businessmen of a particular social level: nine clockmakers, three jewelers, two engravers. During the summer, their numbers rose to seventy-two. Out of sixty members whose professions were recorded, two were businessmen, three were salaried employees, four were members of the liberal professions, the others were all artisans or shopkeepers, though they were in the artistic or luxury trades: thirteen jewelers, twelve clockmakers, six engravers, two sword-cutters, one (metal) founder, one fan maker, one inlay worker and one tapestry maker. There were also other artisans or businessmen: three dry goods dealers, two tailors, two cobblers, a hat maker, a carpenter, a locksmith, a painter, a brush maker and a lemonade vendor. At the beginning of August 1793, the social composition of the societies changed slightly. Out of seventy-one members whose occupations were mentioned, the fourteen clockmakers, fourteen jewelers, and the seven engravers still outnumbered the others, but there were now seven salaried employees, two mechanics and a cook. The complete lack of any social data for the year II unfortunately makes it impossible to discover to what degree the lowest social strata of the *Pont-Neuf* section managed to become members of its Hommes-Libres society.

Of 125 new members admitted to the society of the *Réunion* section between September 23, 1793, and 12 Frimaire, year II, whose occupations were listed, the seventeen clerks and employees formed the largest group. Then came fourteen jewelers and twelve artisans in the luxury trades. The well-to-do middling bourgeoisie was represented by three merchants and eleven shopkeepers, whose particular business was generally not mentioned, three men of private means, five retired businessmen or artisans who lived on their incomes. Eight cobblers were the most numerous among the humbler artisans. The lowest strata of society were represented by four small shopkeepers and two workers whose trades were not listed, two floor-polishers, a mason, a woodcutter, a peddler, a rag-and-bones merchant, and a day laborer. The liberal professions numbered three surgeons and an apothecary, two sculptors, two bailiffs, two solicitors, two scribes and a teacher, to whom could be added a former canon and the vicar of Saint-Méry.

On 23 Nivôse, year II, the membership of the republican society of the *Unité* section stood at 280. Although thirty-six of its members could be classified as merchants, brokers or manufacturers, twenty-eight as employees and only sixteen as workers, or "little" people, the majority of the society's members consisted of 181 artisans and shopkeepers whose social background is indeterminate.

Here again, one must bear in mind the paucity of documentation, and the slender information these documents have to offer; and how much any study of the social con-position of the societies, as of that of the sans-culottes, is bound to lack solid ground. The popular societies were democratized during the autumn of 1793; the sectional societies were more generally open to the humblest strata. Both, however, were dominated by members belonging to the lower middle class of small artisans and shop-keepers, a social stratum extensive enough to encompass the most diverse occupations, and to lead by imperceptible gradations from the respectable poor to the middling bourgeoisie.

Also, as far as politics were concerned, the body of members was less important than the small number of militants who led them. Whatever their membership, society meetings were regularly attended by only a minority of active sans-culottes; they alone were the driving force of the popular movement, the cadres, as it were, of a party.

Certain documents are misleading. Like the general assemblies, the societies admitted the public to their sessions. In the spring of 1793, the Hommes-Libres society, which had fewer than one hundred members, rearranged its meeting hall. Two hundred chairs were brought in, as many women were usually present. But in short course the members of popular societies were caught up in the discrediting of the Society of Republican Revolutionary Women, who often had to be content with mere attendance at the sessions. The same went for the children and young people who gathered at these meetings "in order to learn and become acquainted with revolutionary principles." One can thus explain the large attendance reported by police spies like Bacon, who, on 11 Ventôse, reported large gatherings at the sectional societies in the *Arcis* and *Indivisibilité* sections, and, on 13 Ventôse, large numbers of women at the *Lombards*, *Bon-Conseil* and *Droits-de-l'Homme* societies. On 22 Ventôse, the society of the *République* section declared that its meeting hall had become too small for the increased attendance; it decided to meet henceforth in the Temple of Reason. Although until the spring of the year II, attendance did increase to a certain extent, the members who actually took part in the debates were few; even fewer in the older popular societies. As with regard to the general assemblies, the militant members of the societies consistently exhorted their colleagues to be more conscientious in attendance —for example, on May 25, 1793 (Prairial, year 1), the president of the patriotic society of the *Butte-des-Moulins* section. On 24 Pluviôse, year 11, a member of the society in the *Poissonnière* section decided to hand over a list of people who had missed three consecutive sessions to the membership committee. These appeals went unheard.

According to a denunciation made to the Convention during the autumn of 1793, only fourteen members, including four women, attended the sessions of the Défenseurs-de-la-République society. When it was purged, 7 Frimaire, year 11, the Amis-de-l'Egalité society in the *Réunion* section had 148 members; on October 9, only forty-three members were present at the session, forty-two on October 14, thirty-seven on 19 Brumaire. On 5 Nivôse, sixty-two members attended the inaugural session of the *République* sectional society. The petition presented to the Convention on 28 Ventôse by the society in the *Mucius-Scaevola* section was signed by ninety-five members; however, we do not know whether these signatures were collected during the same session. According to a denunciation made on 11 Prairial, the sessions of the Fraternal Society of the Two Sexes of the *Panthéon-Français* section were only attended by some sixty men and as many women.

These fragmentary statistics are confirmed by the few surviving series of verbatim reports. Among these are the minutes of the patriotic society of the *Bibliothèque* section, which, in 1793, was renamed *Lepeletier*. On November 14, 1790, eighty members voted in the elections for their president. On April 24, 1792, only nine members were present, thus failing to achieve a quorum. On September 17, 1793, they rescinded a by-law stating that eleven members must be present before debate could begin. On September 24, they announced that there were too few people present to hold a meeting. On October 1, seventeen members were present, but the quorum of fifteen was not achieved. On October 19, a member was furious at the small attendance: any member absent for six consecutive sessions would be deprived of his membership. Did this threat have any effect? On 7 Brumaire, the society announced that it would not accept new candidates for membership unless twenty-five members were present. On October 22, forty-two members signed a petition and sent it to the Convention.

On 14 Frimaire, attendance at the *Poissonnière* society was so low that the sessions could not be declared open. On 24 Frimaire, the committee was elected by twenty-five members: on 27 Frimaire, thirty-nine were present at nominations for the membership committee. On 2 Nivôse, forty-seven members elected their president; but on 7 Nivôse, only twenty-eight were present to elect the membership committee. On 14 Nivôse, only thirty-seven were present for a first ballot, forty-five for a second. On 2 Pluviôse, the president was elected by forty-three members, the secretaries by fifty-three. Attendance swelled during the spring crisis, to seventy-eight on 2 Ventôse, seventy-seven on 2 Germinal, only to drop to forty-eight on 2 Floréal.

Attendance at the Hommes-Libres society seems to have been just as low. The attendance sheets rarely list more than twenty names for the month of August 1793, when the society supposedly had one hundred members. Once the moderates had been disposed of, the sans-culottes were more conscientious: thirty-one names were listed on the attendance sheet for 24 Nivôse; after the purge, it counted eighty-five members. The crisis of the winter of the year II mobilized the sans-culottes, and attendance rose: an average of fifty members were present between the last days of Pluviôse and the beginning of Ventôse; at the height of the crisis, the maximum number present was fifty-eight. The confusion that followed the execution of Hébert had its impact on attendance; on 4 Germinal, fifty-five were present, thirty-four on 22 Germinal and

less than thirty during the month of Floréal. The campaign
against the popular societies roused some agitation: thirty-
six members were present at a meeting of the Hommes-
Libres society on 4 Prairial. They too were forced to dissolve their society. Fifty-three names on the attendance
sheets of 14 Prairial indicated both allegiance and protest
by the membership.

During the year 1793, the popular society formed a
fighting force against the moderates; they were then protected by the nascent revolutionary government during
the course of the summer. By autumn, the increase in
the number of sectional societies showed the militants'
concern to maintain their control over political life. There-
after, the sectional societies and the government bureaucracy were at loggerheads: on the one hand there was the
fundamental antagonism between popular power and sans-
culottes democracy, and on the other, between the Jacobin
dictatorship and the revolutionary government.

With an armed force at their disposition, naming their
officers, electing their own magistrates and their committees, the sections formed so many autonomous organs in
the capital. By communication in normal times, by fraternization during crises, the sectional organizations, assemblies, committees and societies duplicated the municipal organization. It was a powerful force, which threatened to displace the revolutionary committees, and which
tended to destroy the social balance upon which the
revolutionary government was founded, to the benefit of
the sans-culottes. Brought to power in order to guarantee
the safety of the bourgeois revolution, the government
committees were hard put to tolerate the existence of
popular organizations, which were rapidly getting out of
hand; they deprived the sections of the right to nominate
their commissars, who, salaried and under government
jurisdiction, became officials; they tamed the general assemblies and suppressed the sectional societies. They
thereby lost the support of the sans-culottes, who had

brought them to power. The cadres continued to exist, emptied of all popular content. Jacobin centralization supplanted sectional autonomy. But could the Jacobins, confronted with an adverse reaction, continue in power without sans-culottes support?

VI

DAILY LIFE AMONG
MILITANT SANS-CULOTTES

Strongly entrenched in popular organizations, the militant
sans-culotte devoted much of his leisure time to political
life, even if he did not hold office in his section. He did
not attend Jacobin meetings, partly out of convenience,
but also because their social milieu was not exactly his;
he divided most of his evenings between the sectional
society and the general assembly. To guide the militant,
the societies published the *Political and Patriotic Time-
table of Events for the Next Ten Days*, copied from that
of the Jacobins. Five evenings out of every ten were reserved for the parent society, which was "the only center
of public opinion." The popular or sectional societies
usually met on the second, fourth and seventh days of the
decade (ten-day period replacing the usual week); on the
tenth day, at eleven o'clock, there was often a civic re-
ception. On the fifth and tenth days, the general assemblies held their sessions. "When he has worked hard all
day [wrote Hébert in *Père Duchesne*], the sans-culotte
goes and relaxes in the evening in his sectional assembly,
and once among his brothers . . . one shakes his hand
the other slaps him on the back, asking him how things
are going."

The militant showed himself in his section in clothes
that had become the symbol of his social class, a red cap
on his head, a pike in his hand in times of upheaval.

Even more than the short jacket, known as the *carmagnole*, the red cap became the symbol of the militant sans-
culotte. The headgear of freed slaves, and therefore an

emblem of freedom, the red cap was used as such after 1789. The Swiss from Châteauvieux wore them when they were freed from the galleys. From that time on, although the revolutionary bourgeois did not adopt the red cap, it became a part of the dress of the people. "The view from beneath a red woolen cap fills he who wears it with delight, and woe betides those who try to rag him!" said the *Révolutions de Paris* in March 1792. "His enthusiasm is as respectable as it is reasonable. He has been told that in Greece and Rome the woolen cap was the emblem of freedom and a rallying point of all the enemies of despotism. That was enough for him. Since that moment, every citizen has wanted one of these caps." At about the same time, an attempt to force the Jacobins to wear them as well failed. On March 19, 1792, Pétion and Robespierre opposed its being worn by speakers and by the society's committee. "It would detract," said the latter, "from the only national emblem, the tricolor cockade."

In spite of Jacobin objections, the red cap became mandatory after August 10. It was gradually adopted by the authorities of the various sections. On December 8, 1792 (17 Frimaire, year I), the general assembly of the *Droits-de-l'Homme* section ordered its president to wear one; next day, the *Sans-Culottes* section's general assembly decided that all the officials of the section would wear one. Henceforth, the red cap was to be the sans-culottes' symbol of political power and a target for sarcasm and attacks from the moderates. The *Pont-Neuf* section had given orders that no member could take the floor unless he was wearing one; on April 17, 1793 (28 Germinal, year I), a certain Daubenton spoke without a cap and "spared no words in defiling this symbol of the people's freedom"; he was bound over to the police and banned from the assembly for a year. On April 21, the *Contrat-Social* section took notice of the fact that the majority of presidents and secretaries of general assemblies "wore the red cap of freedom," and decided to do likewise. On May 4, the *Sans-Culottes* section demanded that its president present an address to the Convention on the following day wearing the red cap and trousers.

The victory of the popular movement during the course of the summer of 1793 was also the victory of the red cap. The fashion spread. In the *Beaurepaire* section, Montain-Lambin, health officer and militant, "first substituted the Jacobin costume and particularly the red cap for an elaborate headdress and the apparel of his social class." On 16 Brumaire, at the request of Chaumette, the General Council ordered all its members to wear the red cap. On 16 Brumaire, the *Amis-de-la-Patrie* ordered its treasurer to buy four red caps for its committee. A cartoon of the popular militant of the autumn of 1793 shows him wearing "a red cap on the head, a sword at his side and long moustaches under his nose." To shout, *Down with the red cap!* was reason for suspicion. The attempt by the Society of Republican Revolutionary Women to force women to wear red caps failed. The attempt was denounced on 7 Brumaire before the General Council of the Commune, and on the following day the Convention decreed freedom of dress. On 27 Brumaire, when a delegation of women wearing red caps appeared before the General Council, it was greeted with shouts of *Down with women's red caps!* In a moralizing speech, Chaumette reminded the women that their place was in the home; he was applauded; male chauvinism won the day.

In fact there was a certain amount of confusion about the wearing of the red cap. The sans-culottes wore it out of conviction, others out of prudence or as a form of demagoguery. On 1 Frimaire, the *Halle-au-Blé* section brought to the attention of the General Assembly the fact that several aristocrats were wearing them in order to be able to insult patriots. They urged that anyone who wore his own hair be forbidden to wear a Jacobin-style wig: "Many people wear wigs in Paris and their own hair in the country." The only people who could wear the red cap were those employed by the constituted authorities in the exercise of their duties. The Council banned Jacobin-style wigs, but passed on to the day's order of business, ignoring the second proposal. Discussion was taken up again on the following day, when someone pointed out that the red cap was an object of derision on the part of muscadins and aristocrats. Some thought it degraded the cap to allow all citizens, without distinction, to wear it; others thought everyone had the right to wear it. The Council, which, the day before, had banned the Jacobin-style wig, passed on to the day's order of business —motivated by freedom of apparel. The militants continued to persist, nevertheless, in wishing to regulate the wearing of the red cap. On 10 Frimaire, the *Temple* assembly protested against people dancing, wearing the red cap: it defamed the cap, which should be worn only on government service. In a letter to Hébert dated 2 Nivôse, a militant from the *Chalier* section denounced false patriots who appeared in them: "Indiscriminate wearing of red caps makes it impossible to recognize those worthy of wearing it [sic]"; he suggested that those unable to get written affidavits from their fellow citizens attesting to their worthiness be forbidden to wear it. According to the official observer Pourvoyeur, writing on 5 Nivôse, the public was asked to "keep a watch over the behavior of militants who wear the red cap." "Far from being a symbol of freedom and equality to those who wear it, on the contrary, it has distinct connotations all of its own, and those who wear it think that they can behave like little despots."

The red cap disappeared with the decline of the popular movement; it is mentioned less frequently in documents after Germinal. On 17 Messidor, before the General Council, Payan denounced those who pretended to reach heights of patriotism by wearing the red cap. Opposition to the cap increased after Thermidor. Armonville caused a riot in the Convention on 9 Nivôse, year III, when he appeared on the rostrum wearing his red cap. On 30 Pluviôse in the *Lombards* section, when the general assembly announced that it "disapproved of the red cap," its secretary then carefully removed his cockade.

The pike was as much the emblem of the militant sansculottes as the red cap. It brought to mind the great days of the Revolution; it was a symbol of the people in arms, it was a demonstration of popular sovereignty achieved by insurrection. With pike in hand and wearing the red cap—reminders of the people's power—petitioners appeared before the bar of the Convention or of the Jacobin Club. When on June 25, 1793 (Messidor, year 1), Jacques Roux called upon the Convention to outlaw speculators and to decree the death sentence for monopolists, he added: "The sans-culottes guarantee the enactment of your decrees with their pikes." According to Hébert, "Whenever the aristocrats take a swipe at freedom [the sans-culotte] takes his sword and his pike and races over to the section."

Throughout the Revolution, the pike was celebrated as the weapon of the masses *par excellence*. The patriots took particular care in arming the sans-culottes with it; they were at first ineligible for the National Guard. When war was declared, the creation of a corps of pikemen was considered. On July 25, 1792, the Legislative Assembly having been presented with a *Manual for Citizens Armed with Pikes*, Carnot extolled the advantages of this weapon, suggested that soldiers be armed with it, and that its production be hastened. On August 1, the Assembly authorized the municipalities to have pikes made at the Treasury's expense and to distribute them among citizens able to bear arms and who had no guns. During the summer of 1793, when the sans-culottes were calling for the *levée en masse* (summoning all the able-bodied to defend the country) and demanding that the government speed up the manufacturing of war matériel, the pike once again became the supreme recourse against tyrants. On August 14, the Convention listened to a eulogy in praise of the pike, "the most formidable of weapons," "a terrible and invincible weapon." On September 21, Deputy Lejune declared before the Jacobin Club that "we must make use of our pikes"; "too long has this terrible weapon been neglected; the aristocrats have purposely discredited it, nevertheless it is only with pike in hand that the French people were reborn; it is only the pike of the sans-culottes which gave us our liberty." However, the pike did not be-

come a weapon of war; in 1793 and in the year II it remained the weapon of civil strife. The sans-culottes praised
it and called it the holy pike. The symbol of popular
power, the *pike bearer* became the label of the sans-culottes.
The word *pike*, like the word *carmagnole*, ended by becoming synonymous with the sans-culottes themselves. On
September 12, 1793 (Fructidor, year I), pastry cook Du-
Bois was arrested by the revolutionary committee of the
Lombards section for having shouted, *Down with the
pikes!*

During the Terror, numbers of moderates and aristocrats concealed their innermost thoughts behind the costume of the sans-culotte and the general behavior of the
militant. In Frimaire, year II, an article in *Père Duchesne*
thundered against "the new slogan coined by the spokesman for King George Dandin" for mocking patriots and
caricaturing them as follows: "a pair of baggy trousers,
a small waistcoat, a black wig, a red cap to hide his blond
hair; false moustachios, a pipe stuck in his mouth instead
of a toothpick, large cudgel in place of a cane, swears
neither more nor less than *Père Duchesne* instead of speaking with pursed lips."

Apart from such exterior signs as costume, red cap or
pike, the militant sans-culotte showed himself by his speech
and by a certain behavior toward his fellows: the use of
the informal word *tu*, if not of swear words as *Père
Duchesne* would have liked (although working-class language was still exceedingly coarse), was an essential fea-
ture, indicative of a particular interpretation of social relations.

Social mores became more democratic, keeping time
with the rhythm of the Revolution. The fraternal societies were very influential in this area, and substituted the
term *sir* or *mister* for that of citizen. The Convention
imitated them during its first session. But those who
wanted to destroy prejudice and inequality, and make the
language express the fraternal sentiments which filled their
hearts were still not satisfied. On December 14, 1790,
the *Mercure National* endorsed the familiar *tu* in an

article "On the Influence of Words and the Power of Language." In 1791 the same demand was made. The entry of the sans-culottes into political life during the course of the summer of 1792 was bound finally to impose its use. Once again, the popular societies and general assemblies were influential. On December 4, 1792 (Frimaire, year I), a speaker claimed that "the word *vous* was contrary to the right of equality, that the word had been used purely for the purpose of asserting feudal rights, and that the word *tu* was the only personal pronoun free men should use." The general assembly of the *Sans-Culottes* section banned use of the word *vous*, "a hangover from feudalism," and was adamant concerning the use of the word *tu*, "the only word worthy of free men." On December 8, the *Droits-de-l'Homme* assembly insisted that its committee use the familiar *tu*. At about the same time, a ruling decreed by the popular society of Sceaux declared: "Members will treat each other as brothers, use the familiar *tu*, and they will call each other *citizen*, never using the word *monsieur*." Said the *Chronique de Paris* on the preceding October 3: "If *vous* is suitable to a gentleman, *tu* is suitable for a citizen"; "under the happy reign of equality, familiarity is only the mirror of the philantropic virtues which are in men's souls." Nevertheless, the Girondins were hostile to the popular agitation for the use of *tu*, Brissot declared this *impropriety* useless. Robespierre did not favor it.

In spite of the reservations of certain Montagnards, the triumph of the sans-culottes in 1793 made the use of *tu* usual. The sans-culottes wished to go even further and impose its use. On 10 Brumaire, year II, a delegation of all the popular societies in Paris rose at the bar of the Convention against the use of the word *vous*. "A lot of trouble still arises from this abuse, it casts a slur on the intelligence of the sans-culottes; it preserves the arrogance of stubborn men and flattery; under the pretext of showing respect, it casts aside the principles of brotherly virtue." The popular societies demanded that a law be passed "that will reform this vice"; "thus there will be less pride, less intimidation, fewer social distinctions, more obvious familiarity, more of an inclination toward fraternity. As a result, more equality." Ignoring the fact that this verbal fraternal attitude contained its own inherent dangers, the sans-culottes demanded that those who failed to use the familiar *tu* be declared suspect, "of being flatterers and thus indulging in arrogance, which is the basis of inequality." Although Basire demanded that a decree be issued concerning this matter, the Convention was content with an acknowledgment. On 21 Brumaire, Basire renewed the assault, demanding that a law be drafted. The Convention had already refused to make wearing the red cap mandatory by decree. It passed on to the regular order of business: "Is it not contrary to the laws of freedom," declared Thuriot, "to stipulate the manner in which citizens should express themselves?" Ignoring this, the Directory of the Paris département on 22 Brumaire issued orders to the effect that the familiar *tu* was to be used in its offices and its correspondence: "Henceforth the only language suitable to French Republicans would be the language of fraternity." In making this move, they were imitating the Franciade district. Throughout the year II, the familiar *tu* was in general use in sectional organizations as well as in municipal or national agencies. The use of this word in social intercourse did not pass without incident. The sans-culottes insisted on using the familiar *tu*, often going counter to old habits. On 5 Nivôse, two citizens got involved in a fight at the Café Procope with one of the waiters, an old man who did not address them with the familiar *tu*: "They called him slave"; he apologized. The informer added "that the waiter had observed that there was no law imposing the use of the familiar *tu*, and that no citizen should be allowed to incriminate another for such an absolutely voluntary act."

After Germinal, when the tide of the popular movement began to ebb, people began to express a dislike for the familiar *tu*; the reaction was about to set in. In his *Reflections on the Abuse of Authority on the Part of the Revolutionary Committee of the Temple Section* a certain

Bouin rose up on 1 Messidor against the use of the familiar *tu*, particularly in addressing women. "As it is used today, the use of this word injured the reputation of the Revolution, making it seem as if we were reverting to a state of coarseness and rustic manners, because it is used by a large number of public officials in a harsh and brutal manner which gives offense, humiliating and alienating people rather than winning them over to the present order; this pernicious effect is produced especially among women, in whose opinion the use of the familiar *tu* is in every way unseemly, unpleasant and immoral." On 17 Messidor, Payan denounced before the General Council those who, in order to get the reputation of being good citizens, forced themselves "to speak the familiar *tu* as if willingly."

The reaction accelerated after 9 Thermidor, and the decline of the use of the familiar *tu* was proportionate to the decline of popular influence. On 11 Nivôse, year III, the *Vedette ou Gazette du Jour* declared, "The use of the familiar *tu* is disappearing in conversation and . . . is not used so often in letter writing." A brawl erupted in the Café de Foy on 21 Ventôse because a mere citizen had used *tu* in speaking to a general. The events of Prairial brought an end to the use of the familiar *tu*. It rapidly disappeared, at the same time that the passion for equality diminished.

It was still demonstrated after August 10, particularly in the National Guard. In a regulation dated August 13, 1792, the General Council of the Commune had ordered every rank to wear woolen epaulets. The sans-culottes ridiculed them. During the month of Prairial, year III, cries of "Down with epaulets, down with the wearers of epaulets!" were often the signal for revolt among the companies. The sans-culottes were determined to ban all differences in uniform, and vehemently opposed all attempts at restoring privileged units with special uniforms, such as grenadiers or dragoons. On November 24, 1792 (Frimaire, year I), at the suggestion of the *Halle-au-Blé* section, the *l'Homme-Armé* assembly declared that it would not recognize "any form of distinction save those essential for the high command"; reversion to the rank system in the services would result in "discrimination against the poor," which means "destroying the communal purpose of the military and the principles of equality and fraternity." Equality among the troops was a term often exploited by the militants and popular journalists. In *L'Ami du Peuple* for August 14, 1793 (Thermidor, year I), Leclerc declared that the revolutionary army about to be created should set the example; "commandants, officers and soldiers must receive the same wages, eat the same bread, and the distinction of rank should not serve men's vanity, but only the common good." In Number 311 of his *Père Duchesne*, in Brumaire, Hébert wrote an open letter to a "strapping lad called Tulipe," who had written to him from the Moselle region: "Tell me why generals and their aides-de-camp don't wear the national uniform? Why are they covered with gold braid? Perhaps you will reply that there must be differences between ranks, so that we can recognize our leaders; but should republicans be distinguishable by their fine clothes? . . . if we are all equal . . . we must put a stop to the snob value of clothes and particularly in the Army." The general assemblies made sure that outward evidence of military equality was maintained in the Paris National Guard. On April 15, 1792, the *Quinze-Vingt-Douze* section reminded the commander-in-chief never to forget "that free men gave him his powers, that free men never have to be led as if they were slaves." On 1 Nivôse, year II, the *Cité* section issued orders that every tenth day officers and warrant officers would join the ranks for a meal in their mess.

The most vociferous demonstration of military equality was the obligation to serve; the sans-culottes persistently clamored for the abolition of paying a substitute to serve in the National Guard. On October 30, 1792 (Brumaire, year I), the unit attached to the *Droits-de-l'Homme* section demanded "a law which would deal severely with citizens who refused guard duty, making the observation that in a republic every citizen is a soldier." Service in the National Guard was considered as a sort of school of equality. "Mounting guard oneself would abolish every trace of class distinction, which formerly existed." On November 24, 1792, the *l'Homme-Armé* section declared, "The National Guard was the only organization where the hardworking poor and the idle rich can be thrown together." The sections were persistent. In July 1793, they adopted a petition formulated by the *Lombards* section; it stressed the contradiction between the egalitarian principles laid down in the Declaration of Rights and the practice of buying exemption from service in the National Guard: "Judge for yourself, you lawmakers, whether equality can reign in a country where the rich man can always make the poor man die for him." The Convention refused to get involved; composed of representatives of the bourgeoisie, they could hardly suppress a privilege of wealth.

Not all the sans-culottes' social activities were devoted to political life, meetings of general assemblies and sectional societies, service in the National Guard or patriotic missions. If we are to believe the diary called *Le Journal d'un Employé*, there was a lot of getting together with friends, tavern conversations, evenings at cafés, dinners at inns; they talked politics while drinking tankards of wine, and sang patriotic songs. On the day of rest (there was a considerable difficulty in replacing Sunday with the tenth day, but the militants observed it scrupulously) the sans-culottes went in droves to suburban taverns. Hébert often described the Courtille district, with its trailing vines and cherry trees and its cheerful atmosphere; "on the last day of rest," he wrote in *L'Ami du Peuple*, number 341, in Ventôse, "after having celebrated the Republican Mass in the Temple of Reason with all the sans-culottes of my section, that is to say, after having listened to the most patriotic of speeches, and after having sung at the top of my lungs hymns in honor of freedom, in the evening I happily set out, acompanied by a few good boys, to vespers at that marvelous place, the Courtille." Observers all agree that on days of rest there was general merriment, "even during the most difficult periods." On 21 Ventôse, year II, wrote Perrière, the streets in the Courtille area were crammed with crowds of happy well-dressed people; everywhere one heard the noise of dancing and of instruments playing . . . in singing the carmagnole and all those tunes so dear to freedom, the people were celebrating their civic Lent. The Courtille taverns were not the only places frequented by the sans-culottes; now they often took walks on boulevards formerly reserved for the wealthy. According to Perriére, "From one end to the other, the boulevards were stuffed with people"; on 15 Ventôse, "there were more heads of hair than hats." But what pleased Perrière was that "such poorly dressed people, who would formerly have never dared show themselves in areas frequented by people of fashion, were walking among the rich, their heads as high as theirs . . . there was an air of contentment in the crowd, and a stranger would never have guessed that these people were forced to make many sacrifices on account of the critical situation."

In the absence of statistics and of sufficient contemporary description, it is difficult to get a precise idea of the daily life and standard of living of the average sans-culotte. It was very modest, judging from literary sources, and from a few scattered, though detailed, documents.

Bankruptcy files provide a few figures for artisans and shopkeepers. Among the files of members of the middling bourgeoisie, André Guettier, a currier domiciled in the Petite rue Taranne in the *Quatre-Nations* section, declared bankruptcy on January 28, 1793 (Pluviôse, year I), and valued his assets at 6,000 livres worth of furniture and household goods. Jacques-Antoine Courbin, a master locksmith, residing in the Rue de Bondy, declared bankruptcy on March 24, and listed his assets at 5,000 livres worth of furniture, personal effects, linens and clothes. Lalonde, a wholesale grocer of the Rue Tiron in the *Piques* section, declared bankruptcy on February 14, 1793, and assets of 3,400 livres worth of furniture, utensils, linen and clothes. The household possessions of shopkeepers and tradesmen were more modest. The furnishing of Feuchère, a second-hand clothes dealer living in the Faubourg Saint-Antoine, who declared bankruptcy on January 30, 1793, were valued at 1,234 livres; those of Louis Raimbault, a currier living in the Rue d'Argenteuil, declared bankrupt on April 10, at 1,200 livres. Wine merchant Morville, the younger, residing at the Rue Guerin-Boisseau, who declared bankruptcy on February 14, 1793, had 850 livres worth of furniture and linens; grain merchant Charles Guendre had 830 livres worth of personal possessions when he was declared bankrupt on February 28, Charles-François Madeline, a painter residing in the Rue Saint-Martin, who was declared bankrupt on January 24, possessed 600 livres worth of clothes, furniture and linens. Grocer Arnal, residing in the Rue du Murier Saint-Victor in the *Sans-Culottes* section, declared himself destitute; his furniture and household goods were valued at 353 livres on February 18, 1793.

The verbatim reports of investigations or arrests give a clear picture of even worse poverty in the homes of several sectional militants. Claude Desmarets, a grain porter, named a member of the revolutionary committee of the *Maison-Commune* section on September 15, 1793 (Fructidor, year 1), very soon resigned; he could not support his wife and three children on his yearly indemnity of 1,800 livres. His family lived in one room. His household goods were few: two tables, three beds and a cradle; a chest of drawers, a wardrobe, a sideboard "decorated with very small amounts of faience" and "other small objects which did not warrant being described." The value of the household goods of Descombes, who lived in the *Droits-de-l'Homme* section and who was executed with Hébert, was no more than 400 livres. The family of Ducroquet, monopoly commissar of the *Marat* section, was on the verge of starvation. When Ducroquet, already in debt to the tune of 700 livres, was arrested in the month of Ventôse, his wife had nothing to live on; she borrowed money, then had to rob Peter to pay Paul. In his letter dated 1 Germinal, Ducroquet reminded his wife of the troubles

they had had raising their two children; old shirts would
have to do for the layette of the third, which they were
expecting, or the clothes which Ducroquet's mother was
to send from Amiens.

The sans-culotte, even if he was a commissar, was the
worst off. A republican commissar was paid five livres a
day, or 1,800 per annum; a committee secretary, 1,200;
an office boy, 800. Sans-culotte Girbal, forwarding agent
in the central office in charge of the possessions of émigrés, earned 150 livres per month; on 30 Ventôse, year
II, he spent eleven sols drinking in a tavern; on 4 Germinal,
he dined with friends at five livres, two sols per head;
when he ate at an inn, for lack of time to get home, his
meal cost him thirty-two sols; on 10 Messidor, while out
with his wife in Montmartre, he spent four livres, fifteen
sols for a *bad dinner*. He must have had very little left
for other expenses besides food.

It is difficult to ascertain the exact sum of money a
Paris sans-culotte spent on rent. The sans-culottes were
very much involved in the problems of rent, when prices
rose as inflation increased. There was nothing new about
this crisis. It began when the ancien régime fell. In 1789,
a *Special, Local Statement of Grievances of the Third
Estate* demanded that "restrictions be imposed on the high
cost of rent, so that the petit bourgeois not be forced to
spend half his income on putting a roof over his family's
head." There was already a disparity between the western
section of Paris and those of the east and the center. Nobles, financiers, and wealthy bourgeois lived in sumptuous
mansions surrounded by courtyards and gardens from Faubourg Saint-Germain to the Chaussée-d'Antin. The lower
class, the petite bourgeoisie, shopkeepers, artisans and
journeymen were crammed into the old parts of the city,
in dark, narrow, airless streets. However, the various social
classes were not completely segregated. The same old buildings often sheltered many different social classes, from
bourgeois to journeymen: the poorest lived on the upper
floors; the lower were inhabited by the bourgeoisie. Said
Père Duchesne, "Don't expect to find sans-culottes living

in palaces or above the shops of fat merchants and traders, but in attics . . . if you wish to meet the flower of the sans-culottes, go to the workers' hovels." The family of cobbler Bouty, revolutionary commissar in the *Mucius-Scaevola* section, consisted of four persons occupying a single room on the fifth floor. Cobbler Potet, another commissar, lived with his wife and three children in a single room on the fourth floor at 106 Rue Tiquetonne. Another family, with five members, that of Claude des Marets, grain porter and one-time commissar in the *Maison-Commune* section, also lived in a single room. Living conditions were similar for most popular militants. The poorest class of all, journeymen, workers, day laborers, a floating population always changing address, lived in cheap furnished lodgings.

The first years of the Revolution, in spite of circumstances temporarily favorable to the lodgings business, began a period of acute rental problems. Emigration, economic stagnation, foreign and then the civil war, and repressive measures resulted in a major exodus from Paris of all classes of society. The numbers were at their highest during the spring of the year II, when the law of 27 Germinal forced nobles and foreigners to leave Paris within ten days. One should not exaggerate. Paris did attract large numbers of refugees fleeing civil or foreign wars: Belgians, Rhinelanders, Alsatians, Lyonese. The increasing number of government agencies, such as that charged with the manufacturing of war matériel, had attracted to Paris offices and workshops large numbers of workers and minor officials.

Whatever the extent of the rental problem, the sans-culottes, whose purchasing power was continually diminishing, considered rents excessive. Popular demands for price-fixing extended to rents. Several petitions asked for reductions; some went as far as to suggest a maximum similar to that imposed on basic foodstuffs. Popular demands in this area came to a head during the latter part of the summer of 1793, although it is difficult to ascertain whether conditions had actually worsened. In short, the success of the sans-culottes in other areas gave rise to new demands. On September 5, 1793 (Fructidor, year 1), Citizeness Barbot, who owned a notions shop at 17 Rue Transnonain in the *Gravilliers* section, asked "that a general law be passed placing restrictions on the cupidity of landlords." On September 29, the *Popincourt* section asked the Convention that the statute be based on the sum of money paid for rent by penniless soldiers; on October 1, the *Indivisibilité* section asked for the cancellation of leases signed by young conscripts. On October 16, the *Cité* section solicited the support of the assemblies for a petition for an overall decrease of rents. The petition was adopted by all the sections and presented to the Convention on 10 Brumaire, year II. "The law of the 'maximum' is of considerable assistance to the people: but this great act of justice is lacking in other areas." The sections demanded that all rents be rolled back to the 1760 figures: "For it was in 1764 that the tyrant Louis XV and his perfidious ministers began gambling with the people's livelihoods; when a sudden increase in rents was accompanied by a rise in the price of food." On 17 Brumaire, the *Observatoire* section went before the General Council of the Commune and demanded that it give permission for nationalized houses and vacant houses belonging to émigrés to be occupied by the wives of volunteers, doubtless free of charge. The Convention had only unwillingly placed a ceiling on food prices; it was chary of controlling rents; that would have been an infringement on property rights.

This same concern for preserving the *status quo* accounted for the failure to deal with complaints about "principal" tenants and rented rooms. It was customary to rent an entire house to a "principal" tenant, usually a businessman, shopkeeper or artisan, who used the ground floor for his business or his workshop, lived in an apartment above the shop, and sublet the others. He was responsible to the owner for the rent and upkeep of the building; the subtenants dealt only with him. With his business already affected by price-fixing, particularly if he was a retailer, the principal tenant, who was really only a manager, had difficulty in the year II in securing regular payments of rents, which the landlords still demanded. On 28 Floréal, nine butcher principal-tenants, whose businesses were in jeopardy, asked the Convention to authorize them to cancel their leases. The Legislative Committee refused: all principal tenants would then claim the right, in particular "those who rent out furnished rooms."

The furnished rooms situation was no less critical. At the beginning of the Revolution, people in this business did very well, as the result of an enormous influx of foreigners and people from the provinces attracted to Paris by the events. Leases drawn up between 1789 and 1791 took account of this prosperity. Then came the crises, Revolution, war, then the Terror, and establishments with furnished rooms for rent gradually emptied; furnished sublet occupancy fell by 50 per cent. The principal tenant, hounded by the landlord, occasionally forced to sell his furniture, thereby spelling immediate disaster for his business, demanded the canceling of his lease. On 8 Brumaire, year II, citizens who rented furnished rooms in the Faubourg Saint-Germain complained to the Convention. "It is public knowledge that the condition of people letting furnished lodgings is diastrous, and will continue to be so until peace is declared": security measures have emptied them. Confronted with silence on the part of the Convention and its Legislative Committee, the petitioners soon renewed their assault: "All the Convention's decrees have sought only to divide wealth and assist the sansculottes." Will it force heads of families to sell their furniture "in order further to enrich the wealthy landlords, who by and large are opposed to the Revolution?" On 15 Brumaire, another petition was presented, this time from the Faubourg Saint-Honoré, and similar arguments were used. The struggle went on throughout the year II; several principal tenants held office in sectional organizations. In Floréal, a certain Bazin vehemently denounced landlords, whose incomes "had not diminished at all"; they make "the most industrious and most useful class of people bear the burden of their selfishness." In Prairial, on 4 Thermidor and on 17 Fructidor, the principal tenants renewed their attack. Toward the end of Prairial, the Convention's Legislative Committee declared that the *principles involved demanded* that the petitions be rejected and the leases enforced. Perhaps one might discover some form of indemnity, but how was that to be done without burdening the Treasury?

The problem was in fact insoluble: the government authorities were caught between conceding to popular demands and defending the principle of the *status quo*. Their choice was quite clear: they could not encroach on property rights. The Thermidorian reaction, in allowing émigrés and suspects to return to Paris, solved the problem of furnished lodgings but this caused a grave housing shortage, the first victims of which were the sans-culottes.

The sans-culottes were far more concerned with food shortages than with housing and rent; food absorbed most of their wages or pensions. Bread was the people's staple diet, and their daily wages allowed them to buy little else besides. *Père Duchesne* was pleased to announce that "bread is our primary resource." On February 26, 1793 (8 Ventôse, year I), in bringing the high cost of food to the attention of the Commune, the *Invalides* section declared: "What will happen to the citizen whose family consumes more than ten livres [about ten pounds and ten ounces] of bread a day if it stays at the price fixed by the monopolists?" At about the same time, appeared *The Last Cry of the Sans-Culottes Asking for Bread*, one long complaint which shows the importance of bread in the daily life of the masses. The minimum ration for an adult worker was set at three pounds of bread a day, that of a child at one and one half. During the height of the shortage, on 25 Ventôse, year III, the Convention set the minimum ration for manual laborers at one and one half pounds, one pound for the rest of the population; under normal circumstances, they consumed twice that amount. The importance of bread in the daily diet forced the masses to make certain demands: they wanted to have enough bread, reasonably priced and of good quality. Hence demands for the "maximum" (a ceiling price), the demand for control and continuous complaint of fraudulent practices; the sans-culottes demanded bread made from the pure wheat that the rich used. Hébert exploited this situation in the diatribes of *Père Duchesne*. One gets some idea of the problems confronting a working-class family by looking at the daily wage of the road mender in the *Panthéon-Français* district in Ventôse, year II: he was paid three livres a day, while bread cost three sous the pound and a family of between four and five consumed ten pounds a day. Bread appears to have absorbed a dangerously high percentage of workers' salaries throughout the year II, but unfortunately, for lack of adequate statistical data, we cannot determine exactly how much.

In spite of government and Commune efforts, potatoes still were not much in demand, according to a remark made by a militant in the popular society of the *Amis-de-la-Patrie* section. Yet the Parisian masses consumed considerable amounts of meat. There are several reasons for believing this was so, particularly the large number of butchers, and the general discontent when there were meat shortages toward the end of the winter of the year II. When the *Indivisibilité* section called for the rationing of meat on 30 Pluviôse, it set the daily ration at half a pound per person. The amount of meat distributed was hardly negligible: Girbal, an employee who lived in the *Guillaume-Tell* section, received two pounds on 11 Ventôse for a household of two people; on the eighteenth, he was allowed three pounds of veal. Nevertheless, when the municipality regulated meat distribution, on 29 Germinal, the individual ration was set at about half a pound every five days.

The Parisian masses drank considerable quantities of wine. With taverns for the poorest, cabarets, cafés for those who were better off, drinking shops played an important role in the daily life of the sans-culottes, once again emphasizing the importance of the role played by large numbers of the Paris wine merchants in the popular movement, and accounting for the appreciable number of sectional officials among them. Employee Girbal went regularly to taverns with his colleagues, and carefully recorded what he spent there; he paid great attention to his own stock of wine, which he sought out in the villages on the southern outskirts of the city, at Clamart or Ivry; he bottled the wine himself. The countless complaints about poor blends of wine, and the appointment of official wine testers show the importance the sans-culottes attached to their wine and to its quality. *Père Duchesne* considered water drinking positively disgusting: doubtless Hébert was voicing public opinion. "If we don't keep a close watch on the monopolists," he wrote in Pluviôse, "we will be drinking water like the ducks, which I think is a penance to be reserved for the moderates, aristocrats, royalists and Orleanists."

Literary works also give us some idea of the daily life of the sans-culottes. In *Père Duchesne*, Hébert often described in vivid terms, and not without emotion, the lot "of the brave sans-culotte who lives from day to day by the work of his hands. As long as he has a four-pound loaf in his cupboard and a glass of spirits, he is happy." Where *Père Duchesne* describes the sans-culotte as being happy in his hovel, with his wife and his urchins, as long as he had enough bread, "a little stew" and "a patriotic nip to refresh him when he is dropping with fatigue," Chaumette, tending toward the maudlin, saw the poor man "always bent double under the crushing weight of the most arduous work, sweating out his day only to return to his garret and a piece of hard bread, which he often moistened with his tears." One occasionally comes across indictments of luxury, definitions of the ideal life, simple and frugal; they were not merely imitations of Rousseau; they express a certain popular attitude toward daily living. In his *Conversations between a Citizen of Philadelphia and a French Republican*, employee Maurin attributed happiness to the *natural virtues*: "Let us discuss the home of the patriot. . . . There we find simple manners, a frugal board, a mother who nurses her own child. . . ."

For lack of documentation, it is as difficult to ascertain the material conditions of daily life as it is to ascertain the intellectual level of the average sans-culotte.

Numbers of militants who were employed by the sections did not know how to read or write. Aroused in periods of crisis by shortages and impoverishment, they were nevertheless affected by numbers of ideas which, as if by osmosis, circulated from the more cultivated to the humblest members of society; this explains how Rousseau's theories on popular sovereignty were vaguely shared by men who had never read the *Social Contract*. The popular societies that rallied to the Jacobins played a major role in this area; they made a considerable contribution to the political education of the sans-culottes. Hence the importance which the Montagnards attached to them and the hatred which the reactionaries wreaked on them after Thermidor.

The popular press had far more influence than the number of papers printed would lead us to believe; this occurred because they were read aloud every evening in the popular societies and the general assemblies. Furthermore, during the day, in squares or in the street, workers or passers-by stood around listening to soapbox orators. Varlet was not the only militant to make speeches from a moving platform. On October 15, 1793 (Vendémiaire, year II), two orators standing on platforms read patriotic handbills to a large crowd standing on the Pont-au-Change. A certain Collignon called himself the sans-culottes' public reader. From the beginning of the Revolution, he read in squares and during public spectacles a republican catechism which he had written himself. In October 1793, the *Arsenal* section and the Harmonie popular society demanded that, bearing in mind "the lack of presses for the enlightenment of the people, we ought to organize a verbal news system, by starting a newspaper especially for the people, to be read aloud throughout the country by public officials and readers." Although the *Arsenal's* petition was not granted by the authorities, who mistrusted popular speakers, public readings nevertheless were held in streets and on byways until the year III. On 1 Prairial, at ten o'clock in the morning, a stonemason called Closmesnil sat perched on some scaffolding reading a leaflet considered subversive to more than 100 road menders of the *Panthéon-Français* section; he was arrested. Petitioning on his behalf, his comrades declared that they had chosen him "on account of his fine voice and his willingness to read to them every day during their lunch hour the *Auditeur National,* which we all chipped in on in order to learn together." The *Panthéon-Français* road menders were not an isolated case.

Quite by chance, while at his work or taking a walk, the sans-culotte had numerous opportunities not only to hear the news read aloud, but also to read it himself. Militants posted the manuscript leaflets on billboards. In the *Chalier* section, Montain-Lambin posted a handwritten tract twice every ten days at the entrance of the National Guard barracks of his section, which, according to some observers, attracted large numbers of readers. Posters attracted far more attention than these placards: until Germinal, opposing factions plastered the city with them. The first days of Nivôse saw the walls of Paris covered with posters of Vincent Ronsin, Mazuel and Mailliard. Passers-by stopped and discussed them: thus these notices fostered the political education of the sans-culottes, even of the most ignorant among them.

Did the militants, at least those who had an elementary education, read at home? Probably very little. They scarcely had time, spending their days at work and their evenings at the meetings of popular societies or at sessions of the general assembly. Hébert describes the sans-culotte waking at dawn, sweating *blood and water* to feed his family, returning to his hovel in the evening, after having stopped by for a while at an assembly session. "He dines voraciously, and after his meal, he treats his family to a reading from *La Grande Colère* or *La Grande Joie du Père Duchesne"*: a heartwarming scene. The average sans-culotte had neither the habit nor the time to read regularly, even the popular sheets. The verbatim reports of the evidence seized in raids on known militants during the year II and the year III, rarely mentioned books or collections of newspapers, except for a few scattered copies of pamphlets by Marat or Hébert, or a few patriotic tracts. Most militants did little reading other than these political tracts. The most educated among them did not on the whole seem to have had firsthand knowledge of the political or philosophical thinking of the time; they learned indirectly through the press or from speeches given by the Jacobins or the Cordeliers, and more often than not from discussion in the popular societies. It seems likely that this was how the philosophy of Rousseau came to color the thinking of the most active and aware people among the militants.

However, the level of the literary taste of the better-educated sans-culottes was not particularly high. Long since vanished, the literary works sold by peddlers did, however, play an important part in shaping public sensibility and the national culture. During the eighteenth century, book peddling gradually increased, in spite of particularly severe repressive legislation. Even Malesherbes mentions this fact in his *Mémoire sur la Librairie de 1759*. The Revolution lifted the restrictions on book peddling, abolishing censorship and calling upon the sans-culottes to take part in politics, thus increasing opportunities for selling cheap books. By the year II, religious works, and particularly the lives of the saints, which had always been one of the mainstays of popular literature, disappeared from the book vendors' stalls. Books on magic, on the other hand, seemed to have sold just as well as ever, judging from the popularity of such books as: *Explication des Songes* and *Arts de Tirer les Cartes* (Your Dreams Explained and The Art of Card Reading). Romantic novels abounded. Quantities of political tracts were published. When book vendor Buy's stall was seized in a raid, the revolutionary committee of the *Montagne* section drew up an inventory of his books during the first days of Pluviôse, year II. The masters were represented by the complete works of Racine, *The Maid of Orleans, Les Liaisons Dangereuses* and *Tom Jones*; these works were for a better-educated and already bourgeois public. *Le Souterrain, ou Mathilde* and *Le Conte du Tonneau* were truly popular literature, romance and satire. *Un Moyen de Parvenir* was one of those books on how to overcome poverty, derived from the proverbial wisdom of Poor Richard, which provided book peddlers with a large number of popular works toward the end of the eighteenth century. As for contemporary politics, there was a *Poème pour la Révolution* and two pamphlets whose titles were not listed. The variety of these titles shows quite clearly that the book vendor had at his command a stock of words appealing to various categories of sansculottes, from the fairly cultivated petite bourgeoisie to semi-literate people.

The sans-culottes idealized the simplicity of their daily existence. They built their lives around a system, and condemned those who were not part of it. The militant sansculotte was always prepared to moralize; he tended to confuse his way of living with the practice of republican virtues. As far as he was concerned, private virtue was the necessary condition for public virtue; the two were combined to produce patriotism. The French republican explained to the citizen of Philadelphia that "a decent man was a good son, a good husband and good father; to combine, in one word, every public and personal virtue"; "herein lies the real definition of the word patriotism."

The militants were not content merely to accept Rousseau's ideas. Chaumette denounced vice before the General Council of the Commune and undertook to purge Paris. On September 16, 1793 (30 Fructidor, year I), the Society of Republican Revolutionary Women demanded that prostitutes be detained in national homes in healthy surroundings, be given work suitable to their sex and have patriotic articles read to them twice a day; "in short, we must teach them physical and moral ideals." In an address before the Convention, the *Tuileries* section demanded passage of a law closing gambling establishments and houses of ill repute: "The foundations of a republic lay in its morality. Without morality, there will be no government; without government there would be no safety; without safety there would be no freedom." Throughout the Terror, men *lacking in morals* were often considered suspect, morality being one of the fundamental elements of the Republic, according to a denunciation dated September 1793. On 25 Ventôse, the revolutionary committee of the *Faubourg-Montmartre* section decided on the arrest of a certain Hautavoine because "he is, in short, an immoral man, part of whose income derives from his girls, who lead a scandalous life." In a manuscript leaflet which he posted on the gates of the National Guard barracks in the *Chalier* section, Montain-Lambin announced his intention of "teaching all the citizens their duties"; he made special mention of drunkards, saying that "he who seeks insensibility is not worthy of being a republican," and of prostitution. The tract was very successful. These declamations on morality and virtue were less indicative of general corruption than of the simple and dignified life of the masses as embodied in the militants' clichés. In various pamphlets, Hébert made brief sketches of family life which must, for the most part, have been descriptions of sansculottes. "When he comes home to his hovel at night, his wife gives him a warm embrace, and his little brats come to take him by the hand." Ducroquet's simple letters to his wife are proof of a family life full of tenderness and dignity, even in its poverty.

A life of dignity, but without social prejudice. Common-law marriages were frequent. Some were legalized after the birth of children; many never were. The number of children born out of wedlock and lodged at the Hospice d'Humanité, formerly the Hôtel-Dieu, in the year II, is particularly important. On October 13, 1792 (Vendémiaire, year I), Etienne Pascal, a journeyman farrier, aged twenty-six, and Marie-Louise Buffin, aged seventeen, appeared before the *Bondy* general assembly. "For eighteen months they had been united in the most tender attachment for each other and had a child baptized with their respective names"; they had come before the assembly to prove the "authenticity of their love," meaning by this that they were taking "an oath of their own volition, formal and reciprocal, which would unite one to the other." "Out of respect for morality and for nature's most worthy sentiment," the general assembly ordered that this declaration be inscribed in the registers. It was, nevertheless, an exceptional case, since the simple declaration before one's fellow citizens was considered as superfluous as the legal formalities of marriage. In a petition urging equal rights for natural and legitimate children in matters of inheritance, a sans-culotte, who listed his occupation as master mason, declared somewhat ostentatiously "that he came from a line of bastards and was father of six children whose mother had never been married, which has not prevented the household from running smoothly and the children from growing up as if lawyers and priests had been at work."

The sans-culottes' insistence on demanding equal rights for natural children and common-law wives shows the importance that the masses attached to free unions. The *Bon-Conseil* section complained to the Convention about the law concerning public assistance to the families of soldiers: "It says nothing about those interesting creatures whom barbarous prejudice used to consider illegitimate. It is equally silent concerning citizenesses whose feelings of tenderness had made them fecund, before having fulfilled the wishes of the law, that is to say, by having failed to go through the formalities required to legalize the union." However, during the year ii, the sectional authorities did not distinguish between legitimate and illegitimate wives and children. On 29 Messidor, year iii, a member of the welfare commission for the assistance of soldiers' families in the *Maison-Commune* section pointed out that several orders of the assembly granted assistance "to citizenesses who had not been legally married to citizens who were at the front"; the respectable people won out, and with them, conventional morality; the assembly forbade its commission to grant any assistance to women who were not legally married.

The absence of social prejudice among sans-culottes was increased by a certain sense of solidarity. The word was still far from its contemporary meaning; there were, nevertheless, many examples of this civic virtue which, in popular thinking, was but a result of fraternity. Although some people served on relief committees, a new form of charity—Jacques Roux in the *Gravilliers* section, for instance, or Montain-Lambin, who had declared himself general welfare officer in the *Beaurepaire* section, whose charitable activities even extended as far as finding lodgings for people—the sans-culottes were aware of a mutual responsibility which bound them together. They contributed proportionately more than the wealthiest citizens to public collections, not all of which were made for purely patriotic reasons. This was another source of resentment against the rich. The active solidarity among sans-culottes was often shown by adoption. On October 16, 1793 (Vendémiaire, year II), the *Montagne* section adopted an orphan whose father had gone to the wars; a woman offered to look after him, and the assembly handed him over with confidence. On 30 Frimaire, year II, the *Droits-de-l'Homme* section adopted the child of a captain killed in the Vendée campaign; its mother had just died. Françoise Ravinet, innkeeper, who was known for participation in every great revolutionary day until Prairial, year III, and who was mother of four young children, did not hesitate to adopt a fifth for the sake of humanity. A new code of morality was born.

On account of their life style and their outlook, their social and political experiences and their organizations, the sectional militants formed an autonomous force within the revolutionary movement. Food shortages mobilized the sans-culottes, and their power increased. The revolutionary government and the dominant bourgeoisie felt threatened. Doubtless certain characteristics of the sans-culotte were close to those of the Jacobins. He, too, carried political passion to the verge of fanaticism; his rigid attitude was the source of the heroism which went as far as the ultimate sacrifice. His passionate desire for unity was no less strong. If his behavior occasionally appeared anarchic, the idea of individuality was foreign to him. Like the Jacobin, the sans-culotte drew from the heart of that Revolution, which had destroyed the social structure, the administrative bodies and the communities, a spirit of party and gave to it human warmth; he was among *brothers and friends* in the popular societies and general assemblies. The militant sans-culottes lived in groups and acted en masse.

In the last analysis, the passionate desire for equality appears to be the distinctive trait of the sans-culottes: the *fact* of equality was the necessary complement to the *right* of equality. It was the notion of equality that fed their revolutionary ardor and arrayed it against the aristocracy, and then against the bourgeoisie. This passionate desire for equality sets the sans-culottes apart not only from the Girondins and the moderates, but also from the Montagnards and even the Jacobins, who were equally concerned with class distinctions.

But was the time ripe for a social democracy?

ON THE POPULAR MOVEMENT AND REVOLUTIONARY GOVERNMENT: A SUMMARY OF POLITICAL CONTRADICTIONS

In the last analysis, the events of 9 Thermidor were a tragic episode of class conflict within the former Third Estate. However, in order to give them their just place in history, we must remember that the Revolution was essentially a struggle between the members of the Third Estate and the European aristocracy. In ᷄ this struggle, the French bourgeoisie had the upper hand: how could it have been otherwise? The revolutionary government, created through the union of the Montagnard bourgeoisie and the Parisian sans-culottes, found its reason for existence in defense of the Revolution against aristocracy at home and abroad. It goes without saying that when the Revolution placed the bourgeoisie at the head of the nation, the Montagnards did not condemn it; they were of the opinion that it was a matter of no particular importance to them. With victory their only aim, the Montagnards and particularly the followers of Robespierre were convinced that the Third Estate must remain united, as it was in 1789. Hence their alliance with the sans-culottes, who alone made possible the founding of the revolutionary government during the course of the summer of 1793. And until the spring of 1794 the government played the role of arbitrator in order to enforce a fairer distribution of necessary sacrifices, to keep a firm rein on both the resistance of the bourgeoisie and the popular movement, if they endangered the policy of national defense. The war came first.

The Paris sans-culottes were in agreement with the revolutionary government on the essentials, the hatred of the aristocracy and the desire for victory. They were always in agreement on these two points, so much so that on 13 Vendémiaire and 18 Fructidor they stifled their legitimate rancor, and a number of them helped the Thermidorian bourgeoisie put down the counterrevolution. However, it was only a short time before there was conflict between the revolutionary government and the Paris sans-culottes. Although the conflict was a direct result of the war, it was nevertheless an indication of the existence of two completely irreconcilable attitudes, two different social classes.

On the political front, the war required an authoritarian government and the sans-culottes were fully aware of this, since they had assisted in its creation. But from the first, the demands of war resulted in practices that were contradictory to the form of democracy envisioned by the Montagnards and the sans-culottes. Furthermore, democracy, as practiced by the sans-culottes, tended spontaneously toward a direct form of government, which appeared incompatible with the exigencies of wartime conditions. The sans-culottes had called for a strong government which would eradicate the aristocracy; they were not prepared for the fact that in order to win, this government would be obliged to force them to toe the line.

Their political ideals, vaguely outlined during periods of revolutionary struggle, did not move the sans-culottes toward a form of liberal democracy, as envisaged by the bourgeoisie, but toward a popular form of democracy. This meant control over elected officers, the right of the people to dismiss their elected officers, and certain processes such as the *viva voce* vote or the vote by acclamation; these demands are furthermore indicative of the fact that the sectional militants did not intend to be satisfied with a merely formal democracy. Their struggle tended to give substance to that which had originally been but an idea; they looked upon the Republic as being a democracy in action. For the more enlightened among them, freedom and equality had not been granted once and for all, but had to be won every day; liberty became liberation, equality, social conquest. Thus that general happiness which all held to be the purpose of society would come to pass. Beyond the opposition of circumstances, there was a fundamental contradiction in this matter between the bourgeoisie and the Paris sans-culottes, between sectional militants and the revolutionary government.

In the area of economics and of social relations, the contradictions were no less insurmountable. Robespierre and many other Montagnards stated that peacetime government and wartime government were not the same: a valid statement, not only from the political point of view but also in the area of economics. The conflict of interests between the "haves" who had agreed to support it and salaried men, who had helped to found it, meant that the revolutionary government, which needed both of them, had to play the role of arbitrator.

Being free traders, the members of the Public Safety Committee were far from happy with a controlled economy. They resigned themselves to the situation only because they were unable to do without the price-fixing and conscriptions necessary for supporting a major national war. They agreed to these measures only as expedients to be used only to the day of victory. The revolution which they led, although it had become a democratic one, was still a bourgeois revolution. From this point of view, it was absurd to tax goods without taxing the wages which were part of their net cost; the government was forced to maintain the peace between the leaders of industry, whom they could not do without, and wage earners.

It was even more necessary to maintain a controlled economy in order to avoid the devaluation of the currency. In order to bolster the *assignats* and to maintain at least part of their value in spite of the inevitable inflation (the government was obviously unable to reform the monetary system during wartime), it was necessary to impose a maximum on salaries as well as goods. If the government were to tolerate wage increases, it would have to raise the price of supplies for national defense and for manufacturing war matériel, since the government did not intend to touch private property or profits; that hypothesis was historically absurd from the point of view of a bourgeois revolution. The Public Safety Committee therefore agreed to price-fixing so that the state could finance the defense of the nation, without unleashing disastrous fluctuations in price, profits and salaries, which would in turn give rise to rampant inflation: the *assignat* would have been wrecked and the government thrown out.

This policy was based on the assumption that the alliance between Montagnards and sans-culottes would remain intact. Now, this ran counter to the interests of even the Jacobin bourgeoisie, because it suppressed economic freedom and restricted profits. At least, the Jacobin bourgeoisie continued to defend the Revolution and accepted the dictatorship of the committees. But apart from the manufacturing of war matériel paid for by the state, and apart from the wheat and forage requisitions from the peasants, artisans and shopkeepers, even Jacobins, ignored the maximum: there was bound to be a conflict with salaried men.

Suffering from the effects of inflation and food shortages, the sans-culottes were essentially concerned, as they had been under the ancien régime, with the ratio between wages and prices. When they forced requisition and price-fixing on the Convention, they were not thinking only of national defense: they were even more concerned with being able to feed themselves. The workers were quite naturally inclined to take advantage of the relative scarcity of manpower, in order to get wage raises while ignoring prices. Between the autumn and the spring of the year II, the sans-culottes were the masters of Paris, or were at least feared by the Convention, and thus were able to push for wage increases; contrary to the law, the Hébertist Commune did not tax them. The value of the *assignats* was threatened, while the bourgeoisie expressed their dissatisfaction; government intervened.

After Germinal, the revolutionary government came to the assistance of businesses which, caught between fixed prices and illegal wage increases, were losing money. The Public Safety Committee issued numerous instructions granting price increases commensurate with the maximum price of food set during Ventôse, in spite of the law. These increases would have had no effect if wages had continued. Hence the instructions issued by the Robespierrist Commune on 5 Thermidor, which, however, affected only Paris salaries. But after Prairial, with the harvest due shortly, the Public Safety Committee intervened, urging that the districts restrict wage increases for farm laborers. In the meanwhile, the Commune once again took up the matter of the increase already won by wage earners; the latter considered that the government had abandoned the role of mediator which it had played until that time. The controlled economy of the year ii, not having a class base, was bound to fall. After 9 Thermidor, the edifice crumbled.

It goes without saying that in societies with a bourgeois structure arbitration by the committee would tend to favor the "haves" over the wage earners, the former managing to evade price controls as long as they could provide for private consumers. The Robespierrists would doubtless have corrected the situation if they had been able to. The artisans and the merchants would doubtless have exploited consumers less if there had been enough raw materials in the workshops or supplies in the stores, the sale of which would have guaranteed them a profit which they considered adequate. Journeymen and day laborers had always contended that to maintain their right to exist, prices should be commensurate with wages; they would doubtless have resigned themselves to a ceiling on wages if they could have been sure of getting enough to live on.

But the revolutionary government lacked the means of balancing the supply and demand of merchandise and basic foodstuffs. Methods of production and transportation were inadequate. Neither the concentration of capital nor the rationalization and mechanization of work had been sufficiently modernized for that purpose. The government ran afoul of the economic structures of the period; war further magnified the problem of food supply. The controlled economy of the year II faced insurmountable problems in providing itself with livestock and other farm products. And wouldn't they have to consider the peasant? The lack of transportation facilities created problems even for the delivery of bread, all the more because of the absence of that concentration of flour milling which capitalism had yet to create.

The revolutionary government therefore restricted itself to guaranteeing bread to the population of Paris, without going to the extent of instituting nationwide rationing; as for the rest, it was up to the local authorities and consumers to force merchants and farmers to supply them and at the price fixed by law. Only the Army was allowed to requisition material. When the Paris sans-culotte found himself plagued with shortages, he demanded salary increases and resorted to strikes; the committees banned strikes, as the ancien régime had always done. Thus an insurmountable barrier was erected between the revolutionary government and the popular movement which had brought it to power. The economy was geared to artisan activity and was incapable of adapting itself to a major war effort.

In addition to the conflict between the revolutionary government and the popular movement, contradictions characteristic of the Paris sans-culottes movement also contributed to the downfall of the system of the year II.

Social contradiction existed between Jacobins, nearly all recruited from the lower, middling or upper ranks of the bourgeoisie, and the sans-culottes, if by this we agree with Pétion when he says that these latter consisted only of day laborers and skilled workers. But one cannot consider sans-culottes and wage earners identical, although the latter were most numerous among the sans-culottes. The real situation was more complex. The sans-culottes were not a class as such, nor was the sans-culottes movement a class party. Artisans, shopkeepers and merchants, journeymen and day laborers—along with a bourgeois minority—formed a coalition against ·the aristocracy which represented an irresistible force. However, within this coalition, there was a friction between those who, artisans and merchants, enjoyed incomes from private property or industry, and those who, journeymen and day laborers, had no other source of income save their wages.

The application of the law of the "maximum" brought the contradictions to a climax. Artisans and shopkeepers considered it just and right that the peasants be forced to feed city dwellers; but it was not long before they were to be indignant when they themselves were subjected to controls. Journeymen were complaining too. The *levée en masse* and the civil war depleted the work force, and as a result raised wages; since producers and middlemen would not respect price control, why should workers be victimized? The need to continue with the revolutionary struggle had cemented the unity of the Paris sans-culottes, and for a while they pushed into the background the conflicting interests which were breaking up their ranks; these conflicting interests, however, could not be completely suppressed.

Certain social attitudes further complicated these conflicts. Contradictions among sans-culottes were not exactly the same as those between the "haves" and the producers on the one hand, and salaried employees on the other. Among the last mentioned, there were numbers of master artisans, employees, who, on account of their life style, considered themselves bourgeois and had no intention of being confused with the lower orders, even if they had espoused their cause. On the other hand, numbers of real bourgeois called themselves sans-culottes and acted as such.

The sans-culottes came from all levels of society and therefore had no class consciousness. If they were generally hostile to new production methods, it was not for a common reason. The artisan was afraid of returning to being a wage earner; the journeyman hated the monopolist who raised the price of goods. It would be anachronistic to call journeymen class-conscious; rather, their attitudes were formed by their artisan masters. Concentration of capital had not yet, by gathering them in and around factories, given rise to that concentration of men so favorable to awakening class solidarity and operating the mass conversion which guarantees its surge forward.

Nevertheless, although the sans-culottes lacked class awareness, one cannot deny the existence of a certain class consciousness among wage earners. Subordinate to their masters, they were aware of themselves as a very particular group, distinguishable not only by manual labor and by their rank in the hierarchy of production, but also by their clothing, their diet, above all by their housing, by their pleasures and by their moral code. Also by their lack of education, which the well-born and the wealthy reserved for themselves; it gave the masses a sense of inferiority, and sometimes of powerlessness. The militant sans-culottes often denigrated *men of talent*, yet aspired to master their own destiny by emulating them.

Comprising various elements, not constituting a class, and thus completely without class consciousness, the sans-culottes, in spite of a few feeble attempts at co-ordination, always lacked an effective instrument for political action: a strictly disciplined party, maintaining that discipline by class recruitment and rigid scrutiny of its members. Lack of class cohesion doubtless characterized the revolutionary government; the same was true of the Jacobins. The whole regime of the year II rested on an idealist concept of democratic policy; hence its weakness. The result was disastrous for the popular movement.

Although numbers of militants attempted to discipline the general assemblies and the popular societies, leaders in many sections made the situation worse by fighting for power, sometimes by abusing it when they had it. As for the masses, apart from their hatred of the aristocracy and the summary measures which they planned against it, notably, massacre, they do not seem to have been endowed with much understanding of politics. They had confused anticipations of the advantages to be expected from the Revolution. They demanded price control less out of a desire to save the *assignats* and to insure the production of war matériel, than because they hoped that fixed prices and, therefore, controls would maintain their standard of living. When they realized that in many respects the controlled economy was not working, they withdrew their support and once again began making demands. Would the Paris sans-culottes have stopped demanding wage increases if (an absurd hypothesis) the "haves" and the producers had respected the maximum and not sought to increase profits above the level judged reasonable by the revolutionary government? Highly unlikely. The war demanded sacrifices; one of them was that there should be no war profiteering.

In this sense, indeed, 9 Thermidor was a day that made fools of the sans-culottes. Dissatisfied with the revolutionary government, they were unaware of the danger which its fall would place them in. Ten months later, unable to cope with rising costs and shortages, finally realizing what they had lost, they demanded the return of a controlled economy and rose for one last time, only to be once and for all crushed and swept off the stage of history.

Interior dissension among the sans-culottes was not the only reason for their defeat. The decline of the popular movement was implicit in the dialectic movement of history itself. Underhanded attack by the government committees and the encroaching power of the revolutionary government, the dramatic events during Germinal and the disaffection which followed cannot themselves explain the decline of the popular movement. It was bound to weaken; it grew strong, then as it triumphed, developed tendencies which in the end contributed to its downfall.

And first because of biological factors. Most of the sectional militants had been around since July 14, 1789; they had participated in all the uprisings. Since August 10, their activity had increased. The enthusiasm and excitement engendered by "the great days" entailed a nervous fatigue, which after victory was carried into the daily demands of militant life. Five years of revolutionary struggle had exhausted the political personnel of the sections, who had been the mainspring of the popular movement. The militants, always on the alert, were bound eventually to succumb to fatigue. On various occasions, fatigue forced the leaders of the Revolution to retire from political life for a while, among them, Robespierre during the month of Messidor. Robespierre said that with the war dragging on, "the people were getting tired." The popular movement had lost strength and keenness.

There was also a psychological reason for this. Vigilance seemed superfluous once the civil war was over, when the threat of invasion had been averted, when the day had been won. It was the same for both the people and the bourgeoisie, though the latter had different reasons for being tired. They were interested not only in ending the Reign of Terror, but also in ending the controlled economy, and in regaining control of government and administration. The people aspired to enjoy the fruits of their labors. One cannot from this standpoint interpret as mere maneuver the act of the *Montagne* section in opening a register to record new signatories to the Constitution; many militants considered the Constitution of June 1793 to be a symbol of social democracy; they had always insisted on the right to public assistance, on the right to education. The masses were particularly concerned about the right to exist. Victory being finally certain, there was, if not plenty, at least greater ease in getting food, daily bread being assured. Victory demobilized the popular movement.

The war effort did have a side effect: the sans-culottes became weaker as each month went by. The conscription of three thousand men for the Vendée campaign, then for the Eure campaign, and the general recruitment for the Revolutionary Army, deprived the militants of the greater part of their supporters: the youngest, the most inclined to action, often the most enthusiastic and politically aware, who considered defense of the nation their primary civic duty. In order to measure the vitality of the popular movement, it would be most important to reckon exactly the drain of men resulting from these various drafts. Although one cannot make a complete study, certain documents give us at least an idea of the tremendous loss of men suffered by the Paris sections in 1793. Out of the 3,540 voters twenty-one years old and over in the *Piques* section in the year II, 233 volunteers signed up for the Vendée campaign May 3–17 (Floréal, year I); most of them were sans-culottes, and in the prime of life. On July 17, 1793 (Messidor, year I), the *Finistère* section pointed out that its armed forces consisted of twelve companies, "but they had been so reduced by citizen enlistment, in the line as well as short-time volunteers, that only 942 men between the ages of eighteen and forty were left." This section had approximately 12,000 inhabitants; 3,783 voters over the age of twenty-one were counted in the year II. In July 1793, the sections had difficulty finding men fit to bear arms: the companies were largely manned by men of fifty and even sixty. In the *Quatre-Vingt-Douze* section, 767 (23.7 per cent) of 3,231 men were over fifty years old. In the *Arcis* section, the companies counted 2,986 men, "one quarter of whom are over sixty years old, and will have to be retired." Conscription raised the age level of the men available to the popular movement, thereby weakening the revolutionary ardor and fighting spirit of the Paris masses.

Finally, the dialectic of success itself depleted the cadres of the sans-culottes. Even though they may not have been driven by ambition alone, many sectional militants considered that their activism warranted a reward in the form of a job. There was also a price to be paid for the stability of the popular movement: the satisfaction of personal interests coincided with the need to scrutinize membership. But likewise, success gave rise to a new conformism. This can be seen in the evolution of the revolutionary commissars. Originally, they were the fighting element among the sectional political personnel. Drawn from the humblest ranks of the sans-culottes, they had to be paid a wage if the Revolution were to succeed. Their fear of losing their jobs as well as the encroaching powers

of the revolutionary government soon made them docile
instruments of authority. Throughout the course of the
year II, therefore, many militants thus transformed themselves into employees. This process was a necessary outcome not only of the internal development of the Paris
sans-culottes, but also of increased class antagonism in the
provinces and at the frontiers. The most aware sans-
culottes became part of the state apparatus; the political
activity of the sectional organizations found itself curbed
by the increased demands of national defense. At the same
time, the democratic process was weakened in the sections;
red tape gradually paralyzed the critical spirit and the
activity of the masses. The final result was a decline in
popular control over the machinery of the revolutionary
government, which became increasingly authoritarian.
This bureaucratic rigidity deprived the Paris sans-culottes
of a large portion of their activists.

These various factors, which could be cited on many
occasions other than the year II, account for the weakening
of the popular movement; it soon collapsed.

Nevertheless, we cannot strike a merely negative balance for the popular movement in the year II. Doubtless
it was unable to achieve its own goals, that egalitarian and
popular republic which, in their confused manner, the
sans-culottes yearned for; current events as well as their
own internal contradictions prevented it. The popular
movement nevertheless contributed to the onward thrust
of history by the decisive assistance it gave to the bourgeois revolution.

Without the Paris sans-culottes, the latter would not
have succeeded in such a radical manner. Between 1789
and the year II, the sans-culottes constituted a powerful
weapon of revolutionary struggle and national defense.
In 1793, the popular movement made possible the inauguration of the revolutionary government, thus defeating counterrevolution at home and the coalition abroad.
It was the Thermidorians who gained from the victory;

they could not win a peace, because the controlled economy was abandoned and because the demoralization of troops who lacked equipment paralyzed the Army and allowed the enemy time to prepare for new campaigns. From this, one draws an even better understanding of the achievement of the revolutionary government and the importance of the popular movement of the year II.

Looking farther ahead, the popular movement had no slight effect on history. Its triumph during the course of the summer of 1793 led to the Terror, which destroyed the old society. The upper middle class of the ancien régime, rooted in commercial capitalism and to a certain extent linked to the social and political system of the feudal aristocracy, was not spared either. The artisan and shopkeeper sans-culottes, whose leaders were small independent producers (see the analysis of the members of the Paris revolutionary committees), were, during the year II, the most effective element in the struggle to destroy the old methods of production and the social relations which they entailed. The Thermidorian reaction was both economic and political; by that time, the Terror had cleared the field for introducing new relations of production. Industry was to dominate commerce in the capitalist society which sprang from the Revolution; the commercial capital against which the Paris sans-culottes had fought a bloody battle in the year II was stripped of its autonomy and henceforth took second place to the only productive capital, industrial capital.

As for the sans-culottes themselves, the economic evolution managed to create different classes within their ranks. Among the small and medium-sized producer-merchants who had filled the ranks of the popular movement between 1793 and 1794, some succeeded and became industrialists, while others failed and swelled the ranks of the wage earners. Others were still attached to their workshops and their stores. Economic freedom speeded the concentration of business enterprise, transforming the material conditions of social life, but at the same time altering the structure of the traditional working class.

What their fate might be—for every artisan who became a successful industrialist, how many failed?—both artisan and journeyman suspected, the latter knowing that the machine would increase his risk of unemployment, the former knowing that industrialization would close his workshop and transform him into a wage earner. Throughout the course of the nineteenth century, artisans and shopkeepers clung to their way of life. It would be interesting to find out who played the leading role from June 1848 to the Commune of 1871—the proletariat, or the traditional popular masses; one might be able to chart the decline of the latter in terms of the triumph of industrialism, while at the same time emphasizing one of the reasons for the weakness of nineteenth-century revolutionary activity.

Thus the dramatic character of class struggles during the year II becomes all the more important when one bears in mind their repercussions; at the same time, they make even clearer the basic character of contemporary French national history.

INDEX

Adoption of children, 249
Affiliation, 203 ff.
Age of Enlightenment, 42
Agriculture, 52
Amis-de-la-Patrie section, xxxviii, 11, 17, 34–35, 149, 188; education, 86–87; food, 241; politics, 101, 113, 116, 118; population, 27; red cap, 225; sectional society, 200, 201, 202
Amis du Peuple, 53, 54, 56, 88, 98, 107, 113, 232, 233
Anarchists, 133
Ancard, M., 51
Ancien régime, xxi, xxii, xxix; hostility toward, 3, 23, 92, 143
Anthéaume, M., 5
Apathy, offense of, 148–49
Archives, xxx–xxxii, xxxiii
Arcis section, xxxviii, 48, 54, 152; armed forces, 261; indemnity, 178; politics, 117, 171; sectional society, 215, 217; unity, 148
Aristocracy, xvii, xix, xx, xxii, 6–7, 72, 103, 156; hostility toward, 62, 92; institutions, xviii; mercantile, 14, 16; plot, 159, 160; red cap, 225–27; sans-culottes, xxvi, xxvii, 5 ff., 20, 23, 62, 252; Third Estate, 20, 251; violence, 158, 160
Armies, 18, 25, 75; clothing, 66–71, 231–32; conscrip-

tion, 74, 260–61; control over, 114–15; equipping, 66–69, 77–78
Arming of citizens, 102–3
Arrests, 147–49
Arsenal section, xxxviii, 17, 19, 37–38, 159, 243–44; fraternization, 155; insurrection, 128; politics, 106, 138; popular society, 204; unity, 146
Artisans, 22, 23, 28, 33 ff., 93; class, 7; housing, 236–37; influence, 41, 58; work force, 29
Aspirations—objective conditions, antagonism, 93
Assignats, 27, 28, 29, 49, 64, 65, 77, 253, 254, 258
Assistance, right to, 81–85. See Public assistance
Auditeur National, 244

Babeuf, M., 10, 21
Babillard, 214
Bacon, M., 51, 215, 217
Barbant, Jacques, 17
Barère, M., 172
Barnave, M., xviii–xix; *Introduction to the French Revolution*, xviii *and* n
Barry, Etienne: "Essay on Political Denunciation," 143
Basire, M., 230
Bastille, 24, 37
Beaubourg section, xxxviii, 145
Beaulieu, Boileux de, 123